SHAKESPEARE
AND THE
COURTLY
AESTHETIC

SHAKESPEARE AND THE COURTLY AESTHETIC

GARY SCHMIDGALL

UNIVERSITY OF CALIFORNIA PRESS
BERKELEY · LOS ANGELES · LONDON

University of California Press
Berkeley and Los Angeles, California
University of California Press, Ltd.
London, England
© 1981 by
The Regents of the University of California
Printed in the United States of America

1 2 3 4 5 6 7 8 9

Library of Congress Cataloging in Publication Data

Schmidgall, Gary, 1945–
    Shakespeare and the courtly aesthetic.

    Bibliography: p. 273
    Includes index.
    1. Shakespeare, William, 1564–1616. *The
Tempest.*   2. Shakespeare, William, 1564–1616—
Political and social views.   3. Great Britain—
History—James I, 1603–1625.   4. Great Britain—
Court and courtiers.   5. Courts and courtiers.
I. Title.
PR2833.S3   822.3'3   80-23257
ISBN 0-520-04130-5

FOR VIRGIL WHITAKER

CONTENTS

vii

PLATES

ACKNOWLEDGMENTS

THE READER who discerns in this study the influence of interdisciplinary methods pioneered at the Warburg Institute in London is not mistaken. My initial research was made possible by two generous grants from the Leverhulme Foundation and the Mabelle McLeod Lewis Memorial Fund for support during a year's reading at the Warburg and the British Library. To the staff at each institution, whose efficiency and helpfulness made much possible in a short time, I am grateful. I am also indebted for courtesies extended by the Huntington Library during the final stages of research. A fellowship from the Andrew Mellon Foundation gave me the time to make revisions in the original manuscript. Foremost among my individual benefactors is John Bender, who during my first researches patiently and thoughtfully considered with me the difficulties of the subject. I am also grateful to Stephen Orgel, Ronald Rebholz, Paul Robinson, and Joseph Wittreich for their criticism and encouragement. Four of my colleagues at the University of Pennsylvania gave me the benefit of their close readings and perceptive advice: Roland Mushat Frye, Phyllis Rackin, Humphrey Tonkin, and Robert Y. Turner. My dedication is but slight return for Virgil Whitaker's generosity, affection, and the example of his humane spirit and scholarship.

PREFACE

"TELL ME, ye learned, Shall we for ever be adding so much to the *bulk*—so little to the *stock?* Shall we for ever make new books, as apothecaries make new mixtures, by pouring only out of one vessel into another?" These questions posed in exasperation by the authorial persona in *Tristram Shandy* might well occur to anyone who attempts to keep abreast of Shakespearean studies—even if one stakes out only a portion of real estate within that vast bourn. Anyone who tries to canvass scholarship on the Late Plays, for instance, or even just on *The Tempest,* is likely to find himself wondering as Tristram does at the proliferation of learned commentary. "So thou apprehend'st it, take it for thy labor," says Shakespeare's "churlish philosopher" Apemantus; one sometimes feels the same way toward recent critical approaches to the playwright. The well-intentioned if melancholy efforts of Shakespearean specialists to keep in touch with the state of the art are bound to lead to meditation upon the general problems of writing about the canon, and my efforts were no exception. Plain concern as to whether what follows is bulk or stock— and what author does not convince himself that he has added to the latter?—has led me to certain conclusions about Shakespearean criticism worth mentioning before setting out.

The most obvious worry for anyone writing on the Late Plays is: will his or her readers' patience outlast the critical outpouring? I must own to an increasing sense of being "oppressed with travel" when I consider the plethora of books and articles on these works. As if contemplation of the various "endings" of *The Tempest* were not enough, one sets to wondering—fantasizing, surely, is the better word—about a critical ending, a burying of theoretical batons certain fadoms deep, the utterance of a loud *sufficit.* It is no doubt delusive, and heartless toward posterity, to think such thoughts, but I admit I have thought them. After all, the bromide that each scholarly generation deserves its own versions of Shakespeare covers a multitude of critical sins and repetitions—and reveals very few critical saints. One cannot even speak confidently of "obsolescence" in recent discourse, because that implies progress. And these days it is hard to get a mental purchase on the scattered, inchoate, and proliferating critical goings-on and then be able to say, *this* is progress. One longs sometimes for the grand, focusable gladiatorial combats of the Dowdens, Bradleys, Granville-Barkers, Tillyards, Stolls, Knights, and Wilsons. As it is, the critical forest seems so thickset with growth—not many handsome trees but much shrubbery and brambles—that one often gets the surreal feeling one's feet are no longer touching the fecund Shakespearean earth that nurtured it all.

I am not alone in these thoughts. There was a time, and it was not so long ago, when one could still imagine a brave new world of critical frontiers yet to be explored in the Late Plays. In his overview of 1958 Philip Edwards could write a generally gracious appraisal of what had hitherto been achieved and could hopefully suggest an agenda for the future.[1] Twenty years later F. D. Hoeniger appears with his survey "Shakespeare's Romances since 1958," in a more harsh and disgruntled frame of mind: "Too much writing on the Romances has . . . been repetitious or supererogatory."[2] And he closes by noting that, unlike Edwards, he does not "need" to offer an agenda for future scholarship. The trend is not

---

[1] Philip Edwards, "Shakespeare's Romances: 1900–1957,"*Shakespeare Survey* 11 (1958): 1–18.

[2] F. D. Hoeniger, "Shakespeare's Romances since 1958: A Retrospect." *Shakespeare Survey* 29 (1976): 1–10. A recent, extensive, and selective bibliography of Late Play criticism may be found in *Shakespeare's Romances Reconsidered,* ed. Carol Kay and Henry Jacobs (Lincoln, Nebraska, 1978), pp. 181–215.

good. I wonder rather gloomily what a review article written twenty years hence will conclude.

More optimistically, I hope that a retrospective article written, say, at the turn of the millennium will be able to report that something like critical cloture was finally voted on one perennial issue, and also that commentators finally came to grips with a tease question frequently and enticingly asked about the Late Plays but rarely entertained seriously.

The perennial issue that has contributed perhaps the most bulk to criticism of the Late Plays is the question of genre. *The Tempest* particularly has ignited much dry matter of generic speculation. The possibilities are admittedly boggling: *The Tempest* as romance, morality play, initiation ritual, refinement of the *commedia dell' arte,* topical response to New World voyages, masque, comedy, tragedy, tragicomedy, hymeneal celebration, fairy tale, myth, or autobiographical palinode. Who can deny that every one of these possibilities is reflected more or less in the play? And who can deny that critics, in pressing for these various genres, have often enhanced our appreciation of *The Tempest?* But there is for me a besetting unsatisfactoriness in attempts to categorize the play generically. We have what Gerald Schorin has aptly but not very elegantly called "a mixed-mode categorization problem," and he responds to the challenge as have so many by announcing that "it remains for us to determine the predominant genre of *The Tempest.*"[3] The cruel word is *predominant;* it has forced

---

[3]Gerald Schorin, "Approaching the Genre of *The Tempest,*" in *Shakespeare's Late Plays: Essays in Honor of Charles Crow,* ed. Richard Tobias and Paul Zolbrod (Athens, Ohio, 1974), pp. 176, 180. Rosalie Colie, in her *Resources of Kind: Genre-Theory in the Renaissance,* ed. Barbara Lewalski (Berkeley, 1973), shows the same genre-theorist's imperative need to discern a "dominant" genre: "The process of interpretation of *The Courtier* remains tricky. We still have to decide what kind is dominant in the book" (pp. 113–114). Certain other statements in Colie's helpful study, however, seem to suggest that the search for genre in "problematic" works might be futile or,

critics to produce commentaries that are, so unlike *The Tempest* itself, unbalanced and partial. Thus, a genre or stage tradition, instead of remaining what it invariably is in the play, namely, a component, becomes a determinant. I have not read a single attempt to capture *the* genre of *The Tempest* without a sense of critical failure to encompass the whole play. My heart sinks a little when I see titles that assume a generic category. I would be similarly disheartened to hear of a book titled *Shakespeare's Courtly Plays*.

Generic criticism urges us to fractionate what is, in the case of *The Tempest,* remarkably indissoluble. Such criticism works against the notion that I have of how the play was made, a notion well expressed by L. C. Knights: "The island mirrors, or contains, the world; what we have to do with is not exclusion and simplification but compression and density."[4] Generic critics, who often seem to be working *a priori* from a generic tradition rather than from Shakespeare's text, are typically unable to mount the peculiarly creative response the play requires. They are also the least inclined to the hardest task of criticism—the task that Shakespeare demands more than any other playwright (because he never repeated himself) and the task that *The Tempest* demands more than any other of his plays: the task of treating a work as a thing unto itself, as *sui generis*.

Having said this, it may seem paradoxical to draw attention to yet another genre as a way of communicating my sense of the process of compression or centripetal solidifying of various expressive modes in *The Tempest*. But it will become clear in the ensuing pages that I think the epic may

---

worse, misleading: "Certainly as far as *writers* were concerned, rules were there to take or leave—the Renaissance is rich in uncanonical kinds" (p. 76); "though there are generic conventions all right, they are also metastable" (p. 30). And thus metadependable for critical purposes?

[4]L. C. Knights, "*The Tempest,*" in Tobias and Zolbrod, *Shakespeare's Late Plays,* p. 21.

prove to be the genre capable of summarizing and working
with the resources of Late Play genre criticism—or at least of
putting that criticism in a usable perspective. For the epic is
the genre that least impels us to the fractionation or "crack-
ing" of the play.[5] I would like to mention here briefly the epic
poem that *The Tempest* most resembles in intellectual milieu
and scope (*The Faerie Queene*) and the epic it most resembles
in what might be called its "fiction" and structure (the
Aeneid).

The Tempest can be seen as a kind of reduction of the epic
that still by Shakespeare's dramaturgical magic retains the
larger genre's magnitude and richness of experience. It is as if
Shakespeare had managed to convey the experience of a
cross-country race in the space of a hundred meters. Like *The
Faerie Queene, The Tempest* offers a kaleidoscope of genres.
The various literary and theatrical traditions that critics have
thought to lie behind Shakespeare's play sound much like the
traditions A. S. P. Woodhouse discerned in Spenser's epic

[5]For the purposes of this discussion I speak of the epic as a genre. It is a
difficulty of Colie's study that she does not: "No wonder the epic seemed so
mixed a form in the Renaissance" (*Resources of Kind,* p. 23). Colie's view
would seem to be contradicted by Sir Philip Sidney's weighty testimony in
his *Defence of Poetry:* "All concurreth to the maintaining the Heroicall, which
is not onelie a kinde, but the best and most accomplished kindes of Poetrie"
(*Prose Works,* ed. Albert Feuillerat [1912; rpt. London, 1962], III, 25). Colie
relies, rather, on the concept of *genera mista,* and not often convincingly. It is
not very helpful, for instance, to "stress *King Lear* as a work of *genera mista*"
(p. 123), or to refer to "the clear and frank mixture of genres in the opera" (p.
22). Opera is not so much a mixture of genres as a mixture of expressive
modes, and the same might be said of the epic. If the word *genre* means anything, opera and epic are genres. If any concept in Colie's book is applicable
to epic and, by extension, to *The Tempest,* it is the *genus universum,* which she
describes as "culture as a whole, the total kind" (p. 20). It is possible, I suppose, to follow the genre theorists and call *The Tempest* Shakespeare's closest
approach to Polonius's "tragical-comical-historical-pastoral," but I feel it is
more useful to see it as a work both inclusive and encompassing—as a work
of the *genus universum.* I am tempted to paraphrase Colie's description of *Gar-
gantua and Pantagruel* as "a book of books, and of all kinds of books" (p. 79)
and say that *The Tempest* is a play of plays, and of all kinds of plays.

poem: "There is scarcely a genre that it does not involve or draw on—epic, narrative, chivalric quest, the whole range of allegorical poetry, as the Middle Ages developed it, not to mention pastoral, emblem, idyll, interlude, and masque."[6] The same "involving" and "drawing on" occurred as Shakespeare prepared *The Tempest*. However, our patience with generic criticism of Spenser is much greater, so manifestly difficult is it to hold *The Faerie Queene* in one's head as a whole and integrated structure—if, indeed, Spenser ever seriously expected anyone to try. But the play we must try to grasp as a whole—as a work, to repeat Knights's fine phrase, of "compression and density." Looking at the play as a theatrical condensation of a *Faerie Queene*–like structure is, I find, helpful to this end, even though the final product is utterly un-Spenserian.

The *Aeneid* impresses me as similarly useful—perhaps more so, since Virgil's epic has better maintained its hold on the imagination in the last centuries than Spenser's. In fact, I will be suggesting more fully in chapters three and five what Frank Kermode, J. M. Nosworthy, and most recently Jan Kott have suggested before: the *Aeneid* figures far more powerfully in the background of *The Tempest* than we have hitherto imagined.[7] The possibility that the epic genre is the genre ultimately most relevant to the play and to the Late

---

[6] A. S. P. Woodhouse, *The Poet and His Faith* (Chicago, 1965), p. 21.

[7] Frank Kermode, ed., *The Tempest* (Cambridge, Mass., 1954), pp. xxx–xxxiv; J. M. Nosworthy, "The Narrative Sources of *The Tempest*," *Review of English Studies* 24 (1948): 281–94; Jan Kott, "The *Aeneid* and *The Tempest*," *Arion*, new series 3 (1976): 424–51, and "*The Tempest*, or Repetition," *Mosaic* 10 (1977): 9–36. Kott gives numerous further references in his notes. I should add that Kott and I draw radically different conclusions from our references to Virgil. I was interested also to find that one of F. D. Hoeniger's few positive suggestions for further study of the Late Plays concerned Virgil: "It is time to remind ourselves of the echoes from Virgil, Ovid, and St. Paul. Old voyages and 'wonder,' not only new, lie behind" the plays ("Shakespeare's Romances," p. 5).

Plays appeals to me strongly because the epic is the most inclusive, multifaceted, and spacious of genres. It seems the most appropriate genre to associate with the most inclusive, multifaceted, and (desert island notwithstanding) intellectually spacious of Shakespeare's plays.[8]

The question referred to above as a frequent tease in Late Play criticism was asked, surely not for the first time, by S. L. Bethell in 1947: "Why does Shakespeare in the last phase of his dramatic activity turn to these naive and impossible romances?"[9] The question is often asked, but, since critics have overwhelmingly concerned themselves with finding out *what* the Late Plays are rather than *why* they are, the question is usually raised for rhetorical purposes only. Hallett Smith, for example, puzzles "as to why Shakespeare wrote *Pericles, Cymbeline, The Winter's Tale,* and *The Tempest*" and concludes that "it would have been passing strange if he had not."[10] No answer at all. Barbara Mowat addressed the problem even more recently: "The question now remains: why should Shakespeare have chosen to shape the tactical dramaturgy of the Romances so strangely?"[11] However, near

---

[8]One of Beethoven's late quartets, the monumental and mysterious seven-movement Opus 131 in C-sharp minor, recapitulates the multifaceted artistic unity I experience in *The Tempest.* Maynard Solomon describes the piece in his biography *Beethoven* (New York, 1977): "There are many pressures toward discontinuity at work in this Quartet: six distinct main keys, thirty-one changes of tempo, a variety of textures, and a diversity of forms within the movements—fugue, suite, recitative, variation, scherzo, aria, and sonata form—which makes the achievement of unity all the more miraculous. Beethoven is here pressing dissociation so far that it turns into its opposite—perfect coherence and profound integration" (p. 325).

[9]S. L. Bethell, *The Winter's Tale: A Study* (London, 1947), p. 20. Philip Edwards asked again in the survey article cited in note 1 above, "Why should Shakespeare turn to writing these plays?"

[10]Hallett Smith, *Shakespeare's Romances: A Study of Some Ways of the Imagination* (San Marino, Calif., 1972), p. 20.

[11]Barbara Mowat, *The Dramaturgy of Shakespeare's Romances* (Athens, Georgia, 1976), p. 64.

the end of her book we are disappointed, though not surprised, to learn that it is "impossible to identify what was the
cause . . . in the design and construction of these plays" (p.
117). Mowat nevertheless entertains three explanations that
are worth pausing over:

> It is quite possible that Shakespeare felt that he had
> carried closed form dramaturgy to a variety of perfec-
> tions, and, as a result, became interested in trying to
> create a new kind of dramatic experience.
>
> (p. 117)
>
> [Shakespeare was responding to] renewed interest in
> the fascination of Greek Romance.
>
> (p. 118)
>
> Perhaps Shakespeare first of all wanted to say some-
> thing about life that he had only hinted at before.
>
> (p. 118)

I suppose they have an air of plausibility, but each one rings
false. It is pure whimsy to imagine the first suggestion running through the playwright's mind, even if translated from
professorial jargon into his own tongue. The second possibility is stated too baldly; it begs the crucial questions: who was
fascinated by these Greek romances and how is this fascination discerned? The last suggestion simply does not square
with my sense of how Shakespeare went about writing plays.
He was not a George Bernard Shaw, who set out to "say
something" and then wrote it up for the stage. Shakespeare
says much, but he can rarely be found saying some *thing*. His
plays are rich in messages, but not messages in the upper case
or in neon.

Mowat's question, though, was not really germane to her
critical purposes. The question might be said to have gotten in
her way. I pause over her digressive attempt to provide an
answer because she does what has often been done before:
reason from *what* the Late Plays are to a sense of *why* they are.

What speculation there has been about the reason for their being—and the small amount of such speculation is in itself noteworthy—is rather free-floating. None of Mowat's speculations has anything to do with the facts of Shakespeare's professional life, the exigencies of his company, or the general social and artistic flux that occurred during his active years. This tendency to ignore Shakespeare's working environment is odd, given the universal agreement that he was a shrewd and pragmatic man of the theater. It would stand to reason that some speculation as to the environment in which the man undertook to write his last plays would help us better understand the form they eventually assumed.

Both the broad focus and format of this study require a warning about what I am setting out to achieve. The omnipresence of *The Tempest* may lead the reader to expect a full "reading" of that play to emerge. This will not happen—not least because I think that Shakespeare's protean masterpiece is, of all his plays, the one most easily undervalued in its conceptual totality by thematic simplification. Addressing himself to *Measure for Measure*, Philip Brockbank wrote: "A great play has many kinds of energy, and many elusive significances that are apt to put our own critical discourse upon trial."[12] This view applies with greatest force to *The Tempest*. To gather together its energies and significances would require a critical single-mindedness that my other concerns here render impossible. I have perforce approached the play in a limited way, that is, as a highly politicized literary work and as a piece of very complex art; I did so because courtly art typically set orthodox political assumptions in sophisticated artistic environments.

My study is about the methods of cunning prince-pleasers (a phrase of Puttenham's) who sought to give a grace to

[12]Philip Brockbank, "With a saving grace," *Times Literary Supplement,* 26 November 1976, p. 1470.

greatness (a Jonsonian phrase). *The Tempest* appears throughout the following pages as a convenient and worthy subject—like a lawyer's test case—upon which to focus a discussion of Shakespeare's response (and, by extension, that of his artistic contemporaries) to the pressures of courtly tastes and artistic mandates. If we are to appreciate fully *The Tempest* and other plays like it, we must be aware of their more sophisticated, resonant, and artificial levels of meaning, that is to say, their courtly levels of meaning. We must examine *The Tempest* more closely with respect to the most complex and learned "capacity" for which it was intended. Frederick Sternfeld has written, "*The Tempest* is a courtly work par excellence,"[13] and on such a view of the play this study is founded.

But it cannot be sufficiently emphasized that Shakespeare felt pressures other than courtly ones. Prospero, for instance, radiates much semi-allegorical political energy resulting from courtly influence, and this I discuss at length. But he is a whole theatrical being—a complex and profound figure—because Shakespeare was also responding to the pressures of his perceptions of human nature and of his own status as a creator. Consideration of Prospero's courtly and political aspects left insufficient occasion here to celebrate that pervasive wholeness of conception which is the supreme quality of Shakespeare's art.

This study falls naturally into two parts of about equal length. The first focuses on the outlines of what I call the courtly aesthetic—with special reference to James's first decade on the throne of England. Historical and literary fluctuations in the vitality of courtly art and the place of *The Tempest* within the broad sweep of changing fashions are outlined in

---

[13]Frederick Sternfeld, "Le Symbolisme musical dans quelques pièces de Shakespeare présentées à la Cour d'Angleterre," in *Fêtes de la Renaissance*, ed. Jean Jacquot (Paris, 1965), I, p. 321.

chapters one and two. Shifting from mutable historical circumstances to the continuities of courtly art, I examine in chapter three certain themes of enduring importance in any court—and in *The Tempest*. Selected aspects of the aesthetic that affected the form of royal entertainments are discussed in chapter four: some of these aspects were uniquely part of the artistic revolution that took place in James's first London decade, others were equally Elizabethan and Jacobean.

The concept of the courtly aesthetic is elaborated in the second half of the study through a close look at aspects of *The Tempest*'s imagery, structure, and characterization that suggest the influence of artistic royalism. This approach has yielded what I believe is a suggestive political perspective on the play; it is summarized at the opening of chapter five and elaborated in chapters five through seven. I conclude with a more subjective comparison of *The Tempest* and Velázquez's famous courtly painting, *Las Meninas*.

I spoke earlier of progress. Progress in Shakespearean criticism can be likened to the development of technology available for illuminating the theatrical stage. Over the centuries advances in lighting expertise (which began in earnest in England when Shakespeare was writing the Late Plays) have brought us to computerized lightboards. The array of electronic gear, the kinds, sizes, and sheer number of lights are astonishing; a lighting designer is now necessary in any serious theater, so complex is his art. Critics of Shakespeare are also necessary. His audience did not need illumination because there was, literally, no darkness. There was good Elizabethan daylight. But the passing centuries have inevitably left important aspects of Renaissance plays in darkness. These plays will always require illumination. The ideal event is for critics to make use of their critical gear to light the whole play and, as a corollary, to adjust the levels of illumination according to the priorities of the author. That is, light brilliantly what is important, provide half-light for what is not, and perhaps leave in the shadows what is necessary for the right chiaroscuro effect. But above all, the critic must light the entire play. The failures of Shakespearean criticism can almost all be ascribed to a kind of imbalance in illumination. The critic riding very hard on a thematic motif, an "idea" of the time, a persistent image, or a monistic "reading" is like the lighting designer who favors a dark stage and the strong spotlighting of his action. If the spot flutters or a character steps suddenly into the darkness, then one becomes aware of the mode of illumination and the presence of a fallible technician. Shakespearean criticism quite innocent of such fallibility is rare.

I am repeating a point made a few pages earlier and made often by others—F. D. Hoeniger, for instance: "The best theater criticism is of the kind that keeps the whole play in view."[14] It is very hard, with Shakespeare, to err on the side of comprehensiveness. With The Tempest, it is impossible. The play's extraordinary range of style, characterization, form, and "address" makes it the least amenable to the sweeping but specific manipulation of critical spotlights. I have been happy to pursue the present course because it has given me the feeling that I have kept many, if not all, of the play's important aspects in view—its themes, images, form, historical milieu, its relation to various literary traditions, and its meanings.

[14]F. D. Hoeniger, "Shakespeare's Romances since 1958: A Retrospect," Shakespeare Survey 29 (1976): 8.

· I ·

COURTLY ART
AND *THE TEMPEST*

*I*N HIS TREATISE *The Painting of the Ancients* (1638),
François Du Jon attempted to suggest the complex
knowledge required to create and to understand a worthy
painting:

> Bees . . . . doe sucke out of the juice of severall flow-
> ers such a sweet and pleasing savour of honey, that all
> the wit of man is not able to imitate any such thing:
> and why doe wee then wonder that Picture should
> lacke the helpe of many Arts, which not being sensi-
> bly perceived in the worke, are for all that secretly
> felt, by transfusing into the Picture a hidden force de-
> rived out of many sciences?
>
> (p. 236)

Du Jon's admonition applies to all Renaissance art forms, and
the drama is no exception. Many arts and sciences not strictly
dramaturgical affected playwrights like Shakespeare, and these
influences are often "secretly felt" in their works. More than
a study of the courtly aesthetic or of *The Tempest*, this is a
broad attempt to suggest that the full understanding of a
given Renaissance artistic creation may often require a search
for the "hidden force" transfused into it from other arts—and

1

from art forms associated with different social classes. Renaissance men did not observe the arbitrary academic frontiers that have been hardening over the last two hundred years, and we are now—through the studies of scholars like Erwin Panofsky, Frances Yates, D. J. Gordon, and Stephen Orgel—beginning to realize the naiveté and inadequacy of studies in Renaissance art and literature that are limited by the disciplinary boundaries of colleges and universities. Francis Bacon pressed exactly this point in a well-known passage from *The Advancement of Learning*: "No perfect discovery can be made upon a flat or level: neither is it possible to discover the more remote and deeper parts of any science, if you stand but upon the level of the same science, and ascend not to a higher science."[1] And Bacon later reemphasizes his great early plea for what we now call—not altogether happily, I sometimes think—interdisciplinary studies: "Generally let this be a rule, that all partitions of knowledge be accepted for lines and veins, than for sections and separations; and that the continuance and entireness of knowledge be preserved" (III, 366–67). This is the golden rule of comparatist scholarship.

The study of Shakespeare has heretofore focused upon important recurring themes and images in the plays. Another body of criticism has focused on the influence of the classical or humanist tradition and upon the development from

[1]Francis Bacon, *The Works*, ed. James Spedding (1857–74; facsimile rpt. Stuttgart, 1963), III, 292. Throughout the text, citations from Bacon are made by volume and page number of the Spedding edition. Quotations from *The Tempest* are taken from the New Arden edition by Frank Kermode (Cambridge, Mass., 1954). *The Riverside Shakespeare*, edited by G. Blakemore Evans and others (Boston, 1974), is used for all other Shakespearean quotations. Ben Jonson is cited from *The Works*, edited by C. H. Herford and Percy and Evelyn Simpson (Oxford, 1925–52), by volume and page number. References to the works of Edmund Spenser are from *The Works of Edmund Spenser*, the eight-volume variorum edition of Edwin Greenlaw, et al. (Baltimore, 1938). All contemporary quotations are given exactly as printed in the editions cited, except that the archaic *u*, *v*, *i*, and *j* have been conventionally modernized.

medieval drama to the popular Elizabethan theater. Madeleine
Doran well represents this premier *modus operandi* of her
scholarly generation in the preface to *Endeavors of Art* (Madison, Wis., 1954): "This book is an essay in historical criticism.
It is based on the premise that to know and understand the
frame of artistic reference within which the practicing
dramatists of the Elizabethan and Jacobean periods worked
is to understand better their artistic achievement" (p. vii).
By "frame of artistic reference" Doran meant literary and
theoretical reference; she was in effect standing—brilliantly,
let it be said—upon what Bacon would have called "the level
of the same science." What has occurred in the last decade or
so has been an enlargement of the frame of artistic reference to
include social, political, and pan-artistic influences upon literary figures. Scholars are beginning to acclimatize themselves
to working in a wider-ranging "science." Our knowledge of
courtly art and entertainment has recently enjoyed a remarkable advancement as a result of this trend. Great interest in
courtly art has been reflected, for instance, in a number of medievalist studies, Angus Fletcher's *The Transcendental Masque*
(its first three chapters are as good a prolegomenon for the
study of Renaissance courtly art as I know of), the Inigo
Jones quatercentenary in 1973, the works of Roy Strong and
Stephen Orgel, the *Fêtes de la Renaissance* series edited by Jean
Jacquot, and the facsimile reprinting of many important
iconologies and other texts on fine arts in the Renaissance.
The central purpose of the present study is to encourage an
effort to bring this recently acquired knowledge of the Renaissance courtly aesthetic more directly to bear upon English
literature generally and Shakespeare's works in particular.
That is to say, I will try to give a sense of some of the radical
changes in the ways men of the stage served and exploited
their milieu as England moved from Tudor to Stuart absolutism, from Renaissance to Baroque expression in the arts,
and from feudal oligarchy to commercial aristocracy. This

will require a consideration of the nature of the courtly aesthetic itself; a look at the influence it had in the process of adapting nondramatic literature for the stage; a cursory address to the perplexing matter of the interaction of public, private, and courtly theatrical sectors; and, more specifically, an attempt to imagine the reasons for the turn in Shakespeare's career marked by *Pericles*. Much support for the views of *The Tempest* presented below exists in the other Late Plays, but in order to ease both the length and complexity of this study, I have generally refrained from allusion to pertinent passages in *Pericles, Cymbeline,* and *The Winter's Tale*. I hope the reader will grant that if this or any attempt to illuminate *The Tempest* is convincing, it will be significant in varying degrees for the other Late Plays.[2]

Scholars have tended to overlook the radical change in courtly fashions and entertainments that, in England, took place at about the midpoint of Shakespeare's career. Elizabeth's court was the last for which Castiglione's *Book of the Courtier* is an appropriate introduction. Though some have begun to explore the ramifications of the extensive Stuart revolution in the arts, this remarkable change requires much further study. Shakespeare's Late Plays are in part a response to this revolution, and my concern in what follows is to explore the nature of this response and its artistic consequences. I have chosen *The Tempest* as my cynosure. Prospero, Ariel, Caliban, and Ferdinand all reflect character types prominent in courtly art; the Revels Speech cannot be fully understood but from the perspective of courtly entertainments; the masque-within-the-play of act 4 (perhaps excepting the masque in Beaumont and Fletcher's *Maid's Tragedy*) the only one of the time that has the genuine feel of its real-life courtly counterpart; and the political significance of *The Tem-*

[2]E. M. W. Tillyard has made the same point in reverse in *Shakespeare's Last Plays* (1938; rpt. London, 1964): "The prospect of understanding *Cymbeline* without *The Winter's Tale* and *The Tempest* is poor indeed" (p. 1).

pest owes much to courtly assumptions. Courtly art, in short, can tell us much about *The Tempest* and other plays of the time, and vice versa.

The present book falls under the rubric of milieu studies. Its methods are rather new in Shakespearean scholarship: "milieu" became a subsection in the *Shakespeare Quarterly* bibliography only in 1976. The actual process of applying our increasing knowledge of relevant disciplines to literature is still unrefined. We could have wished for better guidelines, a higher state of the art of multi-disciplinary criticism. But we have to start somewhere.

Clearly, though, the methods can lead us astray. On one end of the spectrum they can degenerate into a highly specific hunt for topical allusions. Such allusions seldom affect our understanding of a Shakespearean play—even on the rare occasions when the allusions can be satisfactorily verified. On the other end, the methods can float away on the ungraspable current of the "ideas of the time"; the connection between literary text and milieu can become as varying to the sense of each reader as Hamlet's cloud is to Polonius. The career of Frances Yates, an important scholar in the "milieu" tradition, is pertinent here. I am obviously in agreement with her perception of the failure of scholars to explore Shakespeare's Stuart milieu: "[The] comparative neglect of the historical climate of Shakespeare's later years corresponds to the general neglect, in the history of Europe as a whole, of the early years of the seventeenth century. . . . It is strange that Shakespearean scholarship seems to have paid so much more attention to the biographical, the literary, or the critical aspects of its vast subject than to investigating Shakespeare's work in relation to the thought movements of his age."[3] Yates's book is a fascinat-

---

[3]Frances Yates, *Shakespeare's Last Plays: A New Approach* (London, 1975), pp. 80, 102.

ing, provocative, and useful one if we keep in mind that it was intended as a preliminary sally to be refined by others "through future work." But many of her speculations are so farfetched that, as one of the first major forays using such methods, her book must be considered unfortunate.

Yates's central thesis itself is problematic: the Late Plays represent "an archaising revival in the Jacobean age. . . . [a return to] the world of Shakespeare's youth and its ideals" (p. 79). Shakespeare was not an idealist, in the first place, so it is hard to see the Late Plays as a *pure* return to "the ideals of Philip Sidney." The playwright was surely capable of recognizing that "you cannot go home again." Nor can one conceive that the revival, if it occurred, was not shaped according to the different artistic and political conditions the Stuarts brought with them. Nor does Yates offer convincing evidence for another main thesis of her book, namely, that Shakespeare was a partisan for the "new science" and therefore particularly interested in refurbishing the reputation of that strange man John Dee. It is hard to travel so far with Yates as to say that, in *The Tempest,* Shakespeare "chose to glorify a Dee-like magus" (p. 95), that "Prospero is clearly the magus as scientist" (p. 97), or that the play is "a reply to the censure [of Dee] by James" (p. 96). And when Yates asks if one "dare assert" that *The Tempest* is a "Rosicrucian manifesto" (p. 130), I at least feel obliged to answer one surely dare not. Shakespeare was not a Rosicrucian and did not write manifestos. In short, Yates's attempts to "relate Shakespeare to the history of the times" seem too boldly specific, too baldly propounded. Such speculations undermine the credibility of the method, and this is especially unfortunate because, even if true, they do not really help us better to appreciate the play. In this respect Yates's ideas remind me of her early study of *Love's Labour's Lost*—a spirited attempt to run down the many likely topical allusions in the play. Her book is unneces-

6

sary to an appreciation of that splendid Shakespearean exploration of the glorious and the criminal powers of words; indeed, it is a menace to such an appreciation.

A constant difficulty and challenge of milieu studies is to state as precisely as possible the relation between artistic or historical circumstances (and their flux) and the literary event. Consider Yates's hypothesis of an Elizabethan revival in the early seventeenth century. There is truth in this, but the truth is stated too simply. She might have spoken more accurately of the revival of a revival. After all, Elizabeth's court in the last years experienced something of an archaising urge itself. Graham Hough, concerned with *The Faerie Queene* (a product of the 1590s), wrote that Elizabeth's court saw a "fusion of a deliberate and indulged archaism with a surviving or revived ideal of conduct."[4] Also puzzling is Yates's mention of the "pervasive influence of Sidney" in relation to *The Tempest*. Sidney's *sprezzatura* does not have much in common with the Late Plays; in fact, the "art" of Prospero is almost exactly opposed to the ideal of *sprezzatura*. Prospero's is a salient and virtuosic art, an art of "vanity" more akin to the "honest haughtinesse and self-esteem . . . (which let envie call pride)" that John Milton was to profess in his *Apology for Smectymnuus* (1642).[5] A revival in Shakespeare's later years would have had to take place in the atmosphere of an entirely new artistic ethos—the ethos of the baroque. Thus Glynne Wickham can, I think justly, assert that *The Tempest* "succeeds in the baroque manner."[6] This may be one way of explaining why

---

[4]Graham Hough, *A Preface to The Faerie Queene* (New York, 1963), p. 223.

[5]John Milton, *Complete Prose Works,* ed. Don Wolfe et al. (New Haven, 1953–), I, p. 890.

[6]Glynne Wickham, "Masque and Anti-masque in *The Tempest,*" *Essays and Studies* 28 (1975): 14. See also Clifford Leech, "Masking and Unmasking in the Last Plays," in Carol Kay and Henry Jacobs, eds., *Shakespeare's Romances Reconsidered* (Lincoln, Nebraska, 1978), pp. 40–59.

the Late Plays are not like the plays of Shakespeare's youth, to
which Yates suggests a return, or to explain why *Love's
Labour's Lost,* for all the superficial parallels, is so utterly unlike *The Tempest.*

The preferable course for a milieu study, according to my
taste, is a middle one. The search for allusions results in an
approach too small for the literary text, and the history-of-
ideas or the pure historical approach becomes too large and
finally floats blimp-like from its moorings in the text. A milieu
study, avoiding these pitfalls, should produce a better ability to
read or experience in the theater what the playwright put into
his play. This is a matter of reading in perspective—a method
exemplified by D. J. Gordon's splendid explication "Rubens
and the Whitehall Ceiling," Angus Fletcher's *The Transcendental Masque,* Stephen Orgel's *The Illusion of Power,* or
Ernest Gilman's *The Curious Perspective,* to name a few excellent studies. With the Whitehall Ceiling, as I believe with *The
Tempest,* a central problem is one of knowing how to experience the political (that is to say courtly) meaning of the work.
Gordon made clear that for us moderns this is not easy: "It is
of course still, even now, notoriously hard for us to believe
that a great painting can have, could ever have had, a political
purpose."[7] After noting that many of the difficulties of de-
ciphering the meanings in the Rubens panels lie in "looking
too precisely for references to specific actions" (read "topical
allusions"), Gordon proceeds to a more general—and still the
most succinct and illuminating—description of what "happens" in the Rubens allegory.

A similar ignorance of political content has hindered our
experience of the Late Plays, *The Tempest* in particular.
Perhaps this is because the more fundamental sense of the
word *political* is seldom met with in Shakespeare studies. The

7D. J. Gordon, "Rubens and the Whitehall Ceiling," in *The Renaissance
Imagination,* ed. Stephen Orgel (Berkeley, Calif., 1975), pp. 24–50.

Late Plays are not normally thought of as political plays—except now and then by radical director/ideologues. There is no reference to them in L. C. Knights's chapter on Shakespeare in *Public Voices: Literature and Politics;* nor in the long chapter on "The Polity" in Norman Rabkin's *Shakespeare and the Common Understanding;* nor in H. M. Richmond's *Shakespeare's Political Plays,* where individual chapters are devoted to the histories, *Julius Caesar,* and *Coriolanus.* The implication is clear: plays with "politics" in them are the political ones. *Political,* however, means having to do with men living together in a *polis*—like the royal seats of Cymbeline's Britain, Leontes's Sicilia, Prospero's Milan, or Shakespeare's London. In this sense all but perhaps the earliest Latin-based plays by Shakespeare are political, and the Late Plays are highly political. I would even venture further that *The Tempest* is the most profoundly resonant political play Shakespeare ever wrote—as chapters five and six will demonstrate.

Others have suspected that we have not been sufficiently aware of the politics of courtliness in *The Tempest.* "In the case of *The Tempest* it is hard to see how anything short of royal resources and a royal sense of occasion could do it justice. Moreover, as contemporary performances and criticism reveal, we have little sympathy with Renaissance dramatic style, and hardly any real knowledge of it."[8] I have from the beginning of my interest in the Late Plays held the same suspicion that Brownlow expresses here. As with the Whitehall Ceiling, there is something in the Late Plays and, most strik-

[8]F. W. Brownlow, *Two Shakespearean Sequences* (Pittsburgh, 1977), p. 184. Glynne Wickham's reiterations in the last volume of his *Early English Stages, 1300–1660* (London, 1957–72) should leave little doubt that more must be learned about the influence of the Stuarts on drama. His conclusions greatly encouraged my work and some are worth reproducing here:

> It is thus the conditions of Court performance that should supply us with most of our data for production methods in the public theatres. They were thus not the exception, but the rule. It is ac-

ingly, in *The Tempest* that *faces* the court and courtly life. We must seek therefore to know more about the influence of the court on early Stuart drama.

My attempt to give outline and color to a unique but both chronologically and geographically diffuse artistic ethos has been necessarily wide-ranging. It is no surprise to me—and I hope will be no surprise to the reader—that I have not re-created the courtly aesthetic fully and "from the life." My methods are too much like those of the identi-kit or composite drawings used by the police to achieve a full re-creation. Before a lively sense of the aesthetic can emerge, researches in many areas beyond my expertise will be necessary. At the threshold of the topic, we still lack superlative biographies of James or his main courtiers. Nor are there any incisive studies of James's court and its sociological constitution. We have not been able to advance clearly and convincingly beyond the important (but problematical) studies of Shakespeare's more elite audiences made by Alfred Harbage and G. E. Bentley. Other approaches must also be brought to bear if we are to

---

cordingly in this direction that I think research should be directed in the years ahead.

(p. 29)

If . . . we persist in regarding performances in the public play-houses as the norm for Elizabethan and Jacobean acting companies . . . we place the cart firmly before the horse, misread the evidence by neglecting its historical context and falsify the artistic principles governing both play construction and stage conventions through-out the period . . . . One reason that may account for the all too frequent submissions to these temptations in recent years is the divorce which has regrettably sundered the study of English litera-ture from that of history and of architecture and the fine arts in the wake of ever-increasing specialization in our educational system.

(pp. 149–150)

All the facts . . . point clearly towards the copying or adaptation of Court precedents in Elizabethan and Jacobean public and private playhouses.

(p. 161)

understand courtly aesthetics in general and James's in particular. One might, for instance, pursue Kenneth Burke's intriguing definition of "the principle of courtship" in rhetoric as "the use of suasive devices for the transcending of social estrangement."[9] We need a closer application to courtly art of the "psychology of pictorial representation" discussed by E. H. Gombrich in *Art and Illusion*. We also need a study of the practical applications and effects of the comparatist aesthetic theories of the Renaissance as set forth, to name one excellent study, in John Steadman's *The Lamb and the Elephant: Ideal Imitation and the Context of Renaissance Allegory*. A better sense of the influence of Biblical allegory, exegesis, and mythography upon the courtly artistic environment would also prove valuable.

In any event, formulating precisely what I have achieved in the task of identification is not easy, since what is "royal" or "courtly" can be nebulous even in the best of times. Yates changed the title of her book for paperback distribution to *Magic and Majesty in Shakespeare's Late Plays,* and the title is now closer to what the book contains. But *majesty* does not help very much; it rather tends to obscure the more subtle emanations of royal power in artistic enterprises. The best way to describe how the courtly aesthetic works in Shakespeare's plays is suggested with reference to another subject by Donald Howard in *The Idea of the Canterbury Tales*. Speaking of the Melibee tale, he writes, "It is the focal point of an 'address to the court' which runs throughout *The Canterbury Tales*."[10] Note that Howard writes of *an* address, not *the* address; Chaucer was no more addressing the court than was Shakespeare. Howard goes on to define this "address to the court" as "not a dramatic unit like the 'groups' [of tales] but a

[9]Kenneth Burke, *A Rhetoric of Motives* (New York, 1950), p. 208.
[10]Donald Howard, *The Idea of the Canterbury Tales* (Berkeley, 1976), p. 315.

recurrent theme, a metastructure, which relies on a developed *engagement* between author and audience" (p. 315). This seems a sensible way of describing the influence of the courtly aesthetic on Shakespeare as well, that is, in terms of a metastructure of courtly preoccupations and significances embedded in his plays. Emphasis must fall on the prefix *meta*. The more explicit and realized the "address" becomes, the more the play loses its identity as a play—or in terms of the courtly aesthetic, the more the play transmogrifies into a masque, processional entertainment, or staged equivalent of a panel from the Whitehall Ceiling. Our interest must rest, as Howard put it, on the "developed *engagement* between author and audience." That cannot be done for the most obviously important and powerful part of Shakespeare's audience, the court, without some knowledge of the aesthetic that court chose to honor and delight in. The ways such knowledge can be expressed vary from the more impressionistic analysis of Enid Welsford in *The Court Masque* to the highly specific drawing of parallels we find, for instance, in Glynne Wickham's interesting article "Masque and Anti-masque in *The Tempest*."

The reader has the right to ask in what tone of voice or frame of mind Shakespeare's "address to the court" is made. I suggest in chapter seven that the address is deeply ambivalent, and this requires comment because one might well feel this very ambivalence makes the address less "courtly." *The Tempest,* like most of Shakespeare's great plays, is a test of the commentator's Negative Capability, for in many respects it seems to make differing, even mutually exclusive, statements. How otherwise could critics have ranged so far apart in seeking the central impetus of the play: is it idyllic (J. D. Wilson), death-centered (F. W. Brownlow), reconciliatory (G. W. Knight), optimistic (R. W. Chambers), pessimistic (J. Kott), or both optimistic and pessimistic (F. Kermode)? This question is rather like the one Norman Rabkin has asked about *Henry V*: is Henry an ideal monarch or a Machiavellian militarist? Rabkin goes on to describe the kind of artistic method evident in *The Tempest:* "I am going to argue that . . . Shakespeare creates a work whose ultimate power is precisely the fact that it points in two opposite directions, virtually daring us to choose one of the two opposed interpretations it requires of us."[11] Rabkin continues: "The kind of ambiguity I have been describing in *Henry V,* requiring that we hold in balance incompatible and radically opposed views each of which seems exclusively true, is only an extreme version of the fundamental ambiguity that many critics have found at the center of the Shakespearean vision" (p. 295).

Now, one can pose a number of questions about *The Tempest* that seem to elicit contradictory answers. In Sidney's terms, is the world of the play a golden or brazen one; is it essentially idealistic or realistic? Is the play a monument to erected wit (a brave new politically healthy Milan) or to infected will (things of darkness, an insistence, as R. G. Hunter writes, on the "indestructibility of evil"[12])? Is the island really the soul of man, or is it the place where a history of the world is reenacted? A most intriguing question about the plot: does Prospero plan all along to act mercifully, or is the beginning of act 5 a true moment of ethical psychomachia and resolution?[13] Finally and most pertinently, is the courtly life de-

---

[11]Norman Rabkin, "Rabbits, Ducks, and *Henry V,*" *Shakespeare Quarterly* 28 (1977): 279. Janet Adelman arrives at a similar conclusion in *The Common Liar: An Essay on Antony and Cleopatra* (New Haven, Conn., 1973), pp. 169–71. See also "Ambivalence: the Dialectic of the Histories," in A. P. Rossiter's *Angel with Horns* (London, 1961), pp. 40–64.

[12]R. G. Hunter, *Shakespeare and the Comedy of Forgiveness* (New York, 1965), p. 240.

[13]The important passage is 5.1.17–30. This seems to me an absolutely crucial question for any reading or production of *The Tempest,* and it is remarkable how divided critical opinion is on the answer. Among those who believe real psychomachia is involved are Dover Wilson (*The Meaning of the*

picted as essentially good or evil in *The Tempest*? I am myself forced to a conclusion like Rabkin's by the consideration of such questions. *The Tempest* is "all of the above." It is neither a golden nor a brazen image of the human soul, the political state, or the history of the world, but an alchemical semistate of both metals. A sense of this ambivalence allows me to suggest that while *Hamlet* may offer the richest verbal experience in the canon and *King Lear* the greatest imaginative experience, *The Tempest* is Shakespeare's most perfectly balanced and comprehensive dramatic structure. Rabkin concludes that the "inscrutability of *Henry V* is the inscrutability of history" (p. 296). *The Tempest* is more inclusive: its inscrutability is the more general inscrutability of human nature and existence.

Tempest [Newcastle-upon-Tyne, England, 1936], pp. 14–18), Robert Egan (*Drama within Drama*, [New York, 1975], p. 111), and L. C. Knights ("*The Tempest*," in Tobias and Zolbrod, *Shakespeare's Late Plays*, pp. 26–27). Among those who think the decision for mercy is all along a *fait accompli* are E. M. W. Tillyard (*Shakespeare's Last Plays*, pp. 53–54), Don Cameron Allen (*Image and Meaning* [Baltimore, 1968], p. 80), and John Fraser ("*The Tempest* Revisited," *The Critical Review* [Melbourne, 1968]: 74).

    I am personally convinced the latter view is the right one. It is persuasively argued by Bertrand Evans in *Shakespeare's Comedies* (Oxford, 1960):

> [Shakespeare] could have represented Prospero in conflict with himself—but he rejects the possibility at the opening of Act V, when Ariel raises the question of punishment or forgiveness for the enemies helpless at Prospero's feet. Clearly, this question could have been made the cause of great inner struggle for Prospero, and had *The Tempest* centered on it dramatic tension would have been assured. But nowhere is Prospero's nature evinced with more finality than in the announcement of his intention—which suggests no struggle, but only that struggle might have been had he been less than he is [5.1.17–30 quoted]. Though until this statement we have ourselves not known Prospero's plans for his old enemies, we have not been made to suppose either that he was himself uncertain or that he had at first intended vengeance rather than forgiveness. Neither the announcement nor anything earlier suggests inner struggle before the decision is reached. Prospero is not Lear, who has to learn his lesson in human sympathy: whatever *The Tempest* is, it is not an account of Prospero's struggle with and final triumph over baser elements in himself.
>
> (pp. 333–34)

As with so many important questions of Shakespeare's personal opinion, we will never know what he thought about James, his court, or the aesthetic that flourished there. As usual, influences emanating from the court were subdued by his hand, and he subdued himself in them. He obviously found usable the courtly taste for the spectacular, for drama in which hard things are made easy (dramatic ease, comic ease, and courtly ease are intimately related), for the sweet delay of gratification, for the stasis of illusion as opposed to the movement of reality. And, as Brownlow has said, one cannot help feeling that royal resources were needed to give *The Tempest* its optimum theatrical potency. There *is* theatrical majesty in the play.

But Shakespeare was no courtly partisan, even in purely artistic matters. Beautiful as courtly art might be, it could also keep men "in false gaze." "What a world of Love and Bee-like Loyalty and Heart-adherence did the Stuarts trick and tyrannize away!" wrote Coleridge.[14] That sad process could hardly have escaped the notice of royal servants like Shakespeare, who were intimately connected with the king's revels. A notable part of Stuart "trickery" lay in the lavish courtly aesthetic that dynasty sponsored; the Stuarts naturally gravitated toward the unreal world of art because the realities of courtly finances, social change, and burgeoning antimonarchical sentiment would scarcely support their wishes. The courtly aesthetic was delimited by reality—the ultimate reality coming in the form of a headsman's axe. The aesthetic is likewise circumscribed in *The Tempest*. All of act 5 is preparatory for a return to the complexity of the real world after the sojourn in the magical, wish-fulfillment world of the island. The end of the play brings the return to a place where wishes, power (including artistic power), and life itself will be limited.

Illusion requires an end, but reality does not. Thus *The*

[14]Coleridge's marginal comment, collected in *Inquiring Spirit,* ed. Kathleen Coburn (London, 1951), p. 321.

15

Tempest, for all the aspects of the play that give one a sense of closure, has no true end. There is nothing in it like the apotheosis of James in the Whitehall Ceiling (Plate 1).[15] There is rather a powerful ambivalence toward courtly life: the reconstituted court in Milan will still disconcertingly mingle Mirandas, Antonios, Ferdinands, and Sebastians. Caliban himself may not be present, but his spirit will be. The question is not so much one of Shakespeare's approval or disapproval of the courtly life or aesthetic *per se.* The only conclusion one can draw—the same conclusion we must draw from *The Faerie Queene*—is that the price of the ideal courtly life is eternal moral and political vigilance. This is something neither Spenser nor Shakespeare undertook to guarantee in his vision of the courtly life.

Very early in the reign of James I, Shakespeare came to write the first of two memorable speeches equating departure from the stage with our inevitable exit from the theater of the world:

> Life's but a walking shadow, a poor player,
> That struts and frets his hour upon the stage,
> And then is heard no more. It is a tale
> Told by an idiot, full of sound and fury,
> Signifying nothing.
>
> (*Macbeth,* 5.5.24–28)

The nihilistic and annihilating sense of "nothing" reverberates with particular force through many of Shakespeare's middle-period plays. In these—one thinks of *Hamlet, Troilus and Cressida, King Lear, Antony and Cleopatra, Timon of Athens,* and *Coriolanus*—all too often only the man "who knows nothing, is once seen to smile" (*Macbeth* 4.3.167). In these

---

[15]D. J. Gordon's essay "Rubens and the Whitehall Ceiling" in *The Renaissance Imagination,* ed. Stephen Orgel (Berkeley, 1975), elaborates on the iconography of the ceiling.

1. *Painting of the Ceiling in the Banqueting House at Whitehall*, 1720 engraving by Simon Gribelin (after Peter Paul Rubens, original installed 1635). Reproduced by permission of the Yale Center for British Art.

Upper central panel: James presides over the crowning (by Minerva or Britannia?) of the new-born Kingdom of Great Britain, which unites England and Scotland. Overhead, putti hold the arms that James assumed when he proclaimed himself King of Great Britain in 1604. At the bottom, the putto setting fire to the arms signifies the king's pacifying power. *Central panel:* James's apotheosis. *Lower central panel:* the pacific king refuses victory through war. *Upper left panel:* Temperance (?) defeats Profligacy. *Upper right panel:* Liberality (?) defeats Avarice. *Lower left panel:* Heroic Virtue (Hercules?) defeats Rebellion. *Lower right panel:* Wisdom (Minerva?) defeats Lust.

works man and his ideals are rendered naked, unaccommodated, and vulnerable by knowledge of the presence of evil.
The spare Elizabethan stage, which inevitably emphasizes the
actor and his lines, served these plays well, and still does. In
keeping not only with *Macbeth* but the other tragedies and
problem plays of the distressed middle period, Macbeth's idea
of the ultimately futile and ephemeral nature of life is suggested in imagery of emptiness and barrenness borrowed
from the stage of the Globe Theater, where the main properties were merely costumes and a few portable pieces of furniture. Macbeth's words are for the era of the speaking actor
—the period in theatrical history perhaps best symbolized by
the sound and fury of the soliloquizing player.

Less than a decade afterward came the palinode in *The
Tempest:*

> Our revels now are ended. These our actors,
> As I foretold you, were all spirits, and
> Are melted into air, into thin air:
> And, like the baseless fabric of this vision,
> The cloud-capp'd towers, the gorgeous palaces,
> The solemn temples, the great globe itself,
> Yea, all which it inherit, shall dissolve,
> And, like an insubstantial pageant faded,
> Leave not a rack behind. We are such stuff
> As dreams are made on; and our little life
> Is rounded with a sleep.
>
> (4.1.148–58)

Prospero bids farewell to a stage far different from the stage of
Macbeth, a stage that has supplied a feast for the eyes, splendor and magnificence.[16] The focus of the Revels Speech is not

---

[16]A passage from Palingenius's *Zodiacus* is often cited as a source for the
Revels Speech. I do not think the case convincing. Palingenius's lines are a
more general expression of the theme *sic transit gloria mundi* and are notably
poor in imagery. The theatrical references in the speech ("revels," "actors,"
"pageant," "rack," and probably "stuff") and the specific images ("baseless
fabric," "cloud-capp'd towers," "gorgeous palaces," "solemn temples,"

upon the single player but upon many "spirits" who have, led
by a great impresario, made a complex artistic "vision" possible. The poor player of a few years earlier now finds himself
surrounded by the imagery of a new mode of dressing and
filling the stage. The present study is an attempt to show how
Shakespeare's changing stage imagery reflects actual changes
in English theatrical fashions during the years intervening between *Macbeth* and *The Tempest*.

Macbeth addresses his farewell to an audience and an
aesthetic we generally associate with Elizabethan drama.
Prospero's speech, however, alludes to another aesthetic tradition based upon the spectacular illusionism of the *trompe l'œil,
coup de théâtre,* and *deus ex machina*. This aesthetic was expensive and required not only sophisticated artistry but sophisticated technologies. Its development was limited to the courts
of royalty or the palaces of wealthy noblemen. Prospero is
bidding farewell in imagery spawned by the courtly aesthetic,[17] and one question that I will pursue shortly is why *The*

"great globe") are Shakespeare's own invention. T. W. Baldwin rightly
places Palingenius in the "dim aura" behind the speech. For a discussion of
the issue, see his *Smalle Latine and Lesse Greeke* (Urbana, Illinois, 1944), I, pp.
673–77. Another possible source frequently mentioned is a passage from Sir
William Alexander's *Darius* (London, 1603). This is subject to the same reser-
vations that apply to Palingenius, though there are a few imagistic parallels.

[17]Indeed, it would be easy to find other speeches from pageants and
masques at court, not only for James but also for Elizabeth and many continental monarchs, that amount to paraphrases of the Revels Speech. One
example is the conclusion to Francis Davison's *Masque of Proteus,* performed
for Elizabeth in 1594:

> Thus on *Shrove-Tuesday,* at the Court, were our Sports and Revels
> ended . . . now our Principality [of the Revels] is determined;
> which, although it shined very bright in ours, and other Darkness;
> yet, at the Royal Presence of Her Majesty, it appeared as an
> obscured Shadow: In this, not unlike unto the Morning-star,
> which looketh very chearfully in the World, so long as the Sun
> looketh not on it: Or, as the great Rivers, that triumph in the Mul-
> titude of their Waters, until they come unto the Sea. *Sic vinci, sic
> mori pulchrum.*
>
> (*Gesta Grayorum,* ed. W. W. Greg [1914: rpt.,
> ed. Desmond Bland, Liverpool, 1968], pp. 88–89)

Tempest, though presumably written for audiences not necessarily courtly, came to be imbued with that courtly aesthetic, not only in the imagery of the Revels Speech but in the texture and form of the entire play.

We are accustomed to think of Shakespeare's early career as having begun primarily with drama and poetry of courtly ambience, though most scholars still place the first historical tetralogy at the beginning. It is clear from the majority of early allusions just where his genius was thought to lie, for we read of "Honie-tong'd *Shakespeare,*" whose characters speak with "sugred tongues," of his "hony-flowing Vaine," and of the "faire blossome" of his lines.[18] When a character in *The Returne from Pernassus,* part one, asks to hear "Mr. Shakspear's veine," he is referred to "Venus and Adonis."[19] This epyllion was his first published work as well as the most popular of all his writings—if editions (ten by 1616 and six more by 1636) are any indication of popularity. In the same passage from *The Returne from Pernassus,* Gullio vows he shall have Shakespeare's portrait "in my study at the courte."

At career's end Shakespeare again turned his attention to the realm of courtly art. Perhaps our attention has not often been drawn to this return because he came back not to Elizabeth's but to James's court. Times and fashions had changed enormously since those palmy days of the sonnets, the long poems, *Love's Labour's Lost, Romeo and Juliet,* and *A Midsummer Night's Dream.* The style of Lyly, Peele, or even Sidney was no longer apt; when Shakespeare came again to write plays with an eye to the court, he had to make adjustments and move in new directions that are apparent in the Late Plays. Scholars and directors have had difficulty in com-

---

[18]These references are from John Munro, ed., *The Shakespeare Allusion Book* (1909; rpt. London, 1932). Respectively, they are by John Weever, "Ad Gulielmum Shakespeare" (1595), I, p. 24; Richard Barnfield, "A Remembrance of Some English Poets" (1598), I, p. 51; William Barkstead, "Mirrha" (1607), I, p. 175.

[19]Munro, *The Shakespeare Allusion Book,* I, p. 68.

ing to terms with these plays, a difficulty that perhaps reflects the playwright's situation: Shakespeare was at the time of writing responding to diverse aesthetic pressures. These pressures came from different sectors of his artistic environment, and I have chosen *The Tempest* as a vehicle for examining these pressures because it uniquely offers the "abstract and brief chronicle of time" that Hamlet says a good play will represent. *The Tempest* is a good abstract, or epitome, in drama of a clearly discernible and chronologically brief segment in the graph of changing fashions I associate with the efflorescence of the early Jacobean court. The play is an epitome because Shakespeare was attempting to satisfy as many different audiences as might gather to see a play between 1609 and 1611. If *The Tempest,* like the other romances, strikes us as difficult, experimental in respect to his former works, a dramatic vision hard to grasp in its constituent parts (however harmonious and charming), and subject to disconcertingly varying interpretations, one reason may be that we have not appreciated the confusion of theatrical realms Shakespeare himself was struggling to transform into a coherent artistic order.

Shakespeare, as must all successful playwrights, recognized the truth of the axiom, "Every writer must governe his Penne according to the Capacitie of the Stage he writes to, both in the Actor and the Auditor."[20] In his last creative years he had to write for auditors of increasingly distinct capacities. The growing profitability of performance at court and the King's Men's expansion into the more sophisticated Blackfriars Theater made writing specifically for a Globe audience no longer wise. The situation called for pragmatism, and nothing could be less subject to cavil than Shakespeare's willingness

---

[20]The printer's address for *The Two Merry Milkmaids* (1620), quoted in F. P. Wilson, "The Elizabethan Theater," *Neophilologus* 39 (1955): 43. Compare Jonson's remark (VIII, 587): "The true Artificer will . . . speake to the capacity of his hearers."

and ability to heed the practicalities of his profession. Samuel Johnson well remonstrated: "Let it be remembered that our authour well knew what would please the audience for which he wrote."[21]

No playwright possessing Shakespeare's acumen, able to "please all" as he had done with Hal, Falstaff, Hamlet, and Iago, and faced with his obvious task of writing plays for performance in varying places—no such playwright would choose to conquer one stage if it was in his power to conquer all. *The Tempest* was his most successful attempt to suspend his dramaturgical skills, so to speak, between competing theatrical fashions. Here is the "friendly Shakespeare" of the "vulger Element," who could set comedians riding while tragedians stood on tip-toe, the "honie-tong'd" Ovidian, the harsh creator of honest Iago (in Antonio), the poet of nature, and the poet of art.

As a writer, Shakespeare faced the problem of dressing his dramatic ideas for increasingly discrete and discreet audiences. Speaking of poetic decorum in his *Arte of English Poesie,* George Puttenham observed, "There is a decency of apparel in respect of the place it is to be used: as, in the Court to be richly apparrelled: in the countrey to weare more plain & homely garments."[22] This decorum is simple enough. Shakespeare, however, was forced by competing theatrical fashions to observe a more complex decorum. Encouraged to write for courtly and public delight, he had to include both rich and

[21]From Johnson's notes on *King Lear* (*Johnson on Shakespeare,* ed. Arthur Sherbo [New Haven, Conn., 1968], II, p. 703). Note also Johnson's comment on *3 Henry VI,* 4.6.70 ("This pretty lad will prove our country's bliss"): "He was afterwards Henry VII . . . Shakespeare knew his trade. Henry VII was grandfather to Queen Elizabeth, and the king from whom James inherited" (II, 607).

[22]George Puttenham, *The Arte of English Poesie* (1589; rpt. London, 1970), p. 238. Compare this passage from *As You Like It* (3.2.45–48): "Those that are good manners at the court are as ridiculous in the country as the behaviour of the country is most mockable at the court."

plain apparel in his plays. The difficulty of framing these diverse and frequently antagonistic elements within a single
work was not quickly or painlessly overcome, as *Pericles* and
Cymbeline indicate. But Shakespeare finally solved it.

My present interest is in one particular source of influence
on *The Tempest*, namely, that exerted by the court of James.[23]
I hope to draw upon a body of drama and related artistic
genres that developed in the first years of James's reign and in
the last years of Shakespeare's activity. This body of dramatic,
semidramatic, and visual creations has not been examined as
such, most obviously because the early reign of James has
evoked little scholarly interest. Frances Yates has justly observed that "attempts to relate Shakespeare to the history of
his times have concentrated mainly on the Elizabethan Shakespeare. Shakespeare and the Jacobean age is a less familiar
topic."[24] Yates's comment brings us to the related problem of
the weakness of our critical terms, specifically the vexing and
ubiquitous epithets *Elizabethan* and *Jacobean*. A serious matter
is at stake here.

Shakespeare is considered an Elizabethan dramatist. But
René Wellek and others have noted that the term Elizabethan
has over the years insensibly extended its reach not only in
chronology but also in content. The term finds use not merely
in drama and literature but in most other fields as well.[25]
Jacobean, on the other hand, has failed to develop accordingly
and still refers primarily to a distinct kind of drama best

[23]The influence of the "popular" aesthetic is beyond the range of this
book and has, at any rate, received far more critical attention. For a good
recent study and an extensive bibliography on the popular tradition, see
Robert Weimann's *Shakespeare and the Popular Tradition in the Theater* (Baltimore, 1978).

[24]Yates, *Shakespeare's Last Plays*, p. 80.

[25]René Wellek, "The Concept of Baroque in Literary Scholarship,"
Journal of Aesthetics 5 (1946): 77–109. Virgil Whitaker's essay "Shakespeare
the Elizabethan," *Rice University Studies* 61 (1974): 141–51, is typical of the
bias in favor of the epithet.

exemplified by Cyril Tourneur's *Revenger's Tragedy* or John Webster's *White Devil*. The term, which has content drawn from plays other than Shakespeare's, is not normally associated with him—even though a third of his plays, among them his greatest, were written after James came to the throne. The critical weakness of the term Jacobean is apparent from perusal of Una Ellis-Fermor's *Jacobean Drama* (1936). Apt as her generalizations are, they require one to ignore Shakespeare's Late Plays. Twenty years later Madeleine Doran again suggested in an interesting way the difficulty of pinpointing the Elizabethan/Jacobean "divide" in the canon. "Some of the greater Jacobeans—Shakespeare (in *Hamlet*), Marston, Tourneur, Webster, and Middleton" were able to develop a "tragedy of evil."[26] One might note, first, that Doran defines Shakespeare as a Jacobean by referring to a play indubitably written while the queen was still alive, and, second, that an obverse of the tragedy of evil would be a "comedy of good"—a phrase agreeably descriptive of the Late Plays. It is thus not so odd that we should feel uncomfortable calling Shakespeare a Jacobean, though in strict truth we must do so. Clifford Leech's trenchant idea that Jacobean writers knew much of hell but little of heaven is pertinent to the so-called Jacobean tragedies of Shakespeare, Webster, Tourneur, and Middleton, but scarcely to the plays that are the focus of this study.[27] For they manifest a strong literary fashion that virtually point by point contradicts our general notion of

[26]Madeleine Doran, *Endeavors of Art: A Study of Form in Elizabethan Drama* (Madison, Wis., 1954), p. 337.

[27]Interestingly, it does not occur to Maynard Mack to discuss the Late Plays in his article, "The Jacobean Shakespeare," in *Jacobean Theatre, Stratford-upon-Avon Studies* 1, ed. J. R. Brown (1960): 11–42. Anne Barton also speaks, necessarily ignoring the Late Plays, of our "underlying and guiding conviction that tragedy is the dominant Jacobean form" ("He that plays the King: Ford's *Perkin Warbeck* and the Stuart History Play," in *English Drama: Form and Development,* ed. Marie Axton and Raymond Williams [Cambridge, England, 1977], p. 70).

Jacobean drama—a literary fashion that is optimistic, constructive, civilized, regenerating, and rich in artifice.

R. W. Chambers long ago exploded the simplistic notion that "under Elizabeth Shakespeare was happy, under James unhappy" or that "the accession of James I ushered in a period of cynicism and gloom, self-indulgence and crime"; and F. P. Wilson, rejecting the insistence on "Jacobean pessimism," followed up with what must be the only sensible approach: "There are differences; to maintain that there is no change would be as gross an error as to maintain that all was change."[28] I think the real difficulty is that there are two dichotomies here: one lies in the more general changes in national mood, in the royal style of governance, and in the economy and efficiency of the monarchy as Stuarts succeeded Tudors; the other lies in the stunning and more abrupt change in Shakespeare's dramatic style marked by *Timon of Athens* and *Pericles*. These two dichotomies do not tally chronologically, convenient though it would be for Shakespearean critics if they did. Nor do they tally in another important way. The third chapter of Ecclesiastes will help to illustrate what I mean:

> To every thing there is a season, and a time to every
> purpose under the heaven:
> A time to be born, and a time to die;
> A time to plant, and a time to pluck up that which is
> planted;
> A time to kill, and a time to heal;
> A time to break down, and a time to build up;
> A time to weep, and a time to laugh;
> A time to mourn, and a time to dance;
> A time to cast away stones, and a time to gather stones
> together;

[28]R. W. Chambers, "The Elizabethan and the Jacobean Shakespeare," in *Man's Unconquerable Mind* (London, 1939), pp. 250, 267; F. P. Wilson, *Elizabethan and Jacobean* (Oxford, 1945), pp. 17–18.

A time to embrace, and a time to refrain from
                                        embracing;
A time to get, and a time to lose.

All of the negative members of these antitheses could be
pointedly marshalled to describe "Jacobean" tragedy, but
they would apply not at all to (early) Jacobean history. Most
Englishmen of 1604 or 1605, remembering the increasing sense
of crisis and uncertainty as Gloriana decayed, would have
applied the constructive side of Ecclesiastes to the new
dynasty. And anyone familiar with the tenor of Stuart praise
and propaganda or familiar with the optimistic mood in England up until the death of Prince Henry in 1612 would agree
that the positive members of the Biblical antitheses apply best
not to the "good old days" of the queen but to the peaceful
Stuart transition. Of course, it is absurdly simplistic to set this
Biblical template against the actual history of the Tudor–
Stuart succession. But it is less absurd—and I think most
suggestive—to set the passage from Ecclesiastes against the
Shakespearean canon—*if* the fulcrum is set, not on 24 March
1603 when Elizabeth died, but some four years later, shortly
after Shakespeare seems to have given up on his *Timon of
Athens* project. For Shakespeare, it appears, there was a season
to write of dying, killing, mourning, weeping, and casting
stones; hence *Timon, Coriolanus,* and the great preceding
tragedies. But a time appears suddenly to have come for writing of healing, planting, giving birth, laughing, dancing, and
embracing. The playwright became more concerned with get-
ting than with losing; hence the Late Plays. This, the most
intriguing watershed in Shakespeare's career, is poorly served
by the terms Elizabethan and Jacobean as they are normally
used. The latter concept needs to be dissociated from its
tragic metier; it needs more critical shape and fullness,
which the following chapters will provide.

26

· II ·

SHAKESPEARE AND THE JACOBEAN ARTISTIC REVOLUTION

*B*EFORE APPROACHING *The Tempest* or the Late Plays generally, one must consider the tenor of literature toward the end of Elizabeth's life and during the first years after the accession of James. This perspective is necessary if we are to understand the dilemma Shakespeare faced as Jacobean theatrical fashions diverged: in a few years he would have to decide whether to employ his talents in public or in private, courtly service—or, by some special dramatic alchemy, in both.

In England just after the turn of the century the terrible wages of royal chastity were finally paid. Every Englishman, like Essex, had to "wrastle with a Queens declining, or rather with her very setting Age (as we may term it), which, besides other respects, is commonly even of it selfe the more umbratious and apprehensive."[1] Fear of an uncertain or contested succession and its likely consequence, civil war, grew steadily. As one Frenchman observed, "All Europe believed that after the death of this great queen Elizabeth, England could only become a theater full of those most horrible and bloody tragedies one might expect in a state totally disordered and

[1] Sir Henry Wotton, "Of Robert Devereux . . . and George Villiers . . . Some Observations by way of Parallel in the time of their estates of Favour," in *Reliquiae Wottonianae* (London, 1651), p. 11.

27

desolated."[2] And the English theater itself was indeed full of "horrible and bloody tragedies" at this time. An English audience perhaps sensed a special import in the dark visions of the *polis* to be found in *Julius Caesar, Hamlet, Troilus and Cressida, The Malcontent,* and *Bussy D'Ambois.*

The historical moment was too oppressive to support the idyllic, optimistic, escapist literature of a complacent court; it was rather a time for facing realities, revulsion, disillusionment, and heroes dressed in black. The tarnishing effect upon the Elizabethan golden age in literature was general. In his *Loves Martyr* (1601) Robert Chester expressed a typical fear that the Phoenix Queen Elizabeth

> will decay,
> And from her ashes never will arise
> An other Bird.

(p. 7)

He goes on to describe the Ovidian courtly palladium as properly devastated:

> *Vesta* she told, her Temple was defiled:
> *Juno* how that her nuptiall knot was broken;
> *Venus* from her sonne Cupid was exiled:
> And *Pallas* tree with ignorance was shoken:
>   *Bellona* rav'd at Lordlike cowardice,
>   And *Cupid* that fond Ladies were so nice.

(p. 1)[3]

---

[2]Thomas Pelletier, *Discours Politicque à tres-hault et tres-puissant Roy Jacques premier* (London, 1603), p. 41, my translation. Thomas Dekker expressed a similar fear in *The Magnificent Entertainment* (1604): "The sorrow and amazement, that like an earthquake began to shake the distempered body of this Iland (by reason of our late Soveraigns departure) being wisely and miraculously prevented, and the feared wounds of a civill sword (as *Alexanders* fury was with Musicke) being stopt from bursting forth, by the sound of Trompets that proclaimed King *James:* All mens eyes were presently turnd to the North" (*The Dramatic Works,* ed. Fredson Bowers [Cambridge, England, 1953–61], II, p. 253).

[3]Robert Chester, *Loves Martyr: or, Rosalins Complaint,* ed. Alexander

The publication of romances falls off sharply in this period, as does the writing of epyllia, a favorite courtly genre. The popularity of the sonnet sequence, another stalwart courtly genre, also shows a marked decline after 1600. And there are distinct signs that creative energy was being replaced by uninspired hackwork in all these courtly forms. This debilitation may be seen, for example, in Chester's sprawling, otiose *Loves Martyr,* in the proliferation of mediocre compendia like *Englands Helicon* (1600), *Englands Parnassus* (1600), *Bel-vedere* (1600), and *Wit's Theater* (1599), as well as in the dreadful epyllion "Transformed Metamorphosis" (1600).

If the literature of the years surrounding the death of Elizabeth is dominated by any sensibility at all, Montaigne personifies it. His desire to judge man "by himself, not by his finery," his celebration of the virtues of solitariness and abhorrence of courtly fashions, his preference for the plain style and plain speaking, and his consistent expression of the littleness, ignorance, and vacillation of man are, broadly generalizing, hallmarks of the two genres most characteristic of the English scene at this time—the verse satire and the stage satire. Such satires, frequently directed toward the courtly aesthetic, could scarcely flourish but at a time when the court was weakening and vulnerable, as in the queen's last years. How vacant, effete, and distant seems the grandeur of Gloriana's court in Jonson's *Every Man out of His Humour,* first of the corrosive stage satires:

Grosart (London, 1878), pp. 7, 1. In his "conclusion" Chester implies that he, offering Ovidian mythological fare, is already out of step with the times:

> For the Satyricall fond applauded vaines,
> Whose bitter worme-wood spirite in some straines,
> Bite like the Curres of Ægypt those that love them,
> Let me alone, I will be loth to move them.
> (p. 133)

The trend Chester here alludes to is perhaps typified in drama by Jonson's "comicall satyr," *Every Man out of His Humour* (1600).

A man lives there [at court], in that divine rapture, that hee will thinke himselfe i' the ninth heaven for the time, and lose all sense of mortalitie whatsoever; when he shall behold such glorious (and almost immortall) beauties, heare such angelicall and harmonious voices, discourse with such flowing and *ambrosian* spirits, whose wits are as suddaine as lightning, and humourous as *nectar;* Oh: it makes a man al *quintessence,* and *flame* & lifts him up (in a moment) to the verie christall crowne of the skie.

(III, 556–57)

It is not difficult to see in this a Jonsonian parody of the kind of courtly vision Calidore experiences on Mount Acidale in book 6 of *The Faerie Queene* (discussed below, pp. 203–207).

The satirical attack was carried out in "Tearms of quick Camphire & Salt-peeter phrases" by many verse writers; even Sir Philip Sidney, more respected than any other courtly writer, was "not exempt for prophanation, / But censur'd for affectation" by Edward Guilpin.[4] Satirists like Donne may have been writing these verses privately before, but only toward the turn of the century did they burst into publication. All in all, this time was aptly characterized by Dekker's sarcastically entitled, gloomy *Wonderfull Yeare 1603.*[5]

Though the widely accepted yet still vague chronology of plays makes generalization risky, one senses that Shakespeare moved with the mood of the times. Succeeding upon the aureate courtly comedies and the plangent glory of *Henry V* (the final martial glow, one might feel, of the defeat of the Spanish armada) is a turning in *Julius Caesar* toward subjects of political dissolution, the fabric of a decaying world, and human degradation.[6] As Granville-Barker suggested, the idealized

[4]Edward Guilpin, *Skialetheia* (1598; rpt. Chapel Hill, N.C., 1974), pp. 64, 91.

[5]See G. B. Harrison's preface to Nicholas Breton's *Melancholike Humours* (1600; rpt. London, 1929), which describes England's grim mood in 1600–03.

[6]In "*Julius Caesar:* Rupture in the Bond," *Journal of English and Germanic*

figure was pushed to the periphery or worse, and he was replaced by characters like Hamlet, with all his "forms, moods,
shapes of grief." "And where now is that fine upstanding
gentleman, Henry V? He is still at hand, and still commands
our unreserved admiration. But his name is Fortinbras, and he
is often (though he shouldn't be) cut out of the play altogether."[7] The plays Shakespeare began to write in these
troubled years undermined that part of his reputation which
marked him as a courtly writer.[8] And so in the last of the
Pernassus trilogy (1601–02; 1606 quarto) we find this remarkable indication of the change: "Few of the university pen
playes well, they smell too much of that writer *Ovid,* and that
writer['s] *Metamorphosis,* and talke too much of *Proserpina &
Juppiter.* Why heres our fellow *Shakespeare* puts them all
downe."[9] Shakespeare, too, began to show himself capable of
a potent mixture of combative cynicism and vigorous, direct,
realistic dramaturgy.

In this period Shakespeare moved more and more into the
public theatrical arena, well described by Thomas Dekker in
The Gull's Hornbook (1609) as a democratic "place . . . so free
in entertainment, allowing a stool as well as to the farmer's
son as to your templar; that your stinkard has the selfsame
liberty to be there in his tobacco-fumes, which your sweet
courtier hath."[10] Most of Shakespeare's characters popular
with the public are found in the plays of the middle period: of
allusions to Shakespearean and Jonsonian characters between

Philology 72 (1973): 311–28, Marvin Vawter argues forcefully that in this play
Shakespeare goes "beyond Hooker to probe the true cause of social perver-
sion and political disharmony."

[7]Harley Granville-Barker, "From Henry V to Hamlet," in *Studies in
Shakespeare,* ed. Peter Alexander (London, 1964), p. 85.

[8] "The sweet wittie soule of *Ovid* lives in mellifluous and hony-tongued
Shakespeare" (Frances Meres, "Palladis Tamia" [1598], in John Munro, ed.,
The Shakespeare Allusion Book [London, 1932], I, p. 46).

[9]*Ibid.,* I, p. 102.

[10]George Dekker, *The Gull's Hornbook* (1609), ed. R. B. McKerrow
(1904; rpt. New York, 1971), p. 49.

1601 and 1680, twenty-four of the twenty-five most frequently mentioned are from middle-period plays (*Julius Caesar* to *Coriolanus*), and there are no clear allusions to characters from the Late Plays.[11]

With this drift toward the public theatrical arena Shakespeare's style changed accordingly, acclimating to public theatrical fashions: Anthony Scoloker wrote in 1604 that "to come home to the vulgars *Element,* like *Friendly Shakespeare's Tragedies,* where the *Commedian* rides, when the *Tragedian* stands on Tip-toe: Faith it [an epistle to the reader] should please all, like Prince *Hamlet.*"[12] From "honey-tongued" to "friendly" Shakespeare in barely six years—these epithets help us distinguish the early and middle periods of the playwright's career.

An overview of the middle-period plays makes clear a movement toward a public theatrical aesthetic: more literalness, more "realism," more individualized groping for a hold upon the complexities of existence and morality. These traits were antagonistic to the courtly aesthetic, the concern of which was to express the ritualized simplicity of the social structure and to display the richness and complexities of art itself. There is also progressively less prettiness, less of the insulation of romance in the middle-period plays. Social certainties and self-confident heroes and heroines are replaced with characters torn by inner psychic turmoil. Such is the burden of a comment made by Walter Pater on *Measure for Measure:*

> The old "moralities" exemplified most often some rough-and-ready lesson. Here the very intricacy and subtlety of the moral world itself, the difficulty of

[11]See G. E. Bentley's *Shakespeare and Jonson* (Berkeley, 1945) and a recent and critical reexamination of Bentley's compendium of allusions, David Frost's *The School of Shakespeare* (Cambridge, England, 1968).

[12]Munro, *The Shakespeare Allusion Book,* I, p. 133.

seizing the true relations of so complex a material, the
difficulty of just judgment, of judgment that shall not
be unjust, are the lessons conveyed.[13]

Most of the plays from *Julius Caesar* to *Coriolanus* explore the
central dramatic *agon* of good versus evil that Pater finds in
Measure for Measure.

A key word for the middle plays is *diminution*. Their
seeming purpose is often to bring men and their ideals to
nothing, to extinction. As a culmination of this period we
have the devastating trio of *King Lear, Timon of Athens,* and
Coriolanus. The first dramatizes Montaigne's admonition to
judge man "by himself, not by his finery. . . . Measure him
without his stilts; let him put aside his riches and honors, let
him present himself in his shirt."[14] Shakespeare goes further
and presents Lear naked and unaccommodated. In *Timon* he
portrays not only the folly of a rich man but also the death of

[13]Walter Pater, *Appreciations* (1889; rpt. London, 1924), p. 182. Patrick
Cruttwell makes similar comments in his examination of Shakespeare's
change of style from his early to middle plays in *The Shakespearean Moment*
(London, 1954). See especially his second chapter, "Donne and the 'New-
Found Methods.' " Cruttwell observes in the middle plays a greater desire to
"encompass . . . complexities and incongruities" and an abandonment of
"virtually all those variegated forms of 'poetic diction' which the earlier
Elizabethans, each in his own way, all submitted to" (p. 56). The reluctance of
critics, noted by Cruttwell in 1954, to examine changes of fashion in detail
seems still apparent: "It is fashionable to sneer at 'fashions' in poetry; but the
truth seems to be that to be 'fashionable' (that is, to feel what style is possible
here and now) is more important than critics and reviewers . . . are inclined to
allow" (p. 71).

That *The Tempest* is a romance-based play may be one reason critics
have seemed encouraged to treat it wholly apart from its historical context, as
witness Coleridge: "*The Tempest,* I repeat, has been selected as a specimen of
the romantic drama; i.e., of a drama, the interests of which are independent of
all historical facts and associations" (*Coleridge's Writings on Shakespeare,* ed.
Terence Hawkes [New York, 1959], p. 203). Coleridge could not have been
more wrong.

[14]Michel de Montaigne, "Of the inequality that is between us," *The
Complete Essays,* trans. Donald Frame (Stanford, Calif., 1957), p. 190.

the courtly ethic; in this play he performs an anatomy on that great courtly virtue, magnanimity. *Timon* is, in short, the bleak obverse of *The Book of the Courtier*. Finally, in *Coriolanus* we have what one commentator has aptly called a description of the death of the metaphor of the body politic.[15] Here is the final victory of the many-headed monster that any court, or courtly aesthetic, sought to keep firmly subjugated. In *Coriolanus* rhetoric is, as Montaigne disparagingly put it, "an instrument invented to manipulate and agitate a crowd and a disorderly populace, and an instrument that is employed only in sick states, like medicine."[16] We are far from the courtly use of rhetoric to create beautiful, artful illusions and ideals, as in the hands of Sidney or Spenser.

The effect of these cynical and satirical middle-period works is to question the values of society, diminish respect for ideals and the men who hold them, and bring heroines and heroes from all to nothing. "O, see the monstrousness of man" (*Timon of Athens,* 3.2.72) might well serve as a pass-phrase for this time in Shakespeare's career.

I come now to a crucial question. After the turn of the century Shakespeare turned away from the gentility and civilization of the Court of Navarre in *Love's Labour's Lost* and the Court of Athens in *A Midsummer Night's Dream* to create the grim courts of *Hamlet, Macbeth, King Lear,* and *Timon*. Could such a playwright ever regain an edenic vision of the courtier's life (a sense that life at court is potentially good and desirable)? Could an imaginative courtly paradise thus lost ever be regained? We know that the answer is a qualified yes (qualified for reasons discussed at the end of chapter seven), but we have not sought adequately to understand why the

[15]David Hale, "*Coriolanus:* The Death of a Political Metaphor," *Shakespeare Quarterly* 22 (1971): 197–202.

[16]Montaigne, "Of the vanity of words," *The Complete Essays,* p. 222.

astonishing recovery of political optimism in the Late Plays took place. What happened to cause Shakespeare again to write plays infused with courtly morality and the courtly literary aesthetic?

The sources of this change become manifest, I believe, if we consider certain artistic events that can be quite precisely dated: 8 January 1604, 15 March 1604, 5 January 1605, and 30 August 1605. On these dates performances took place in the presence of the new English monarchs that radically changed Shakespeare's—and countless artists'—working environment. These performances served to announce the reestablishment of a vital court in London, and the form they took made immediately clear that the level of magnificence, complexity, and expense of courtly art under James would be far higher than under Elizabeth.[17]

On 8 January 1604 the first Jacobean court masque, Daniel's *Vision of the Twelve Goddesses,* was mounted. It was performed at Hampton Court "by the Queenes most Excellent Majesty, and her Ladies" and marks the beginning of the full-fledged masque's relatively short (about thirty-five years) though brilliant English lifespan. The masque was certainly the most intriguing, immense, and costly artistic fashion at court in the early years of James's reign, and as the quintessential expression of the courtly aesthetic, the masque inevitably influenced other genres.[18] It will figure often in the following pages.

James's inaugural entry into London, delayed by the

[17]An extensive bibliography for this area of research is David Bergeron's *Twentieth-Century Criticism of English Masques, Pageants, and Entertainments: 1558–1642* (San Antonio, Texas, 1972).

[18]Fuller awareness of the nature of the English masque has been made possible by the appearance of *Inigo Jones: The Theatre of the Stuart Court* (Berkeley, Calif., 1973), by Stephen Orgel and Roy Strong. See also Angus Fletcher's *The Transcendental Masque: An Essay on Milton's Comus* (Ithaca, N.Y., 1971).

plague, took place on 15 March 1604. To celebrate the event seven magnificent triumphal arches were erected in the streets of the City of London, and the king progressed through each one on his way to Whitehall. These immense baroque edifices announced a new courtly aesthetic to all London (Plate 2). The lavish arches—"théâtres des rues"—might well stand now as an indication of the kinds of gorgeous palaces and solemn temples that were to find their way into the masque and the drama, if only as poetic images. As Dekker implies, here was rhetoric for the eye rather than the ear: "These were the Mutes, and properties that helpt to furnish out this great *Italian Theater:* upon whose Stage, the sound of no voice was appointed to be heard."[19] The neoclassical architecture of these arches is similar to that reproduced on the scene-cloth of the court masques, as anyone familiar with the stage designs of Inigo Jones would recognize. At least one observer noted the similarity of these public edifices to more private courtly entertainments: "During these triumphes, shee [London] puts off her formall habite of Trade and Commerce, treading even Thrift it selfe under foote . . . [and] becomes a Reveller and a Courtier."[20]

The fifth of January 1605 saw the performance of the first collaborative effort of the greatest English masque designer, Inigo Jones, and the greatest English masque poet, Ben Jonson. To these men we owe a debt for much of our knowledge and interest in the masque as an art form; one must look to their collaborations for the sophistication and development of the basic masque form until the Civil War ended such extravagance. The *Masque of Blacknesse,* by its success at court and especially in the eyes of Queen Anne, crystallized the fun-

[19]Dekker, *The Magnificent Entertainment,* in the *Dramatic Works,* II, p. 265. Shakespeare was in all likelihood present, for the "Booke of Accoumpte of the royall proceedinge" lists him as receiving four and a half yards of scarlet cloth for his livery. See *Collections,* vol. 2, part 3, *The Malone Society* (Oxford, 1931), p. 78.

[20]*Ibid.,* p. 281.

2. "The Device called *Nova fœlix Arabia,*"
engraving by Stephen Harrison. From *Arches of
Triumph* (London, 1604). Reproduced by
permission of the Huntington Library, San
Marino, California.

The triumphal arch was erected for the entry of James into
London, 15 March 1604. In "the most eminent place" stands
Fame with her trumpet. The five Senses sit in a semicircle surrounding a wine-giving "Fount of *Vertue.*" At the foot of the
fountain lie "*Detraction* and *Oblivion,* Sleeping till his Majesties
approch."

damental qualities—and ambitions—of the most important entertainments at the Stuart court.

Finally and most importantly for the present study came a performance presented to Queen Anne by the University of Oxford (on the occasion of a visit by James) of a play called *Arcadia Reformed*. The date was 30 August 1605. This play, called a "Pastorall Trage-comedie" in its 1606 quarto, was written by the inventor of the first Jacobean masque, Samuel Daniel. It is significant because it apparently was the first play designed for the special delight of the Stuart court.[21] In fact, the period of courtly efflorescence I shall be postulating between 1605 and 1615 is framed by Daniel's two courtly plays. The latter, *Hymen's Triumph,* was presented by Anne at her palace in the Strand for the nuptials of Lord Roxborough in 1614. It too is billed in the 1615 edition as a "Pastorall Tragicomaedie." Both plays are conscious attempts to render English versions of the exceedingly fashionable Italian courtly plays *Aminta* and *Il pastor fido* (to which I will return shortly). Between the dates of the Daniel plays the Jacobean courtly aesthetic flourished. As we shall see, this aesthetic began to impinge upon the demands of the public stage, which was less subject to flux, and began to attract more attention from artists and writers.[22]

[21]Inigo Jones seems to have been present at Oxford in some backstage capacity. Henry Paul suggests in *The Royal Play of Macbeth* (San Marino, Calif., 1950), p. 23, that another play performed during James's visit, Dr. Gwinn's *Tres Sibyllae,* heavily influenced Shakespeare's first play for his new king.

[22]Courtly art and literature are subject to fluctuations caused by historical events, royal patronage, royal domestic relations, economic exigencies, foreign affairs, and so on. Public fashions were seriously affected, it would appear, only by the plague, and were on the whole more stable. Andrew Gurr writes in *The Shakespearean Stage: 1574–1642* (Cambridge, England) that "one group of theatres, the Curtain, Rose and Swan before 1600 and the Red Bull and Fortune afterwards, retained a fairly consistent repertory throughout the whole seventy years [i.e., 1574–1642]" (p. 155). Gurr refers here to theaters with a clearly "public" clientele.

The four events just described signified a new courtly flowering toward the end of Shakespeare's middle period. The pendulum was swinging back in favor of artistic life at court. One of James's first official acts was to abolish the players' old patents and renew them in the name of himself, his wife, and his son Prince Henry. Shakespeare was one of the nine named players in the patent for his company. The average number of performances at court jumped from three a year under Elizabeth to thirteen a year under James, and Bentley has calculated that the money received from preference at court jumped as markedly.[23] Almost all commentators from E. K. Chambers through F. P. Wilson, G. E. Bentley, Alfred Harbage, Frederick Sternfeld, and Glynne Wickham have emphasized that the survival of drama in this period was largely due to royal protection. John Webster made the same point when he slyly rebutted the argument that players were a social menace by alluding to this royal patronage: "Rogues are not to be imployde as maine ornaments to his Majesties Revels."[24]

With the success of the masques at court, with the revival of his *Love's Labour's Lost* in 1604, with the successful performance of a pastoral tragicomedy for the queen in 1605, with her specific request for a spectacle like Jonson's and Jones's *Masque of Blacknesse,* and with the appearance in 1608 of Fletcher's sophisticated *The Faithful Shepherdess* (loved by the learned, hated by the groundlings), we can begin to imagine the dilemma Shakespeare confronted about the time of *Timon of Athens* (1607–08) and *Pericles* (1608–09). Two modes of drama seemed to be developing and diverging, and these were largely antagonistic to each other: the public and the courtly.[25]

[23]G. E. Bentley, "Shakespeare and the Blackfriars Theatre," *Shakespeare Survey* 1 (1948): 38–50.

[24]John Webster, "An excellent Actor," *The Overbury Characters,* in *The Complete Works,* ed. F. L. Lucas (1927; rpt. London, 1966), IV, p. 43.

[25]The difference was then, as now, often seen in terms of the repertories

The first—in which Shakespeare had already proved his excellence—was the theater of denigration, decadence, and cynical sensationalism, which had been vigorous for some years. He could have continued this fundamentally tragic dissection of complex existential questions and avoided the burgeoning pressures to produce works more concerned with the common themes, forms, and complacencies of a revitalizing court. He could have continued writing his tragedies, which have been called "the greatest anti-romantic structures ever created."[26] In that event, he would have found himself in the company of what we now think of as Jacobean dramatists—those men whose plays were full

> Of carnal, bloody, and unnatural acts,
> Of accidental judgments, casual slaughters,
> Of deaths put on by cunning and forc'd cause.
>   (*Hamlet,* 5.2.381–83)

He might have continued to produce plays characterized by the sense of defeat, preoccupation with death, mood of uncertainty, hypothesis of an evil world order, Satanism, and

---

of different theaters. As late as 1640 the partisanship was still strong between lowbrow and highbrow audiences. In a commendatory verse for an edition of Shakespeare's poems, for instance, Leonard Digges warns that the stage for which Shakespeare wrote (pertinently for the present thesis, Blackfriars is singled out) ought not to be sullied with wretched doggerel plays:

> But if you needs must write, if poverty
> So pinch, that otherwise you starve and die
> On Gods name may the Bull or Cockpit have
> Your lame blancke Verse, to keepe you from the grave:
> Or let new Fortunes younger brethren see,
> What they can picke from your leane industry.
> I doe not wonder when you offer at
> Blacke-Friers, that you suffer.
>   (Munro, *Shakespeare Allusion Book,* I, p. 456)

See also Clifford Leech's discussion of private and public audiences in *The John Fletcher Plays* (London, 1962), pp. 7–11.

[26]Howard Felperin, *Shakespearean Romance* (Princeton, 1972), p. 62.

Machiavellianism described by Una Ellis-Fermor in her study of Jacobean drama.

Shakespeare would have continued where he appears to have left off in *Timon of Athens,* his most vitriolic attack upon the vices of courtly life and art. *Timon* is Shakespeare's look behind the idealistic façade of courtly luxury, an anatomy of all the "glib and slipp'ry creatures" who surround the powerful and wealthy. The central topic of the play is the decay of civility—in a sense, the impossibility of establishing Castiglione's profoundly congenial courtly atmosphere when greed, sycophancy, and ingratitude are or seem universal. In Timon's Athens there is nothing of that greatest courtly value—"true friendship" (1.2.18). There is only bloodless cynicism and "politic love."

Timon of Athens attacks a courtly aesthetic that thrives on illusion, escape from reality, flattery, and prodigal expense. There is hardly a more brutal assault upon the central courtly art form, the masque, than the speech of Apemantus upon Timon's masque of amazons:

> What a sweep of vanity comes this way!
> They dance? they are madwomen.
> Like madness is the glory of this life,
> As this pomp shows to a little oil and root.
> We make ourselves fools to disport ourselves,
> And spend our flatteries to drink those men
> Upon whose age we void it up again
> With poisonous spite and envy.
> Who lives that's not depraved or depraves?
> Who dies that bears not one spurn to their graves
> Of their friends' gift?
> I should fear those that dance before me now
> Would one day stamp upon me. 'T 'as been done;
> Men shut their doors against a setting sun.

> (1.2.132–45)

Apemantus was certainly not alone in asking, "What needs these feasts, pomps, and vainglories?" (1.2.242). It is a question worthy of that most serious-minded and pomp-despising courtier Fulke Greville. Like Apemantus in Timon's court, Greville was out of favor in James's first euphoric years.

This play's "whirlwind of furious ejaculation," as Strachey phrased it, seems to have come at an inauspicious time. Whether because Shakespeare's depiction of a prodigal hero, well-meaning but nevertheless duped, treaded too near James, whether the sudden flood of poor Scots knights into London is shadowed in Timon's entourage, we can say the tenor of the play would have been found at the least too sharp-tongued and mean-minded for courtly consumption. The play must have lost its footing as it was being finished— if indeed it was finished.[27] For it seems not to have been performed in Shakespeare's lifetime and was not printed until the 1623 folio. As James's court gained momentum, as the new Revels Office grew accustomed to Stuart tastes, as the court burgeoned in size and outward splendor, as the theme of national as well as courtly unity of Scots and Englishmen was propagated, and as the king's political maneuvering within and without England came to require more pomp and circumstance, we might plausibly speculate that Shakespeare (or his company) was not anxious to push the fortunes of *Timon of Athens*. No play that questioned "feasts, pomps, and vain-

---

[27]Una Ellis-Fermor argues strongly that the play was not completed in "Timon of Athens: An Unfinished Play," *Shakespeare the Dramatist and Other Papers,* ed. Kenneth Muir (London, 1961): "It is as an unfinished play, then, that I should like to consider it, a play such as a great artist might leave behind him, roughed out, worked over in part and then abandoned; full of inconsistencies in form and presentation, with fragments (some of them considerable) bearing the unmistakable stamp of his workmanship scattered throughout" (p. 159). Ellis-Fermor does admit that her study leaves us "as far as ever from real knowledge of the cause of the play's collapse" (p. 176).

In matters of chronology I have generally relied on the conclusions of E. K. Chambers, *William Shakespeare* (Oxford, 1930), I, p. 270.

glories" could hope for much approval at a court that was thriving on just such fare. We may well wonder if it was finally rejected at some point in just the way Timon rejects that deflator of courtly vanity, Apemantus:

> Nay, and you begin to rail on society once, I am sworn not to give regard to you. Farewell, and come with better music.
>
> (1.2.244–46)

Shakespeare must have concluded (or someone for him) that entrepreneurial madness lay in pursuit of the attitudes toward courtly life expressed in *Timon of Athens:* he chose to return with "better music" in the form of the Late Plays. Shakespeare, in short, must have decided to accommodate the second of the two diverging theatrical modes: that of spectacular, decorative, and romantic courtly fashion. I find it plausible to imagine that he saw that the artistic mood of the time was changing and that different aesthetic fashions were catching on among the courtly avant-garde. These changes must have encouraged him to alter his dramatic style.

To find an expression of the new fashion, Shakespeare could not have done better than to peruse the commendatory poems prefixed to the 1609 quarto of *The Faithful Shepherdess.* The courtly plays of 1604–15 that I hope to associate with *The Tempest* can be described in much the same terms used by George Chapman to praise Fletcher's play:

> Your poeme onely hath by us applause,
> Renews the golden world; and holds through all
> The holy lawes of homely pastorall;
> Where flowers, and founts, and Nymphs, and
>   semi-Gods,
> And all the Graces finde their old abods:

43

Where forrests flourish but in endless verse;
And meddowes, nothing fit for purchasers:
This Iron age that eates it selfe, will never
Bite at your golden world.[28]

Chapman was one of the pillars of courtly art in the period, and the qualities he applauds in the play show to what extent *The Faithful Shepherdess* serves as a touchstone for courtly dramatic taste. Here a theatrical Apollo, like James the bringer of a new golden age, has ascended; here is optimism, courtly idyll, escapism, and learned pleasure in the artificial. At least in the environs of Whitehall the brief but harsh literary iron age of 1600–04 had passed; rose-colored spectacles were again put on; the acid-tongued Hamlets, Malevoles, and Macilentes formerly at stage center were again (like Antonio, Sebastian, and Caliban) the outcasts, the impotent, the speechless. Idealized heroes and heroines regained the spotlight. The times had changed and some writers were being asked to celebrate the complacent joys of peace and confident sociality. The court was becoming more ebullient.

This period in English history was conducive to courtly art, which requires a certain hothouse climate of peace, abundance, and positive royal support. The first decade or so of James's reign was relatively untroubled. Confrontations between king and parliament had not yet become unblinkable, nor had James's prodigality, not to say profligacy, though worriedly noted by his closest counselors, yet become widely sensed or outwardly troubling.[29] Whatever the shortcomings

[28]Francis Beaumont and John Fletcher, *The Dramatic Works of Francis Beaumont and John Fletcher*, ed. Fredson Bowers (Cambridge, England, 1976), III, p. 493.

[29]From Howes's "Historicall Preface" to Stow's *The Annales, or Generall Chronicle of England* (1615 edition) we have this: "The effectes of this Alteration [i.e., James's accession] were in all respects cleane different from all former chaunges, and was no lesse wonderfull to all other Regions, then beneficiall to the English Nation: who in a moment hadde their Kingdome setled, the Crowne rightly established, the Clergie cherished, the Nobilitie advanced, their Common Lawes continued, and the people resting in all Tran-

of the monarch, they were mitigated in anticipation of the
accession of "the most famous and hopefull" Prince Henry.
Indeed, the first major catastrophe of the reign was Henry's
sudden death in 1612.[30] Until then, however, the initial joy of
a peaceful succession was more or less maintained. In this atmosphere developed the sophisticated plays of which *The
Tempest* is the most important example. This atmosphere is
captured in the preface to Richard Brathwaite's *Sonnets or*

---

quillitie, enjoying their auncient Customes, Lawes, and Liberties, in as good
and as ample manner as either their hearts could wish, or is enjoyed by any
other Nation" (sig. ¶8r).

Except for the first few euphoric years, James's reign was not happy.
However, it was not until about 1610 and thereafter that the serious flaws in
his ruling powers, his dismal parliamentary relations, and his lack of acumen
in economic affairs became obvious. Parliament was often "very much dis-
tasted and stricken dumb" by the king's demands and pronouncements. In
1610 a move to open the king's beloved question of union with Scotland was
whistled down, and by the same year funds were scarce enough to require
curtailment of the ceremonies for Prince Henry's investiture as Prince of
Wales: "The rest of the ceremony that belongs to the Prince is to be performed in as private a manner as may be for the King in this time of necessity
when he is so pressed to the Parliament is not willing to undergo any needless
expense" (*A Second Jacobean Journal*, ed. G. B. Harrison [Ann Arbor, Mich.,
1958], p. 208).

In *The House of Commons, 1604–1610* (New Haven, Conn., 1971), Wallace Notestein concludes that "by 1614 he was a weary old potentate, disin-
clined to effort, and still happiest in the field, where the deer were said to have
been driven before him" (p. 505). A few years later, we learn from Nichols,
"divers accidents gave him a general apprehension of danger. And though he
bore it with unusual patience, yet it seems he was not so confident of himself,
but he prepared to settle things, as if he were to leave all" (*The Progresses,
Processions, and Magnificent Festivities of King James the First* [London, 1828], III,
p. 533). This physical decline, together with the death of the two members of
the royal family most supportive of artistic endeavors, Anne and Henry,
would seem central to an explanation of the decline of courtly vitality after
about 1615. Prince Henry's role as patron of the new courtly aesthetic,
though brief, appears to have been consequential. Roy Strong writes that
Henry "attempted between 1610 and 1612, between the age of 16 and 18, to
transform the aesthetic milieu of his father's court" (*The English Icon:
Elizabethan and Jacobean Portraiture* [New York, 1969], p. 56).

[30]As late as 1828 Nichols could describe Henry's death as "the most
melancholy event" of James's reign (*Progresses*, II, p. 469).

45

Madrigals of 1611. Brathwaite associated peace especially with the progress of the musical art (and this was a period rich in works about music), but his point holds for all forms of artistic endeavor:

> *Janus* hath now shut up his Temple, our civil warres be now ended, union in the sweete harmony of minde and conjunction hath prevented the current of ensuing faction, we may now sit downe under our Beech tree and make a vertuous use of an experienced necessity. . . . We may now make a good consort, since the jarring strings of discord be reduced to so pleasant harmony.[31]

The Tempest and the Late Plays were written in such a period of public calm. It is no coincidence that their effect is, as Brathwaite put it, to reduce the jarring strings of discord to a pleasant harmony, for it is in such a time that men of state and wealth are inclined to appreciate this art of repose and optimism.

We can imagine Shakespeare observing the revitalization at court, the increasing profitability of preferment there, the decidedly romantic and pastoral tastes of the new queen, the ravishing enticements of Inigo Jones's new scenic inventions, regarding himself as a dramatist with yet a few more plays in him, and deciding to change his dramatic style:

> I find my zenith doth depend upon
> A most auspicious star, whose influence
> If now I court not, but omit, my fortunes
> Will ever after droop.
> (*The Tempest*, 1.2.181–84)

---

[31]Richard Brathwaite, "The Epistle Dedicatorie," *Sonnets or Madrigals* (London, 1611), sig. E₄ʳ–E₅ᵛ. Dekker expressed the same idea for the Lord Mayor's shows and triumphs: "*Triumphes* are the most choice and daintiest fruit that spring from *Peace* and *Abundance*" (*Dramatic Works*, III, p. 230).

One might further speculate that, still essentially obliged to the public stage at the time he wrote *Timon of Athens* (the King's Men had not begun to make use of Blackfriars until late 1609), Shakespeare felt constrained to exploit the new courtly fashions in a way that would not offend a public audience. He felt the pulse of the times: an audience that greeted the brusque, unpretentious, "public-ized" romance *Mucedorus* (first extant quarto 1606, but generally felt to be an earlier play) with enthusiasm and hated *The Faithful Shepherdess* would be fair game for a *Pericles*. And indeed it was: his next play was very well received. Two quartos of *Pericles* appeared in 1609, and by 1635 a sixth edition was printed. No other Shakespearean play was more often reprinted during the early 1600's.

That *Pericles* was written essentially for the public stage cannot be overemphasized. While it partakes of many stylistic features of the later, more "courtly" efforts—dance, music, spectacular scenes, romance panoply, greater poetic finish—it is a play designed for popular approval. Some critics are beginning to see subtleties in the play, but these were caviar to the general public that first applauded it. That learned snob who did not miss much, Ben Jonson, called *Pericles* a "mouldy tale." He rightly sensed that the play is a version of courtly romance the *profanum vulgus* could grasp and enjoy. It is telling that, even before a quarto of *Pericles* appeared, one George Wilkins had the idea of printing a prose narrative of the play's action, calling it *The Painfull Adventures of Pericles Prince of Tyre*. The result is a work far more akin to Greene than to Sidney and the more sophisticated romancers.

As has often been remarked, *The Tempest* shows strong resemblances to the episodic romance literature—though certainly these are not as marked as in *Pericles*. As a way of suggesting what in general structural terms the two plays owe to romance material, I would like to draw attention to an episode from the third book of *Primaleon*.[32] The difference between "plebeian" and "courtly" romance in the theater is reflected in *Pericles* and *The Tempest,* and an excerpt from *Primaleon* will help suggest how. This episode begins in the thirteenth chapter, the synopsis of which is: "How *Primaleon* and *Prince Edward* fought a cruell combat at Sea, and how in the end being inchanted by the Knight of the inclosed Island, they were boren thither without any feeling or understanding" (p. 73). Though the similarities between the episode and the action of *The Tempest* are remarkable, my desire is not to suggest a possible source. Rather, I am concerned to show that the play has all the earmarks of a typical romance episode in the progress of its action.

The episode, about one hundred pages long, opens with the following series of events:

> Primaleon had surely been slaine in the place, if at that time the Knight of the inclosed Island had not come thither, who leaping out of his barke into that where they fought, strake upon the mast of the ship with his booke that he held in his hand, which he had no sooner done, but all those that were in the ship lay as if they had beene dead, without any feeling at all. The Knight was a good Magician, and caused two sailers that came with him, to enter into the ship . . . so in short time they arrived at the inclosed Island, and there the Knight that was lord thereof, caused all that were in the ship to be taken forth, they feeling nothing, because they were inchanted, and laid them in divers faire roomes, where every one being put apart, he healed them of their wounds.
>
> (p. 77)

[32]*The History of Primaleon of Greece:* Spanish edition, 1534; French editions, 1572, 1577, 1579, 1609; English editions, 1595–96 (Books I and II), 1619 (Books I, II, and III). Quoted below from the English translation by Anthony Munday (London, 1619).

Thus commences a complex series of awakenings, separations, and carefully orchestrated confusions on the island. In
the course of these we learn more of present interest about the
magician: he admits that he has "alwayes beene more addicted
to my booke then to armes"; he has been deposed from his
rightful inheritance; he has no sons and two daughters; and he
is very concerned about the continuance of his dynastic line.
The episode ends with peace made between the usurpers and
the knight, the celebration of various nuptials, and rejoicing:
"The Archbishop rose out of his seate, and sodainely es-
poused them together: by the meanes whereof, the joy was so
great, that all men thought upon nothing else, but upon pleasure and delight" (p. 169). The usual courtly entertainments
and feasting follow this climax.

As the knight presides over the events in *Primaleon,* so
does Prospero preside over the action of *The Tempest.* Prospero and the Knight of the Enclosed Island function to give
the play and the romance episode their respective central plots
and to fill those plots with various marvelous events. Romance literature depends upon such characters whose powers
over heroes and heroines have a supernatural source, for on
this very wonder-producing eventfulness was based the appeal of the romances—and much courtly art.[33] Their control
of the seafaring parties necessarily makes them the controllers

[33]An enchanted island and a magician's staff come to the mind of François Ménestrier (1631–1705)—the first great student of courtly art—when he
describes the romance as a rich source for masque subjects in *Des Ballets anciennes et modernes selon les règles du Théâtre* (1682; rpt. Geneva, 1972): "The
allegories of romance . . . are composed as are the romances, of marvelous
events, and quite without verisimilitude, because their effects are attributed to
enchantment . . . Thus in the year 1664 the King, wishing to give the Queen
and all his court the delight of some quite uncommon festivities in the gar-
dens of Versailles during the pleasant days of May, took as the subject of the
festivities the delights of the enchanted Isle" (p. 75; my translation). See
Northrop Frye's relevant and valuable discussion of the "Myth of Summer:
Romance" in *Anatomy of Criticism* (Princeton, 1961), pp. 186–206.

of the imaginative event, the producers of its marvels. The episode from *Primaleon* manifests the major themes of courtly *theatralia spectacula:* the invariably happy end, the nuptials that heal dynastic breaches and bind contending forces, the reestablishment of right rule. Inventors of courtly entertainments naturally found frequent inspiration in episodes such as this.

Dramatists, too, felt the influence of the popularity of romances among the cultivated. Shakespeare is one of many who had the possibilities of romance thrust upon him. What is undigested, discursive, and spectacular—what is very like *Primaleon*—in *Pericles* becomes taut and cumulatively effective in *The Tempest* because (like a masque inventor) Shakespeare chose a *single* romance sequence of events for his action. *Pericles* amounts to a theatrical synopsis of the entire *Primaleon; The Tempest* represents the dramatization of one segment of the work. *Pericles* is both a superficial and kaleidoscopic transformation of romance for the stage, whereas *The Tempest* is a carefully focused, richly allusive, "artificial" stage version of romance.

The apparent crudeness of *Pericles,* then, may not be solely attributable to mixed authorship or even to simple artistic failure. For a playwright wedded at the time (whether happily or not) to the public stage and yet simultaneously aware of the possibilities of taking courtly tastes into account, *Pericles* is a plausible production. Though its body, as it were, may seem courtly, its soul is plebeian. *Pericles* is the first work on a brief continuum spanning Shakespeare's last years and shows the gradual transfer of his allegiance to a more ambitious aesthetic. This, I recognize, is all highly speculative, but the question of Shakespeare's motivation for writing the Late Plays has received too little speculative examination.

Pericles can be usefully compared, not with Shakespeare's later plays, but with Heywood's *Rape of Lucrece,* another popular version of an essentially aristocratic subject, which enjoyed success at the plebeian Red Bull Theater. The timing and extent of this play's popularity, incidentally, closely parallel *Pericles:* a first quarto appeared in 1608 and four more by 1638. Also, Heywood's play seems to date from an earlier version of about 1594 and therefore qualifies with *Pericles* as a "mouldy tale."

The Rape of Lucrece is worth attention, not only because there is a courtly analogue in Shakespeare's epyllion, but because this play shows most of the limitations of the public theater when essaying the adaptation of a courtly theme.[34] These defects are shared by *Pericles:* facile plotting, finger-pointing, and much earth-treading verse. Heywood's poetry rarely rises to the occasion of his famous story as Shakespeare's does. Rather, attention focuses on unsubtle dramatic characters. Two-dimensional figures populate the play: Tullia as a mixture of Tamburlaine and Lady Macbeth (compare Dionyza in *Pericles*), Tarquin as a depraved tyrant (compare Antiochus), and Lucrece as a paragon of chastity and innocence (compare Marina). The action suffers from the confusion of two plots, Tarquin's tyranny and his son's rape of Lucrece. Both devolve into the common public form of revenge tragedy. As in many public plays, the playwright focuses upon the unsalubrious life at court, and the play ends, in a manner reminiscent of *Titus Andronicus,* amid

> . . . broken speares, crackt swords, unboweld steeds,
> Flaude armors, mangled limbs, and batter'd casks,
> Knee deepe in blood.[35]

The cast is decimated after "much effusion and large waste / Of Roman blood" (p. 253), the main interest being the typical hurly-burly of bare-stage marshalling of armies. Again typical of the public stage, special effects and properties are simple:

[34]While Irving Ribner concludes *The Rape of Lucrece* is "a pedestrian imitation of *Macbeth,*" he makes a strong effort to appreciate the play in *Jacobean Tragedy: The Quest for Moral Order* (London, 1962), pp. 59–71.

[35]Thomas Heywood, *The Dramatic Works* (London, 1874; rpt. 1964), V, p. 250.

A Table and a Chaire covered with blacke.

(p. 234)

Enter Tarquin with an arrow in his brest.

(p. 249)

Alarum, Brutus all bloody.

(p. 249)

The many songs that dot the action are lascivious fare that might well fit in the brothel scenes of *Pericles;* they utterly ruin the gravity of the action. Finally, the spectacle—the ceremony of Apollo's priests and the march-past of the "pride of Roman Chivalry"—is poor business requiring, like *Pericles,* little in the way of special effects.

The Rape of Lucrece represents a "public" version of a courtly theme. What had provided Shakespeare with scope for extreme poetic finish was turned by Heywood into the "lame blancke Verse" well known at the Red Bull. In Heywood's hands the story became a pretext for what the public audience loved best: bombastic dialogue, sensational events, a giddy pace, and bawdry. These characteristics, incidentally, are akin to the "furious vociferation" and "scenicall strutting" that Jonson associated with Marlowe's plays (Jonson, *Works,* VIII, 587). The difference between Shakespeare's poem and the play is the difference between the courtly and plebeian aesthetics.

Pericles, too, is a public version of a prominent courtly genre. The play distills the action, the bare essentials of the morality and characterization of the refined romance of, say, a Sidney, into a form as palatable to the public taste as Heywood's play. We get close to the kind of thinking that may have passed through the minds of Shakespeare and Heywood as they prepared these plays for the public stage, by turning to a treatise on play writing that appeared in Spain in 1609, Lope de Vega's short apologia, *The New Art of Writing*

Plays. Lope de Vega was, like Heywood in England, the most prolific playwright of his time, and what he says about public taste and acquiescence to its demands is illuminating. Of artistic rules he writes: "When I have to write a comedy I lock in the precepts with six keys, I banish Terence and Plautus from my study that they may not cry out at me."[36] Concerning the unity of time he advises, "Let it take place in as little time as possible, except when the poet is writing history in which some years have to pass; these he can relegate to the space between the acts, wherein, if necessary, he can have a character go on some journey; a thing that greatly offends whoever perceives it" (p. 201). To those like Ben Jonson who would carp at such plays, Lope de Vega adds sharply: "But let not him who is offended go to see them" (p. 201). Shakespeare and Heywood might well have retorted in such a way to critics of *Pericles* and *The Rape of Lucrece.* Of the public taste for constant action, he warns: "Considering that the wrath of a seated Spaniard is immoderate, when in two hours there is not presented to him everything from Genesis to the Last Judgment, I deem it most fitting, if it be for us here to please him, for us to adjust everything so that it succeeds" (p. 201). A true pragmatist, he concludes, "Since the crowd pays for the comedies, it is fitting to talk foolishly to it to satisfy its taste" (p. 198). Lope de Vega, Heywood, and Shakespeare—among other dramatists of the time—could write for all kinds of audiences as theatrical circumstances and fashions changed.[37] Professional exigencies as much as ability or inclination dictated whether they talked foolishly or learnedly to their au-

[36]Lope de Vega, *The New Art of Writing Plays* (1609), p. 198. All quotations are from the translation by William Brewster, included in *Dramatic Theory and Criticism,* ed. Bernard Dukore (New York, 1974).

[37]Those unaccustomed to think of Heywood as an erudite writer should refer to his Lord Mayor's shows and to his play *Loves Mistress: Or, The Queenes Masque* (1634; 1636 quarto), for which the scene designer was no less than Inigo Jones.

ditors. *Pericles* was designed to satisfy a public taste for romance, and it succeeded.[38]

Lope de Vega believed that playwrights who wrote "artistically" for the public stage would die "without fame and guerdon," and in 1607–08 Shakespeare must have sensed the inverse of the Spaniard's dictum—that a playwright who

[38]Critics have tended to look upon the play in much the same ridiculing way that Cervantes's Canon from Toledo looked upon the romances. The Canon's criticisms cover most of those commonly leveled against *Pericles*:

> They have composed them of so many members, as it more probably seemes, that the authors intended to frame *Chimeraes* or monsters, then to deliver proportionate figures, most harsh in their stile, incredible in exploits, impudent in love matters, absurd in complements, prolixe in battels, fond in discourses, uncertaine and senselesse in voyages, and finally, devoide of all discretion, art and ingenious disposition.
>
> (*The Historie of the valorous and wittie Knight-Errant, Don Quixote,* trans. Thomas Shelton [London, 1612], p. 552)

To the public audience all this was to the good, but to men well-versed in the rules of art—like the Canon or, one might add, Chapman and Jonson—plays like *Pericles* deserved reproach. Jonson, with tongue in cheek, put himself in the Canon's party when he suggested (VIII, 205) that Vulcan could well have burned "the whole summe / Of errant Knight-hood" in his library.

The Canon tried to apply his views on romance to the popular stage. We learn that he has on occasion attempted to argue the players out of performing lowbrow works like, one would imagine, *Pericles* or *The Rape of Lucrece:*

> I have sundry times indevoured to perswade the Players that their opinion was erronious herein, and that they would attract more people and acquire greater fame by acting artificiall Comedies then those irregular and [im]methodicall Playes [*las disparatadas*] then used: yet are they so wedded to their opinion, as no reason can wooe, nor demonstration winne them from it.
>
> (*Don Quixote,* p. 555)

The actors naturally refused the Canon, because they were sure of their audience, just as surely as the Red Bull dramatist knew he was dealing with an audience "to whom symmetry, restraint, form, and congruity were less intelligible than sentiment, tragical speeches, ribaldry, and the rest of the *olla podrida* of the plebeian theatres" (Arthur Clark, *Thomas Heywood* [1931; rpt. New York, 1967], p. 220).

failed to write artistically for a *sophisticated* audience would find his fortunes ever after drooping. It would follow that as refined artistry increased we could assume a more sophisticated intended audience, and this is precisely the trend manifested in Shakespeare's plays beginning with *Pericles* and ending with the collaborative effort *Two Noble Kinsmen* (1613).

The task of characterizing this trend is not easy. The essential quality of this revived sophistication is caught by that fictional Spaniard so familiar with the clash of lowbrow and highbrow theatrical tastes, Cervantes's Canon. The Canon complains that plays written according to rules of decorum and art "serve onely for three or foure discreete men (If so many may be found at a Play)." The rest of the audience "remaine fasting, by reason they cannot conceive the artificiall contexture" of such plays (*Don Quixote,* p. 555). Artificial contexture—Shelton's translation of *artificio* is suitably, inevitably vague—is one of the distinguishing features of an elitist aesthetic. Artificial contexture is the product of thinking that more is more. It was essential to courtly connoisseurs, who encouraged the artistic heightening of experience, the ornamentation of moral and political orthodoxies through all available fictional means. George Chapman, an appropriate spokesman for this elitist bias, had occasion to defend artificial contexture in the Epistle Dedicatory to his translation of the *Odyssey* (1612):

> If the Bodie (being the letter, or historie) seemes fictive, and beyond Possibilitie to bring into Act, the sence then and Allegorie (which is the Soule) is to be sought—which intends a more eminent expressure of Vertue, for her lovelinesse, and of Vice, for her uglinesse, in their severall effects, going beyond the life than any Art within life can possibly delineate. Why then is Fiction to this end so hateful to our true Ignorants?
>
> (II, p. 5)

This aesthetic neoplatonism was crucial to the design and effect of other elaborate Jacobean entertainments (compare the neoplatonic content of Jonson's introduction to the masque *Hymenaei* quoted below). With new technology at their command, the poets' and artists' search for the "more eminent expressure" of courtly and royal virtues led to more and more stupendous fictions. With increasingly sophisticated knowledge of the ancients, new Continental fashions, the startling introduction of stage perspective into England, and the importation of scene-moving apparatuses, the powers of the fictionalists increased immensely under James.

These newly won capabilities led to the creation of "spectacles of state" clothed in what Henry Peacham called "the most excellent Ornaments, Exornations, Lightes, Flowers, and Formes" of poetic and architectural rhetoric.[39] These spectacles, based upon solid, not to say rampant, learning, were very carefully contrived. Dekker's report of the preparations for the 1604 triumphal arches suggests their superficial richness:

> By this time Imagine, that *Poets* (who drawe speaking Pictures) and *Painters* (who make dumbe Poesie) had their heads and hands full; the one for native and sweet Invention: the other for lively Illustration of what the former should devise: Both of them emulously contending (but not striving) with the proprest and brightest Colours of Wit and Art, to set out the beautie of the great *Triumphant-day*. . . . Many dayes were thriftily consumed, to molde the bodies of these Triumphes comely, and to the honour of the Place: and at last, the stuffe whereof to frame them, was beaten out. The Soule that should give life, and a tongue to this *Entertainment,* being to breathe

[39]Henry Peacham, the Elder, *The Garden of Eloquence* (1593; rpt. Gainesville, Florida, 1954), title page.

out of Writers Pens. The Limmes of it to lie at the hard-handed mercy of Mychanitiens.[40]

This same care for the "brightest Colours of Wit and Art" marked the invention of the Lord Mayor's shows and, most importantly, the court masques. As Dekker implies, the truly admirable spectacles were designed outward from an inner "idea" or "hinge"; the soul of the courtly spectacle dictated its form. Visual complexity, ideally, was intended to display not only opulence but also intellectual mastery and political power. In their blend of visual magnificence with deep learning and sound morality, masques epitomized the courtly aesthetic. As the inventor most alive to the necessity that learning be the masque's heart, Ben Jonson deserves the quotation of his credo. Its emphasis on spectacle, the reference to the audience for which it was intended, the concern for the hidden meanings of the work, the sense of occasional interest as well as of something monumental and lasting—all are features of the courtly aesthetic:

> The most royall *Princes,* and greatest *persons* (who are commonly the *personators* of these *actions*) [are] not onely studious of riches and magnificence in the outward celebration, or shew . . . but curious after the most high, and heartie *inventions,* to furnish the inward parts: (and those grounded upon *antiquitie,* and solide *learnings*) which, though their *voice* be taught to sound to present occasions, their *sense,* or doth, or should alwayes lay hold on more remov'd *mysteries.*
>
> (*Hymenaei,* VII, 209)

I have dwelt fleetingly upon the arches and the masque because these provide the aesthetic's clearest and most elaborate statements of method. These statements, however, are valid for all contemporary genres in their general philosophy sim-

[40]Dekker, *Dramatic Works,* II, pp. 257–58.

ply because the courtly treatment of any genre required sophistication. A courtly audience would expect polish and allusiveness from an epyllion, a tragicomedy, a verse epic, a sonnet, an impresa, a triumphal arch, or a masque. The courtly preference for images of wit rather than images of nature amounted to a general levy upon artists and writers.

Though the masque did provide many effects for stage writers to borrow as best they could, if only through allusion or imagery, and though its influence upon theatrical fashions is beyond doubt, it is perhaps wiser to approach Shakespeare's Late Plays from a specifically theatrical tradition in order to trace their relation to the courtly aesthetic. Our look at this tradition might for present purposes begin with Torquato Tasso's pastoral tragicomedy *Aminta,* indubitably the product of a courtly environment and a work of seminal importance for the genre. *Aminta* received its first performance in 1573 under the auspices of the Duke of Ferrara in his palace of Belvedere—a court famous for tournaments, festivals, and pageantry. Its success was immediate and spread rapidly; a contemporary noted that the play was recited the next year by "several Knights of Urbino."[41] "From Tasso's time," Ernest Grillo has written, "the pastoral drama became a fashionable spectacle and acquired the favour of the cultivated classes until 1585, when, with Guarini's *Il pastor fido,* it attained its highest development" (pp. 18–19).

Guarini's play brought courtly drama to a new high in "artificial contexture." This *tragicommedia pastorale* appears to have been performed first at Turin in 1585–86. Between 1590 and 1602 it received twenty Italian editions alone. Guarini (who attended the first performance of *Aminta* and consciously emulated Tasso) took fully ten years to write *Il pastor fido.* For the 1602 edition he added about 130,000 words of annotation to his 5,575-line play. Aside from their amusing

[41]Quoted in Ernest Grillo's edition of Torquato Tasso's *Aminta* (London, 1924), p. 17.

self-indulgence, these annotations are interesting as an appreciation of elegant theatrical composition. There is surely no more ample expression of delight in the artificial contexture of the courtly aesthetic by so deep-dyed a courtly aesthetician. The style of *Il pastor fido* is dominated by an extraordinarily contrived potpourri of classical *sententiae*, well-wrought Petrarchisms, luminous streakings of neoplatonic love theory, and speeches of great length and dense ornamentation—a lavish poetic style.[42] Indeed, like *Aminta, Il pastor fido* is rather a poem than a play.[43]

The influence of these two plays on English theater was considerable.[44] *Aminta* was published in English in 1591, and

[42]Guarini explains in the third person how he follows ancient practices, how he adheres or departs from verisimilitude, and how clever his effects are. Remarks such as "un episodio molto leggiadro," "i moti sono studiati con numero, & armonia," "con bellissima circonlocutione," and "metafore belle e proportionate" sprinkle his annotations. One of his last notes deserves partial quotation: "Si può vedere quanto perciò sia singolare l'eccellenza del Pastor fido, havendo il suo facitore saputo si ben produrre la maraviglia, dov'ella è si malagevole da trovarsi, che s'alcuno Poema Eroico si ritrova, che habbia questa qualità del mirabile, non è da farsene maraviglia, potendo esso con le parole finger cose impossibili, & lontane dal verisimile" (*Il pastor fido* [Venice, 1602], p. 255ʳ). This last statement could well serve as the expression of the driving desire of most courtly art—the creation of marvelous miracles—or to use a Shakespearean phrase, the creation of "a notable passion of wonder" (*The Winter's Tale,* 5.2.15–16).

That *Il pastor fido* was accepted as courtly drama in England is made clear in a passage from Jonson's *Volpone:*

> All our *English* writers,
> I meane such, as are happy in th'*Italian,*
> Will deigne to steale out of this author [Guarini] . . .
> He has so moderne, and facile a veine,
> Fitting the time, and catching the court-eare.
> (V, 73–74)

[43] "In these strange plays, the poetry of love was supposed to overshadow its vehicle" (David Orr, *The Italian Renaissance Drama in England before 1625* [Chapel Hill, North Carolina, 1970], p. 98). Orr's book is an excellent study of Italian influence, cursorily touched on here.

[44]Note this statement from Marvin Herrick's *Tragicomedy* (Urbana, Illinois, 1955), p. 126: "The pastoral play which evolved from the eclogues and romances was an aristocratic drama that flourished best in Italy and France, not so fruitfully in Spain and England."

Il pastor fido appeared in translation in 1601. While some Italian influence appears to be present in the plays of Peele and Lyly, not until James was on the throne did tragicomedy truly catch hold. In fact, the author of the first courtly tragicomedy of the Jacobean period, Samuel Daniel, is known to have traveled to Italy and to have met Guarini.[45] Daniel's *Arcadia Reformed* (printed in 1606 as *The Queenes Arcadia*) was performed for Anne in 1604. The play, a copy of Guarini's model, constitutes a beginning of the trend in Jacobean courtly dramatic tastes that was to lead to *The Tempest*.

The influence of Tasso and Guarini is next felt in Fletcher's *The Faithful Shepherdess*. His argument for the genre, ornate language, and artificiality of the play's texture makes obvious Fletcher's debt to Guarini's *Il pastor fido*. And the praise in the play's commendatory verses draws him within the courtly aesthetic:

> Such elegant proprietie
> Of words. . . .
> > Nathaniel Field

> A Poeme and a play too! why tis like
> A scholler that's a Poet. . . .
> > George Chapman[46]

The Faithful Shepherdess is the high point in the English imitation of Guarini's dramaturgy. Judged by the standards of the plays Shakespeare had just written, by the astringent, terrific Jacobean tragedies and the Marston and Jonson stage satires, Fletcher's play might well seem a "problem" one that "remains floating in a void."[47] But seen as a manifestation of an

[45]Orr, *Italian Renaissance Drama*, p. 8.

[46]Francis Beaumont and John Fletcher, *The Dramatic Works*, III, pp. 489, 492. The commendatory poems seem to me a crucial expression of the courtly aesthetic.

[47]Marco Mincoff, "*The Faithful Shepherdess:* A Fletcherian Experiment," *Renaissance Drama* 9 (1966): 163–77. Clifford Leech speculates at length on the relation of *The Faithful Shepherdess* to *The Tempest* in *The John Fletcher Plays* (London, 1962), pp. 158–68.

alien courtly aesthetic introduced into England at a time when its own court was just beginning to revitalize along Continental lines, the appearance of *The Faithful Shepherdess* becomes quite plausible.

Fletcher's pastoral ignited the sudden and brief efflorescence of "artificial" plays by Shakespeare and Beaumont and Fletcher between 1608 and 1615. Of the non-Shakespearean plays of this period, Beaumont and Fletcher's *Philaster* is intriguing, in fact crucial. It appeared sometime during the two years before *The Tempest* was written and, like Shakespeare's play, was performed by the King's Men at both the Globe and Blackfriars.[48] Shakespeare must have been familiar with it.

In his excellent edition of *Philaster,* Andrew Gurr makes many comments on the play that relate it to a courtly audience:

> One cannot stress too much that Beaumont and Fletcher were literary gentry, that they wrote to a bookish rather than a theatrical specification, and that they expected their audiences to understand their works as they understood Sidney and Spenser, at large and not only in the mighty lines. They wrote for the Fulke Grevilles of their day.[49]

The similarities between *Philaster* and *The Tempest* are fundamental—similarities in basic structure, diffidence toward characterization, in moral crux, elitist preoccupations, and the circumstances of their premieres. *Philaster* was obviously written with Blackfriars in mind, since the acquisition of this theater had taken place only the year before; it seems

[48]Critical debate centers on whether *Philaster* predates *Cymbeline* and *The Winter's Tale*. That it predates *The Tempest* seems not to be questioned. Andrew Gurr, in an introduction to his edition of Beaumont and Fletcher's *Philaster* (London, 1969), speculates that it was written "between late 1608 and early 1610" (p. xxvii).

[49]Gurr, in the Introduction to Beaumont and Fletcher's *Philaster,* p. lxvii.

likely that in preparing his next plays for that new audience Shakespeare would have paid close attention to this play.[50]

Gurr's remarks on *Philaster* are also similar to an array of critical observations that have been made about the Late Plays; these observations indicate, it seems to me, the presence of the courtly aesthetic.[51] The burden of these observations is that in the Late Plays the dramaturgy changes from one of realism (the mirror up to nature), linear plotting, and attention to character development, to a new dramaturgy of highly

---

[50]Gurr's remarks on Blackfriars tastes are especially relevant: "Masquing and dancing were another Blackfriars feature tied to the music and spectacle. There are thirteen masques in eleven boy company plays at the Blackfriars ... In that period, up to 1608, the King's Men had masques only in *The Revenger's Tragedy* and *Timon,* where they are integral to the story in a way few of the boys' masques are. After 1608 even if we discount the vision of Jupiter in *Cymbeline* there are masques in *The Tempest, Henry VIII,* and eight Beaumont and Fletcher plays. It became a conspicuous feature of the King's Men's plays. Dances too were rare at the Globe but common in the boy company plays, and after 1608 we find one in *The Winter's Tale,* two in *The Tempest,* and one in *Two Noble Kinsmen"* (*Philaster,* p. xxxix). Gurr's inference, with which I agree, is that Shakespeare responded immediately and consistently to Blackfriars conventions. I would emphasize more specifically that in writing *The Tempest,* Shakespeare might have been influenced by the full-fledged masque in *The Maid's Tragedy,* acted by the King's Men at Blackfriars about 1610.

[51]The theory I am in effect arguing here was laid out in a different context by Angus Fletcher in *The Transcendental Masque:* "To the extent that Renaissance English drama becomes more artificial and courtly as it develops, the natural standard ... will be replaced by more sophisticated criteria" (p. 45). Many commentators, in widely differing contexts, have observed the markedly artificial texture of the Late Plays. See, for example, David Orr, *The Italian Renaissance Drama in England before 1625;* Arthur Kirsch, "*Cymbeline* and Coterie Dramaturgy,"*English Literary History* 34 (1967): 285–306; Cyrus Hoy, "Artifice and Reality in the Decline of Jacobean Drama," *Research Opportunities in Renaissance Drama* 13 (1970): 169–80; Marco Minicoff, "Shakespeare, Fletcher, and Baroque Tragedy," *Shakespeare Survey* 20 (1967): 1–15; Dieter Mehl, *The Elizabethan Dumbshow* (Cambridge, Mass., 1965); Douglas Peterson, *Time, Tide and Tempest* (San Marino, Calif., 1973); Howard Felperin, *Shakespearean Romance* (Princeton, 1972); Joan Hartwig, *Shakespeare's Tragicomic Vision* (Baton Rouge, Louisiana, 1972). On the "courtly" aspects of *Henry VIII,* see John D. Cox, "*Henry VIII* and the Masque," *English Literature History* 45 (1978): 390–409.

self-conscious artistry (the mirror up to art), scenic impact rather than cumulative momentum, and more themes from romance.[52] The result is theater more poetically than dramatically moving.[53]

The Tempest, I think, is rich in the artificial contexture the Canon of Cervantes speaks of. Its charms are those of noble ideas, scenic marvels, and poetic elegance. Shakespeare in this play heightens human experience by transforming it into poetry that goes, as Chapman put it, "beyond the life." Guarini expressed the same idea when he displayed pride in having created "cose impossibile, & lontane dal verisimile" ("impossible things, and far from probable"). This intentional artificiality is merely one instance of the artistic vanity generated by the tastes of learned, aristocratic, and royal beholders. *The Tempest*—like the courtly "vanity" of Prospero's art in act 4—is more a vanity of Shakespeare's dramatic art than any play he wrote.

Shakespeare's Late Plays; the two likely Shakespearean collaborations *Henry VIII* and *The Two Noble Kinsmen;* Samuel Daniel's two tragicomedies *Arcadia Reformed* and *Hymen's Triumph;* Beaumont's *Knight of the Burning Pestle;* Fletcher's *Faithful Shepherdess;* and Beaumont and Fletcher's

[52]A convenient brief characterization of this late turnabout in Shakespeare's career exists in Arthur Kirsch, "*Cymbeline* and Coterie Dramaturgy." In his discussion Kirsch generalizes most of the points that have been made about the Late Plays. He observes that their most distinguishing feature is a "deliberate self-consciousness." He notes a "discontinuous action emphasizing scenes rather than plot," that *Cymbeline* is "frankly experimental," that "most of the features of the play are precisely those which are most typical of self-conscious tragicomic dramaturgy." Kirsch also quotes Harley Granville-Barker on the "new Euphuism in the verse" and upon "this art, which deliberately displays its art."

[53] "In a sense the collaborators, and Shakespeare with them, were writing 'literary' drama for the first time. Their plays are distinct from earlier romantic stories. . . . The difference lies in the shift of priorities from the designs either of comedy or of character-centered tragedy to the Sidneian scheme of moral paradigms or patterns of situation" (Gurr, *Philaster,* p. lx–lxi).

Cupid's Revenge, Philaster, and *A King and No King*—these plays most obviously share a self-conscious and complex artificiality. They are rich in language and visual panoply while weak in the organization of conflict and the control of dramatic impact or suspense.[54] They show the rise of the court as a competitor with the public stage for the services of certain dramatists, Shakespeare being the most prominent.[55] A comparison of *Pericles* with *The Tempest* or *The Two Noble Kinsmen* shows a greater preoccupation with the artifice of his

[54]It is tempting to cast this change in dramatic fashion as a confusion of the "dramatic" with the "masque-like," that is to say, the blending of the more traditional plotted drama with the ritual or celebratory staging of courtly entertainment. The growing confusion between the dramatic and the masque-like is set out strikingly in the prologue for a strange work (both a play and a masque) called *The World tost at Tennis,* by Thomas Middleton and William Rowley (1620). It was billed as "A Courtly Masque" but performed "divers times" by the Prince's Players:

> This our device we do not call a play,
> Because we break the stage's laws to-day
> Of acts and scenes: sometimes a comic strain
> Hath hit delight home in the master-vein,
> Thalia's prize; Melpomene's sad style
> Hath shook the tragic hand another while;
> The Muse of History hath caught your eyes,
> And she [that] chaunts the pastoral psalteries:
> We now lay claim to none, yet all present,
> Seeking out pleasure to find your content.
> You shall perceive, by what comes first in sight,
> It was intended for a royal night:
> There's one hour's words, the rest in songs and dances.
>   (Middleton, *The Works,* ed. A. H.
>   Bullen [Boston, 1885], VII, p. 145)

It is interesting that this description of the "play" shows a move away from traditional dramatic structure and rules toward the "concupiscence of dances" criticized by Jonson and the "pied ridiculous antics" that annoyed Chapman.

[55]The tastes at court must have been especially influential at the time Shakespeare was preparing the Late Plays, for in both the winter of 1608–09 and 1609–10 the King's Men received payment from the Revels Office for private rehearsals during plague time. In 1610 Heminge received 30 pounds "for himself and the reste of his companie beinge restrained from publique playinge within the citie of London in the time of infection duringe the space of six weekes in which time they practised privately for his majesty's service" (Chambers, *The Elizabethan Stage,* IV, pp. 175–76).

plays, as well as the more careful treatment of important courtly themes: the re-creation of a golden age, the establishment of a firm dynastic line, the education of a magnanimous ruler, and the nature of a healthy court. Rather than sequester himself in misanthropy, Shakespeare chose to return "with better music" for a more sophisticated audience. His colleague, John Marston, the supreme playwright of stage invective, was perhaps unwilling or unable to struggle with the new fashions; in 1609 he sold his interest in the Blackfriars and retired to become a country clergyman.

Contemporary references to the courtly flowering I have postulated are rare, as indeed is our general knowledge of the exact makeup of the audiences at court and at the coterie theaters. But there are some clues that a distinct fluctuation took place. Thomas Heywood's play *The Foure Prentises of London* offers one. When first written in about 1599, this work was by all odds intended for the kind of audience that populated the Red Bull. It amounts to a rollicking travesty of Tasso's *Gerusalemme liberata*. Godfrey of Bulloigne becomes a mercer, and the concern of the play is to see what "London prentises can do" on a crusade. Warburton was probably right in suspecting that the far more sophisticated *Knight of the Burning Pestle* was meant to ridicule the tastes exhibited in this Heywood play. At any rate, it was not printed until 1615, by which time the artistic flowering of the Jacobean reign had reached its height. In his preface to the printed version Heywood makes this apology:

> Yet understanding (by what meanes I know not) it was in these more exquisite and refined Times to come to the Presse, in such a forwardnesse ere it came to my knowledge, that it was past prevention, and then knowing withall, that it comes short of that accuratenesse both in Plot and Style, that these more Censorious dayes with greater curiosity acquire, I

must thus excuse. That as *Playes* were some fifteene
or sixteene yeares agoe it was in the Fashion.

(*Dramatic Works,* II, pp. 161–62)

Michael Drayton's *Collected Poems* offers a similar intimation
of fluctuation in literary tastes—but in reverse. In his dedication to the 1619 edition Drayton admits that his poems were
written during what he calls the "Muse-nursing Season"
under Elizabeth in the 1590s. In 1619, however, with James's
court distinctly losing its vitality after the death of Anne and
with the king's own failing health, Drayton worries about the
reception of his courtly fare:

> Thus much I will say, to mine owne disadvantage,
> (should they hap to be unwelcome to these Times:)
> That they were the fruit of that Muse-nursing Sea-
> son: before this frosty *Boreas* (I meane the worlds
> coldnesse) had nipt our flowery *Tempe;* that with his
> pestilenciall Fogs is like utterly to poison the *Pierean*
> Spring, doe not *Apollo* mightily protect it.[56]

Another way of isolating the "courtly" drama of 1604–15
is to look at a later period in English history when the court
was thriving amid relative peace, as well as under another
pleasure-loving queen. Not surprisingly, England's next
period of courtly vitality saw the revival of many works
prominent in the first flourishing years of James's reign. In
this period of 1630–35—which parallels the opening years of
Charles's "Personal Rule" without Parliament—occurred a
remarkable recrudescence of old courtly plays.[57] Beaumont
and Fletcher's *Cupid's Revenge* was reprinted in 1630 and 1635;
their *Philaster* appeared in 1628, 1634, and 1639; *Il pastor fido*

[56]Michael Drayton, "To the Noble Sir Walter Aston," *The Works,* ed.
J. W. Hebel (Oxford, 1961), II, p. 2.

[57] "Although Charles I ascended the throne in 1625, no great series of
court entertainments began to be staged until the years of Personal Rule"
(Roy Strong, *Splendour at Court: Renaissance Spectacle and the Theatre of Power*
[Boston, 1973], p. 224).

was reprinted in 1633; *The Knight of the Burning Pestle* in 1635; *The Faithful Shepherdess* in 1629 and 1634; and *The Two Noble Kinsmen* in 1634. At the next remove, *Love's Labour's Lost* received a 1631 quarto, along with a 1632 reprinting of "sixe Court comedies" by Lyly. The prefatory matter to this last edition indicates another courtly fluctuation had occurred:

> It can be no dishonor, to listen to this Poets Musike, whose Tunes alighted in the Eares of a great and ever-famous Queene: his Invention, was so curiously strung, that *Elizaes* Court held his notes in Admiration. Light Ayres are now in fashion; And these being not sad, fit the season, though perchance not sute so well with your more serious Contemplations.
>
> (A_3^{r+v})

Front matter from other plays of this period indicates a trend toward spectacle, dance, and music such as marked the first decade of the century. In fact, a remark made in James Shirley's *Changes, or Love in a Maze* (1631–32)—

> Your dance is the best language of some comedies,
> And footing runs away with all; a scene
> Express'd with life of art, and squared to nature,
> Is dull and phlegmatic poetry
>
> (*The Dramatic Works and Poems*
> [London, 1833], II, p. 339)

—nearly paraphrases Jonson's criticisms of plays like *The Winter's Tale* and *The Tempest*:

> The Concupiscence of Daunces, and Antickes so raigneth, as to runne away from Nature, and be afraid of her, is the onely point of art that tickles the *Spectators*.
>
> (V, 291)

This may well amount to the first critical comment upon *The Tempest*; it appears in the "Address to the Reader" of the 1612 quarto of *The Alchemist*.

One playwright of the 1630s sought to turn the tide against such spectacular, culinary drama. He warned in his Prologue:

> A Strange Play you are like to have, for know,
> We use no Drum, nor Trumpet, nor Dumbe show;
> No Combate, Marriage, not so much to day,
> As Song, Dance, Masque, to bumbaste out a Play;
> Yet these all good, and still in frequent use
> With our best *Poets;* nor is this excuse
> Made by our *Author,* as if want of skill
> Caus'd this defect; it's rather his selfe will:
> Will you the reason know? There have so many
> Beene in that kind, that Hee desires not any
> At this time in His Sceane, no helpe, no straine,
> Or flash that's borrowed from an others braine.[58]

Such in large part is the superficial nature of the courtly plays of the earlier period we are examining. This may explain why in 1634 *Cymbeline, The Winter's Tale,* and *The Faithful Shepherdess* were revived at court and all "likt," while Jonson's *Tale of a Tub* (a public comedy that takes courtly entertainments in vain) was revived and "not likt."

Periods of marked artistic efflorescence at court—one each, it appears, for the reigns of Elizabeth (*circa* 1588–98), James (*circa* 1605–15), and Charles (*circa* 1630–35)—affected the fortunes of playwrights. Shakespeare's Late Plays ought to be viewed against these fluctuations in courtly taste and with a more perspicuous sense of the nature of art at court. This chronological sketch has been necessarily brief; much remains to be discovered about the fluctuations of artistic fashions in this period. But this does provide at least a rudimentary historical frame of reference for the following attempts to identify aspects of the courtly aesthetic itself.

[58]Thomas Heywood, *The English Traveler* (1633), in *The Dramatic Works of Thomas Heywood* (1874; rpt. London, 1964), IV, p. 6.

THE COURTLY AESTHETIC:
THEMES

A COURTLY AESTHETIC is born, flourishes, and fades—often paralleling the rising and declining vigor of the reigning monarch or dynasty. The power it exerts over the imagination of a court or even an entire nation fluctuates according to historical circumstances, changing fashions, and the technical development of the arts. But because Renaissance courts were based upon similar social and political foundations, the themes of courtly art were not so subject to change. Playwrights, like other artists, paid careful attention to those themes particularly congenial at court. Behind the comically squeamish preparations by the tradesmen for performance at the Court of Athens in *A Midsummer Night's Dream* lies a general truth, namely, that certain subjects and modes of expression would please and others displease, affecting future royal preference. We can be sure that Shakespeare's calculations for a possible courtly performance went beyond Bottom's desire to avoid garlic breath and to find clean linen for Thisby. This positive censorship, not to mention the strict negative censorship dispensed by the Master of the Revels, helps to explain *The Tempest*'s remarkably conservative, orthodox expression of many common courtly themes.[1]

[1]The crucial moral themes of *The Tempest* are Renaissance commonplaces. Most of them can be found in La Primaudaye's popular moral treatise, *The French Academy* (London, 1614):

Ignorance of a mans selfe . . . and the want of knowledge where-

(Though its dramatic form, that is, the way Shakespeare clothed and presented these time-honored themes, was theatrically revolutionary.) These themes are the subject of the present chapter.

CIVILIZATION

The central and most general preoccupation of courtly art is the praise and encouragement of a healthy *civitas* or *polis*.[2] As with other great examples of the civilizing intellect in literature like Virgil's *Aeneid*, Tasso's *Gerusalemme liberata*, and Spenser's *Faerie Queene*, *The Tempest* explores the poetic possibilities of *social* behavior. Its forward-looking intent is to inspire the audience, as Aeneas was inspired by his father's prophecy: *incendit . . . animum famae venientis amore* ("he fired his soul with love of fame that was to be").[3] Victor Hugo

---

fore and to what end he is borne, is the cause of error, of evil.
(pp. 11–12)

Reason is the medicine of the soule.
(p. 31)

The best revenge and most honorable victorie, which wee can carrie away from our enemies, will be to surpasse them in diligence, bountie, magnanimitie, good-turns, and in all vertuous actions.
(p. 359)

It is the property of a great and noble minde to be milde, gracious, and readie to forgive . . . it is a greater point of Magnanimitie to surmount the common nature of men by a wonderfull divinitie of the soule, than to follow after that which beasts are able to do better than we.
(p. 364)

[2]The purpose of courtly art is, as one commentator said of the *Aeneid*, to make civilization poetical, to make it attractive. Brooks Otis's *Virgil: A Study in Civilized Poetry* (Oxford, 1963) is an examination of perhaps the first great example of civilizing art.

[3]P. Vergilius Maro, *Aeneid* (6.889), H. R. Fairclough translation (New York, 1930). The prophetic speech of Anchises and the closing prophecy of Cranmer in *Henry VIII* perform similar functions in communicating their authors' civilizing ideals.

made this point about *The Tempest:* "There is in *The Tempest* the solemn tone of a testament. It might be said that, before his death, the poet, in this epopee of the ideal, had designed a codicil for the Future. In this enchanted isle . . . we may expect to behold Utopia, the promised land of future generations, Paradise regained."[4] Hugo mistakenly calls the play utopian. Its ideal of social harmony was meant to be achievable. The uplifting sweep of act 5 ought to be seen as merely a highly fictionalized romance equivalent of the plangent final scene of *Henry VIII*. Of Cranmer's prophetic last speech, Henry observes, "Thou speakest wonders"; in his final actions Prospero *works* wonders. Though cast in the distinctive dramatic terms of romance and chronicle, the political or "civilizing" miracles of *The Tempest* and *Henry VIII* are essentially alike.

We may wonder about the mixture of propaganda, wish-fulfillment, sycophancy, optimism, cynical realism, and profound desire that produced the visions of Virgil, Tasso, Spenser, and Shakespeare. But to call them utopian misses the point. They render a brave new world, not out of the innocence or naiveté of a Miranda, but out of Prospero's deep awareness of the fierce, pent-up internal forces that always threaten civilization. Just as Gonzalo's utopian jesting is made properly ridiculous by Shakespeare's careful phrasing and by the nasty wit of Antonio and Sebastian, so is Miranda's innocence undercut by Prospero's sharp irony:

MIRANDA   O, wonder!
  How many goodly creatures are there here!
  How beauteous mankind is! O brave new world,
  That has such people in't!
PROSPERO   'Tis new to thee.

          (5.1.182–85)

[4]Quoted in the New Variorum Edition of *The Tempest,* ed. H. H. Furness (1892; rpt. New York, 1964), p. 358.

Her exclamations beg for puncture. Such innocence is harmless enough on the uninhabited island, but Prospero's plans are for Milan and Naples where men must consort with each other.

To generalize, civilizing art focuses on man in society; humanizing art perforce deals with man alone. This dichotomy is suggested by a look at Shakespeare's canon. Those plays in which life at court is seen as potentially pleasant and desirable (*Love's Labour's Lost, A Midsummer Night's Dream, Twelfth Night, The Tempest*) fall into the category of civilizing art; plays that are antiromantic, anticourtly, isolating, and humanizing in the Montaignesque sense of the word (*Hamlet, Timon, Lear*) fall into the latter category. Tasso makes something of this distinction in his explanation of *Gerusalemme liberata*. He observes that the *Odyssey* and the *Divina Commedia* are allegories of the inner, contemplative man; hence, Homer and Dante showed their heroes "not to be accompanied of the armie, or of a multitude of followers" but alone or with a companion. The middle-period Shakespearean tragedies focus on man alone, and they are thus akin to these two epics of the "dark" journey. On the other hand, the *Iliad* and the *Aeneid* represent allegories of the active, civil life of their heroes. Consequently, "*Agamemnon* and *Achilles* are described, the one Generall of the *Grecian* Armie, the other leader of many troupes of *Mirmidons,* and *Aeneas* is seene to be accompanied when he fighteth, or doth other civill actes."[5] Until the last minutes of the play, all of Prospero's important acts are civil ones; the play in effect sets forth an elaborate civilizing process. In his own definition of the allegory of his epic, Tasso called this process an "Operation Political." According to Tasso the "Operation Politicall" can proceed only when "many [are] together and to one end working" (A_3^r), and this is what—under Prospero's skillful leadership—

[5]Torquato Tasso, *Gerusalemme liberata,* translated by E. Fairefax as *Godfrey of Bulloigne, or The Recovery of Jerusalem* (London, 1600), sig. A_2^v.

happens in *The Tempest.* The end of Tasso's epic is a state of "politike blessednes" (A$_4$^{v}) here on earth, for his fictional Jerusalem is intended to signify "the Civill happines . . . which is a good, verie difficult to attaine unto, and situated upon the top of the Alpine and wearisome hill of virtue; and unto this are turned (as unto the last marke) all the Actions of the politicke man" (A$_3$^{r}). Prospero's is the arduous task of the political man: to orchestrate the beings on the island into a renewed political context, foster the practice of various political virtues (chastity, obedience, loyalty), and ultimately reap the benefits of civil happiness. This is the supreme if implicit goal of courtly literature and is accomplished through the creation of fictional metropolises like Virgil's Rome, Tasso's Jerusalem, Spenser's Court of Faery, the Troynovant (i.e. London) of the poets, and Shakespeare's renovated Dukedom of Milan and Kingdom of Naples.

The Faerie Queene, and most especially book 6, presents such an ideal social construct (and the very real dangers that threaten it). This book is an English equivalent of *The Book of the Courtier,* whose explicit purpose is to describe the nature of the perfect courtier, his "civill conversation" and "goodly manners" among men. A central lesson of Tasso's *Gerusalemme* is that "Reason commandeth Anger, not imperiously, but curteouslie and civillie" (A$_4$^{v}), and this is a main lesson of book 6 of *The Faerie Queene* as well. The focus of the two— "civil happiness" and "civility" respectively—is the same. Throughout the book "Conteyning the Legend of Sir Calidore, or Courtesie," *grace* is clearly a social concept:

> These three [Graces] on men all gracious gifts
>   bestow,
> Which decke the body or adorne the minde,
> To make them lovely or well favoured show,
> As comely carriage, entertainement kinde,
> Sweete semblaunt, friendly offices that binde,
> And all the complements of curtesie:

> They teach us, how to each degree and kinde
> We should our selves demeane, to low, to hie;
> To friends, to foes, which skill men call Civility.
>
> (6.10.23)

But like *The Tempest,* book 6 does not blink at evil. It shows, rather, what is necessary to keep the forces that ruin the courtly peace in "bondage strong." In the Blatant Beast are shown the aberrations of civility, how they can be checked, and—in the last darkening stanzas—how easily they can become potent again. The forces of destruction, like the winds of Aeolus that set in motion the tragic events of the *Aeneid,* cannot be extinguished, only circumscribed and controlled by constant vigilance.

As a play urging civilized behavior (Prospero's isle is "uninhabited," "barren," "desert"—a place never considered for permanent domicile, except by Caliban), *The Tempest* is like the greatest of all civilizing literary works, the *Aeneid.* Both poets were deep-dyed in the orthodoxies of their times, and nothing they left us gives the impression of the renegade or heretical. As civilizing intellects they were eager for the preservation of the established order. At least in their literary expressions, they respected the resident power structure and were convinced of the efficacy of their ruling monarchs. The *Aeneid* indicates that Virgil took the Augustan spirit of regeneration seriously,[6] just as Shakespeare voiced often, with a glowing force that bespeaks sincerity, the benefits of Stuart

---

[6] "It seems quite plain that Virgil was himself a convinced Augustan. He was clearly inspired by his theme: he believed in his own 'ideology.' He really saw in Augustus the type of man who could bring peace out of fratricidal war, order from anarchy, self-control from selfish passion, in a sense, an 'age of gold' from an age of iron. He also saw in Rome the paradigm and goal of all historical activity, in Roman *pietas, virtus,* and *consilium* the only hope of peace and social order, of humane behaviour associated with strong government" (Otis, *Virgil,* p. 389).

government we now know were largely illusory. Shake-speare, like all Englishmen of the time, feared a devastating civil war, placed hope in a strong, magnanimous ruler, and desired peace and stability—all sentiments felt in Augustan Rome and prophesied by Virgil. *The Tempest* expresses these feelings, projecting an English version of political *pietas* (Ferdinand, Ariel, Gonzalo, Prospero) and *consilium* (the prudent acts of act 5).

The endurance of Aeneas has a civilizing meaning: "Aeneas is the *hero* in that he looks beyond such tragedy [of self-sacrifice for the Roman ideal] to a peace that will in some sense overcome it and, at the least, serve to mitigate it. In a word: Virgil is a civilized poet."[7] In the *Aeneid* the hero is unhappily suspended between a past *aurea saecula* and the promise of a renovated Trojan society in Italy; the story of the epic is his struggle to attain this political goal. Prospero finds himself in a similar position, exiled from his homeland and depending upon an auspicious star that promises a happy outcome. Indeed, *The Tempest* is a highly compact version of Virgil's epic of a lost civilization rewon: the *Aeneid* focuses on a *Troia recidiva, The Tempest* on a Milan *recidiva.*

The literature of civilization centers upon positive moral constructs—*pius* Aeneas, "noble" Calidore, "good" Prospero. Evil exists in it only to be restrained or converted. The literature of civilization presents a most majestic vision of civil tranquillity. It sets out to prove that men—and most importantly, men at court—can live in harmony. It does so by portraying figures like Calidore, Ferdinand, or Ariel who are willing to perform obediently all "sanctimonious ceremonies"—as well as figures like Allecto, the Blatant Beast, or Caliban who subvert society but who are in the end themselves subjected.

---

[7]*Ibid.,* p. 393 (original emphasis).

THE GOLDEN AGE

Ever since Virgil alluded to his sovereign as bringer of a golden age, this theme has served the creators of flattering courtly art: "This, this is he, whom thou so oft hearest promised to thee, Augustus Caesar, son of a god, who shall again set up the Golden Age amid the fields where Saturn once reigned" (6.791–94). With Saturn or his feminine counterpart Astraea the Renaissance associated a return to peace and abundance such as Anchises predicts for the Trojan *reliquiae*.[8] One of the tasks of the courtly writer was to show his ruler as the creator of a new golden era.

The theme of the golden age returned, sophisticated by Virgil and popularized by Ovid and countless others, became a commonplace of courtly art in the Renaissance. The Italian plays *Aminta* and *Il pastor fido* both contain an initial chorus "O bella etá de l'oro" and then proceed to show how a golden age is alchemically derived from a present iron age. George Chapman chose just this conceit when he praised an English attempt to follow Tasso and Guarini, Fletcher's *The Faithful Shepherdess:*

> This Iron age that eates it selfe, will never
> Bite at your [i.e. Fletcher's] golden world.
> (Beaumont and Fletcher,
> *The Dramatic Works,* III, 492)

But we must look to courtly entertainments and masques for the theme's most brilliant embodiment. In these works poets and artists sought to symbolize their monarch's aureifying powers:

[8] "The Platonickes . . . called the time wherein hee [Saturn] lived the golden age, as a time, entertaining quiet, concord, and true content." Vincenzo Cartari, *The Fountaine of Ancient Fiction,* trans. R. Linche (London, 1599), sig. D₃ᵛ. See also Frances Yates, *Astraea: The Imperial Theme in the Sixteenth Century* (London, 1975).

> 'Tis he [James], that stayes the time from turning
> old,
> And keepes the age up in a head of gold.
> That in his owne true circle, still doth runne;
> And holds his course, as certaine as the sunne.
> He makes it ever day, and ever spring,
> Where he doth shine, and quickens every thing
> Like a new nature.
>
> (Jonson, *Oberon, Works,* VII, 353)

The overall result of such imagery, as we shall see, was the congenial, idyllic, vernal, and bright superficies of the courtly aesthetic.

The conceit is embodied in George Peele's 1591 Lord Mayor's Show *Descensus Astraeae,* which features the descent of the stellified Astraea (Elizabeth), who introduces

> happie times
> That do beget such calme and quiet dayes,
> Where sheep and shepheard breath in such content.[9]

The same crux is worked out elaborately in Jonson's Masque *The Golden Age Restored* (1615). Having effected the banishment of Iron Age, Astraea looks out upon the court of James and concludes:

> What change is here! I had not more
> Desire to leave the earth before,
>   Then I have now, to stay;
> My silver feet, like roots, are wreath'd
> Into the ground, my wings are sheath'd,
>   And I cannot away.

> Of all there seemes a second birth,
> It is become a heav'n on earth,
>   And *Jove* is present here,

[9]George Peele, *The Life and Works of George Peele,* ed. David Horne (New Haven, Conn., 1952), pp. 214–15.

I feele the Godhead: nor will doubt
But he can fill the place throughout,
   Whose power is every where.

This, this, and onely such as this,
The bright *Astraea's* region is,
   Where she would pray to live,
And in the midd'st of so much gold,
Unbought with grace or feare unsold,
   The law to mortals give.
                (*Works,* VII, 428–29)

As Jonson's editors, Herford and Simpson, trenchantly add, "*Iam redit et Virgo, redeunt Saturnia regna,* for James was on the throne" (VII, 420). James was flattered in Virgilian terms as early as the triumphal procession of 1604. In one arch invented by Jonson a figure carries the motto *Redeunt Saturnia Regna;* Jonson explains the allusion: "Out of *Virgil,* to shew that now those golden times were returned againe, wherein *Peace* was with us so advanced, *Rest* received, *Libertie* restored, *Safetie* assured, and all *Blessednesse* appearing in every of these vertues her particular triumph over her opposite evill" (VII, 100). James succumbed to the occupational hazard of Renaissance kings and began to believe such flattery.

Prospero participates in the symbolic process expressed in these citations from Chapman, Peele, and Jonson. He is both a prophet (Anchises) and a bringer of political regeneration (Aeneas). His political career should be associated with the setting and reascent of other Renaissance figures like Apollo, Saturn, and Astraea, upon whom the health of a civilization was often made symbolically to depend—and who often in political allegories achieved a return to political stability. Behind the fictional aura of Prospero lies the cyclical allegory of the Golden Age. He has ruled in a former time of peace; his actions are necessary for its reappearance; and this very reappearance signals the relinquishment of his powers.

Unlike the royal withdrawal in *King Lear,* Prospero's occurs *after* the trials by storm and *after* the forces of evil have been discerned and (at least temporarily) enervated. As Prospero's magic loses its potency, a new golden age dawns. Through the emphasis of the masque, Miranda and Ferdinand become the prospective focus of a new harmony. Miranda in effect becomes the equivalent of Venus, a source of renewed fertility in the two dynasties. Her reappearance upon the tide in Naples shall be at least symbolically reminiscent of Venus's miraculous birth from the waves. Hence the resonance of Gonzalo's lines,

> O, rejoice
> Beyond a common joy! and set it down
> With gold on lasting pillars.
>
> (5.1.206–8)

With gold on lasting pillars—it is the phrase of a civilized man, and perhaps there is no better for capturing the aureate, civilizing action of the play. Its hint of glory, permanence, and celebration reflects the tenor of act 5. Gonzalo's speech celebrates the central fact of the play, that from the chaos of the opening storm has come a new world of order where every man is his own, not usurped by the neurosis of passion or the corruption of ambition. We feel, to use Chapman's phrase, that a golden scepter will again be stroking the strings of civil government.

DYNASTY: THE IMPERIAL THEME

Because the "peace of the presence" depends upon the unbroken, lineal transference of the royal prerogative, courtly art is the art of fathers and children. It should not surprise us that the first consideration in the minds of Shakespeare's countrymen—perhaps as vital as James's actual mode of rule—was the promise of a peaceful succession. This anxiety was the more natural after the agonies of doubt that swept England in Elizabeth's last years, since

> barren Princes
> Breed danger in their singularitie,
> Having none to succeed, their claime dies in them. [10]

Men of the Renaissance displayed a genealogical interest for reasons clear enough: their lives and livelihoods often depended upon genealogical quirks and obscurities. So it was that Puttenham singled out as a particularly apt occasion for "poeticall rejoysing" the birth of noble children: "the comfort of issue and procreation of children is so naturall and so great, not onely to all men but specially to Princes, as duetie and civilitie have made it a common custome to rejoyse at the birth of their noble children." [11]

In his book *The Royal Play of Macbeth*, Henry Paul demonstrated Shakespeare's extreme care to exploit James's preoccupation with his own ancestry: "James was a genealogist. Only one who keeps in mind the passionate interest which this learned king had in his royal ancestry (from which he deduced his alleged divine right) can understand certain parts of the play." [12] And Paul especially emphasizes the importance of the dynastic concept: "It is not only an imperial dynasty that is pictured [in *Macbeth*], but a dynasty which to its great advantage had since the days of Robert Bruce produced a line of nine Stuart kings who had taken the throne of Scotland in direct *lineal succession*. This may conveniently be thought of as the *Stuart theme*." [13] From James's own writings

[10]Thomas Heywood, *The Rape of Lucrece*, in *Dramatic Works* (1874; rpt. London, 1964), V, p. 188.

[11]George Puttenham, "Of the solemne rejoysings at the nativitie of Princes children," *The Arte of English Poesie*, eds. Gladys Willcock and Alice Walker (1936; rpt. London, 1970), p. 49.

[12]Henry Paul, *The Royal Play of Macbeth* (New York, 1950), p. 152.

[13]*Ibid.*, p. 168. The heading of this section is borrowed from the chapter of Paul's book (pp. 162–82) relevant to genealogy. The chapter on the

and speeches the significance of dynastic continuity is manifest. In *Basilikon Doron* he admonishes Prince Henry to "enjoy . . . this whole Ile, according to Gods right and your lineall descent," and he thanked his first parliament for "receiving of mee in this Seate (which GOD by my Birthright and lineall descent had in the fulnesse of time provided for me)."[14]

The poignantly speechless dejection of Alonso at the loss of Ferdinand is suggestive of the dejection of England on the death in 1612 of Prince Henry—the "Glory of knights, and hope of all the earth" (Jonson, *Prince Henries Barriers,* VII, 328). Because Henry had already proved himself a salient personality, vigorous in body and resolute in mind, great expectation attached to his eventual accession. He was Britain's "best hope, and the world's delight; / Ordain'd to make thy eight Great *Henries,* nine."[15] Sir Charles Cornwallis, who knew Henry personally, observed princely attitudes that have seemed welcome in the light of the kings's preferment of dubiously endowed favorites:

> Hee oftimes protested that neither fantasie nor flattery should move him to conferre upon any a superlative place in his favour, but would to the uttermost of his understanding, measure unto all according to the merit of their services, as holding it not just to yield unto affections, or rather second respects, that which is onely due to vertue and deservings.[16]

The picture Cornwallis paints ("To conclude of this Prince,

"Dramatic Personae" is also fascinating in its analysis of Shakespeare's care for genealogical niceties. Paul concludes that Shakespeare's concerted effort in *Macbeth* was "to remind his king of the glories of the Stuart dynasty" (pp. 180–81).

[14]James I, *The Political Works of James I,* ed. Charles McIlwain (Cambridge, Mass., 1918), pp. 22, 269.

[15]Michael Drayton, *Dedication to Poly-olbion* (1612), *Works,* ed. J. W. Hebel (Oxford, 1961), IV, sig. iv*.

[16]Sir Charles Cornwallis, *A discourse of the most Illustrious Prince Henry* (1626 MS, published London, 1641), p. 26.

did hee not all things well?") is akin in its undoubted bias to
Shakespeare's Ferdinand.[17] Likewise, the father's sorrow over
Ferdinand's drowning is reflected in these words written by
the Earl of Dorset to Sir Thomas Edmonds: "To tell you that
our Rising Sun is set ere scarce he had shone, and that all our
glory lies buried, you know and do lament as well as we, and
better than some do, and more truly, or else you were not a
man, and sensible of this Kingdome's loss."[18] Many were to
feel something of Alonso's sorrow a few years after *The Tempest* first appeared. The excellencies of the "hopefull Prince"
(so lavishly expressed, for instance, in Jonson's *Barriers* and
the masque of *Oberon*, in which Henry participated) were
soon to be buried, not to be regained as in Shakespeare's play.

At the heart of the concept of dynasty is the belief that
historical continuity must exist for the cumulative momentum of civilization to develop.[19] Continuity makes direction

[17]Sir Charles Cornwallis's *The Life and Death of our Late most Incomparable and Heroique Prince Henry* (1641; rpt. London, 1738) contains a more
lengthy and adulatory description of the Prince. Cornwallis's peroration is
worth quoting:

> What should I say more of him? over and above all these things,
> hee had a certaine kind of extraordinary unspeakeable excellency,
> my fraile penne and dull style not being able to expresse the same,
> gathered (out of question) by him long agoe from the plentifull
> Garden of the King his Fathers all admired *Bazilicon-doron*, long
> since in his youth dedicated unto him.
>
> (p. 101)

[18]Printed in John Nichols, *The Progresses, Processions, and Magnificent Festivities of King James the First* (London, 1828), II, p. 490. Nichols lists thirty-
two elegies and funeral pamphlets for Henry (II, pp. 504–12).

[19]The present topic draws our attention again to Virgil's epic. Reuben
Brower has well called it "a drama of fathers and sons" in *Hero and Saint:
Shakespeare and the Graeco–Roman Heroic Tradition* (New York, 1971), p. 93.
The *Aeneid*'s crucial fiction is the genealogical myth that traces the line of
Augustus and Julius Caesar back to Aeneas and thus to the divine birth of
Venus—much as James traced his own ancestry back 300 years before Christ.
The two prophetic set-pieces (1.257ff. and 6.765ff.) are plangent tracings of
the dynastic antecedents of the Roman emperors, an endless chain of fathers
and sons coursing through *magnos volvendis mensibus orbis*. The sense of *pietas*
which binds father and son provides some of the most profound moments in

and progress possible. Dynasty works "the peace of the presence" through the long stretch of the historical continuum
and gives order to human energies. Aeneas's benediction as he
leaves Hesperia (*maneat nostros ea cura nepotes*, "May that
charge await our children's children" [3.505]) might have

the epic. Aeneas's reunion with his father in Hell is perhaps the single most
affecting indication of the dynastic theme. After their emotional meeting,
Anchises leads his son through Hell. He is the "presenter" to his living de-
scendant of their posterity's golden future. Aeneas once and for all learns the
lesson of dynastic *pietas*, and it is only proper that he should learn it from his
father:

> Come now, what glory shall hereafter attend the Dardan line, what
> children of Italian stock await thee, souls illustrious and heirs of
> our name—this will I set forth, and teach thee thy destiny.
>
> (6.756–59)

The history of the future inspires Aeneas with "love of fame that is to be" and
the strength to confront the labor awaiting him in Latium.

A popular method of inspiring James's subjects with love was comparison with Aeneas. This was no doubt encouraged by James's choice of a line
from Anchises's prophecy as his motto at the close of *Basilikon Doron:*

> And being content to let others excell in other things, let it be your
> chiefest earthly glory, to excell in your owne craft: according to the
> worthy counsel and charge of *Anchises* to his posteritie, in that sub-
> lime and heroicall Poet, wherein also my dicton is included . . .
> *Parcere subiectis, & debellare superbos.*
>
> (*Political Works*, p. 52)

Shortly before *The Tempest* was written, the connection between the Augustan and Jacobean reigns figured prominently in Jonson's *Haddington Masque*
(1608). There, Venus praises her son Aeneas in terms meant specifically to
apply to James. Jonson explains this intention in a note:

> *Aeneas*, the sonne of *Venus*, *Virgil* makes through-out the most
> exquisite patterne of *Pietie, Justice, Prudence*, and all other Princely
> vertues, with whom (in way of that excellence) I conferre my
> Soveraigne, applying, in his description, his owne *word* [i.e. *Basil-
> ikon Doron*], usurped of that *Poets: Parcere subiectis, & debellare
> superbos.*
>
> (VII, 256)

Another dynastic aspect of *Aeneid* 6 is worth noting. This is the fulsome
praise (6.860–85) of the boy Marcellus whom Augustus had chosen to suc-
ceed him. The boy died in 23 B.C., universally lamented. Both James and
Augustus saw their intended successors die before them.

served as an epigraph for *The Tempest,* had Shakespeare taken
to the Jonsonian habit of supplying one. Underlying Prospero's fatherly love for Miranda is a strong sense of her dynastic importance:

> I have done nothing but in care of thee,
> Of thee, my dear one; thee, my daughter, who
> Art ignorant of what thou art.
>
> (1.2.16–18)

Prospero's care has been for the heiress of the usurped dukedom, as he proceeds to explain. The conversation in which
Aeneas learns the lessons of political *pietas* from his father is
reflected, less prepossessingly to be sure, in the initial inter-
view between father and daughter:

> PROSPERO   Thy father was the Duke of Milan, and
>   A prince of power.
> MIRANDA   Sir, are not you my father?
> PROSPERO   Thy mother was a piece of virtue, and
>   She said thou wast my daughter, and thy father
>   Was Duke of Milan; and his only heir
>   And princess, no worse issued.
>
> (1.2.54–59)

By the beginning of act 4 we are better able to grasp the nature of Prospero's devotion, when he says to Ferdinand,

>   I
> Have given you here a third of mine own life,
> Or that for which I live.
>
> (4.1.2–4)

Prospero is living for the union of Naples and Milan, and the
time when he can retire, sure of political order and a noble line
to perpetuate it.

Even more strikingly victimized by the rupture of the
dynastic bond is Alonso. Until the discovery of his son in act
5, Alonso exhibits the reticence of grief. His only two

speeches of importance in the first four acts express his genealogical concern:

> Would I had never
> Married my daughter there! for, coming thence,
> My son is lost, and, in my rate, she too,
> Who is so far from Italy removed
> I ne'er again shall see her. O thou mine heir
> Of Naples and of Milan, what strange fish
> Hath made his meal on thee?
>
> (2.1.103–9)

Worse than a son, Alonso has lost an heir. Following Ariel's speech browbeating the "men of sin," Alonso makes a remarkable response. He feels guilt, not for supplanting Prospero, but for ruining his own lineage:

> Methought the billows spoke, and told me of it;
> The winds did sing it to me; and the thunder,
> That deep and dreadful organ-pipe, pronounc'd
> The name of Prosper: it did bass my trespass.
> Therefor my son i' the ooze is bedded; and
> I'll seek him deeper than e'er plummet sounded,
> And with him there lie mudded.
>
> (3.3.96–102)

Just how close to his mind the dynastic concern lies is forcibly shown in act 5. Having resigned his dukedom to Prospero and still unaware of Ferdinand's salvation, Alonso learns that Prospero has lately "lost" a daughter. In a speech compact of hopelessness and wishful thinking, he replies:

> A daughter?
> O heavens, that they were living both in Naples,
> The King and Queen there! that they were, I wish
> Myself were mudded in that oozy bed
> Where my son lies.
>
> (5.1.148–52)

85

When by a "most high miracle" this wish is granted, the concern is primarily to heal the broken dynastic lines. Gonzalo as usual steps in with the right words: "Look down, you gods, / And on this couple drop a blessed crown!" (5.1.201–202). To which Alonso adds, "I say, Amen."

Prospero, however, is the central father-figure in *The Tempest*. He is as Ferdinand describes him,

> So rare a wonder'd father and a wise
> Makes this place Paradise.
>
> (4.1.123–24)

We first meet him as "my dearest father," teaching his daughter about the lineage she bears. We leave him hoping

> to see the nuptial
> Of these our dear-belov'd solemnized;
> And thence retire me to my Milan, where
> Every third thought shall be my grave.
>
> (5.1.308–11)

The last line has struck a puzzling note for some, I think, because we have failed to see the reflection of Anchises in Prospero. After Anchises shows Aeneas "what glory shall hereafter attend the Dardan line," his task as *pater familias* and *pater patriae* is done. He inspires his son to fulfill his destiny, dismisses him in a beautifully understated scene, and returns to the land of the dead. Prospero's reference to the grave makes better sense when we realize that his main concern is now soon to be resolved. The line of the "right Duke of Milan" has been secured; he may now begin to pay attention to himself and his books. The troublesome "grave" amounts neither to an odd morbidity nor to the playwright's own sense of his weakening constitution, so much as to an indication that the correct priorities have been observed: the responsibilities of a conscientious leader have given way to the preoccupations of a man. Their dynastic function performed, Anchises and

Prospero are free to return to or face the land of the dead. *The Tempest,* too, is a drama of fathers and children.

The theme of dynasty also looms large in *The Winter's Tale* (see 4.4.547–50; 5.1.130–34; 5.1.168–78—speeches reminiscent of Alonso's). Leontes' turn-about, one might add, finally results from news of his son's death (3.2.146). Polixenes notes that a father's joy "is nothing else / But fair posterity" (4.4.408–9), and the importance of posterity is implicit in the precedence of Leontes' speech:

> The wrong I did myself; which was so much
> That heirless it hath made my kingdom, and
> Destroy'd the sweet'st companion that e'er man
> Bred his hopes out of.
>
> (5.1.9–12)

Explicit and implicit statements of the importance of the dynastic theme dot the play (1.1.34–45; 1.2.34, 163–67, 337; 2.2.25; 3.2.135; 4.4.550–51; and especially 5.1.24–29). Glynne Wickham has even suggested that *The Winter's Tale* was Shakespeare's contribution, full of courtly allusions, to an important dynastic event, the investiture of Henry as Prince of Wales and Heir Apparent in 1610.[20]

The fatherly pride of Prospero and Alonso at play's end is also prominent in the king's reaction to the brilliant dynastic prophecy uttered by Cranmer at the close of *Henry VIII:*

> O Lord Archbishop,
> Thou hast made me now a man! never, before
> This happy child, did I get any thing.
> This oracle of comfort has so pleas'd me
> That when I am in heaven I shall desire
> To see what this child does, and praise my Maker.
>
> (5.4.63–69)

---

[20]Glynne Wickham, "Shakespeare's Investiture Play," *Times Literary Supplement,* 18 December 1969, p. 1456.

Cranmer's speech is most certainly an "oracle of comfort," and the comfort derives from a flourishing dynasty predicted for James:

> So shall she [Elizabeth] leave her blessedness to one
> [James] . . .
> Who from the sacred ashes of her honor
> Shall star-like rise as great in fame as she was,
> And so stand fix'd . . .
> . . . He shall flourish,
> And like a mountain cedar reach his branches
> To all the plains about him. Our children's children
> Shall see this, and bless heaven.
>
> (5.4.43−55)

THE PERFECT RULER

Temperance

Because courtly art depends for its vitality upon a strong monarch, and because it often addresses the monarch directly, it is concerned to lay before its audience the ideal of the perfect ruler. Sidney, Spenser, and most Elizabethans thought this was Virgil's primary object in the *Aeneid,* and a similar concern to describe the perfect ruler is notable in *Gerusalemme liberata, The Faerie Queene,* and the *Arcadia.* Indeed, much courtly literature amounts to a thinly disguised mirror for princes.[21] The manner in which Prospero is set forth conforms not only to this literary tradition but to the way James himself was praised and flattered. The crux of his portrayal lies in the

[21]Roy Strong thoroughly demonstrates the importance of idealized rulers in his study of Renaissance courtly festivals: "Renaissance mirrors, like court festivals, endlessly parade the illustrious figures of antiquity as *exempla* of virtues and vices for the ideal ruler. Working under the aura of a pervasive Neo-Platonism, the heroes of antiquity—Augustus, Alexander, Aeneas and a host of others—became 'Ideas' of a particular virtuous or vicious abstraction made flesh" (*Splendour at Court: Renaissance Spectacle and the Theatre of Power* [Boston, 1973], p. 52).

concept of temperance, and the play's admonition to princes is the same as Hamlet's to the players: "In the very torrent, tempest, and, as I may say, the whirlwind of your passion, you must acquire and beget a temperance" (3.2.5–7).

Of the four moral virtues (prudence, justice, and fortitude being the others), temperance was the most important in the Renaissance ethical system. Without temperance within and among men, none of the other virtues could exercise their power, and without the tempering of multiple forces—be they humors, family members, or social classes—order was impossible. For the Renaissance, temperance meant order: "To live in Temperance, is to order and dispose every thing according to the right use whereto it was appointed."[22] Temperance also meant unity:

> Therefore the wise men have most religiously observed two beginnings of things; the one of evil, divisible, imperfect, manifold, called *duallitie,* or *Binarius numerus.* Another of good, indivisible, perfect, and in name, and nature, always one, called *unitas.* If *Duallitie,* or *Binarius,* as cause efficient beare sway, then in the aire it breedeth intemperature; if in citties, families, or kingdomes, wars, and discorde; if in the body, diseases; if in the minde of men, vice, and wickednes. But where *union* possesseth chiefe place, her fruites are, to the aire wholsome temper; to citties, families, & kingdomes, mutual love, and joye; to the bodie health, and strength; and to the minde, vertue, & godlines.[23]

La Primaudaye summarized the importance of temperance when he wrote, "this vertue of temperance comprehendeth in it all the other vertues: that through her a harmony, concor-

---

[22]Jean de Cartigny (John Carthenay), *The Voyage of the Wandering Knight* (1607; rpt. ed. Dorothy Evans, Seattle, Wash., 1951), p. 106.

[23]John Thornborough, *The Joyfull and Blessed Reuniting* . . . (London, circa 1604), p. 11.

dance, and conjunction of them all is made."[24] This is the temperance Prospero commands at the end of *The Tempest.*

Caliban, Sebastian, and Antonio represent the forces of evil, duality, and intemperance.[25] The remembrance of Caliban's plot "distempers" Prospero during the wedding masque, and this malaise is overcome by a process of tempering his temptation to revenge—obeying the ideal of Portia's speech in *The Merchant of Venice.* Prospero functions as a *moderator* in the scheme of the play. He intervenes in the action, comments on its progress, orchestrates the groups of characters—all with the ultimate purpose of tempering those under his control. Prospero embodies the very definition of *temperare* (Latin: to temper) described by Leo Spitzer:

> Accordingly *temperare* would mean an intervention at
> the right time and in the right measure, by a wise . . .
> "moderator" who adjusts, adapts, mixes, alterna-
> tively softens or hardens (wine, iron, etc.). Any pur-
> poseful activity which proceeds with a view to cor-
> recting excesses was called *temperare.*[26]

The Renaissance expressed this idea through the theory of the four humors: "As shee [Nature] hath in naturall mixtion reduced the fowre contrary Elementes into a temperate and

[24]Pierre de La Primaudaye, *The French Academy* (London, 1614), p. 170.

[25]The moral "seascape" of intemperance is reflected in *The Tempest* and in this passage from Thomas Walkington's *Optick Glasse of Humors* (London, 1607): "Without this knowledge of our bodily nature, we are like to crasie barkes, yet ballist with prizelesse marchandise, which are tossed too and fro upon the maine of ignorance so long, till at length we bee shattered against the huge rocke of Intemperance" (sig. 6ᵛ–7ʳ). La Primaudaye, too, hints at the moral behind the storm in *The Tempest:* "as the windes torment and tosse that shippe which they have seazed upon, now here now there, and will not suffer it to be guided by her maister: so Intemperance moouing and compelling the soule to disobey reason, suffereth her not to enjoy tranquillitie and rest, which is an assured haven of harbour from all windes" (*The French Academy,* pp. 179–80).

[26]Leo Spitzer, *Classical and Christian Ideas of World Harmony* (Baltimore. Md., 1963), p. 82.

agreeing conformitie . . . so shoulde wee by temperate discretion bee willingly united with our neighbour friends into one corporation," wrote Thornborough in his treatise on the union of England and Scotland.[27] The end result of *The Tempest*'s action is this "one corporation"—a social structure in which Tasso's civil happiness and Spenser's civility can flourish.

By the power of his nobler reason Prospero is able to overcome vengeful fury. For the Renaissance such political temperance was golden. The full title of Walkington's tract on the humors hints at this idea: *The Optick Glasse of Humors or The Touchstone of a golden temperature, or the Philosophers stone to make a golden temper.* Thornborough makes even more explicit the connection between the exercise of temperance and the achievement of a golden age:

> The Poets call this latter age *Ferrea:* let us which live in it prove them Poets, not Prophets, that so being joined to our golden head [i.e. James] in all obedience and dutie, in all love and zeale to our countrie, and in Unitie among our selves, we may live a blessed life in the golden age of our happy time, and shew our selves well tempered, not of brittle but of better clay.[28]

The political thought of *The Tempest* focuses upon Prospero as the ideal ruler, and he is ideal because he finally comes to practice temperance:

> O, in what Safetie Temperance doth rest,
> Obtaining Harbour in a soveraigne Brest!
> Which, if so praisefull in the meanest Men,
> In pow'rfull Kings how glorious is it then?[29]

[27]Thornborough, *The Joyefull and Blessed Reuniting* . . . , p. 54.

[28]John Thornborough, *A discourse* . . . (London, 1604), pp. 34–35.

[29]Michael Drayton, *Englands Heroicall Epistles* (1619), *Works,* ed. J. W. Hebel (Oxford, 1961), II, p. 156.

Very glorious in Prospero's case, for from it flow his humane and merciful gestures in act 5.[30] Prospero is a textbook study of the nature of the temperate ruler, and *The Tempest* is a dramatic expression of the idea that every man, every citizen, and especially every ruler must seek that "mediocrity, which Cicero calleth the best of things" (La Primaudaye). Thus, the climactic speech of the play—

> Though with their high wrongs I am struck to th'
> quick,
> Yet with my nobler reason 'gainst my fury
> Do I take part: the rarer action is
> In virtue than in vengeance: they being penitent,
> The sole drift of my purpose doth extend
> Not a frown further.
>
> (5.1.25–30)

—is very similar to the moral crux of other literary monuments to the Renaissance desire for temperate rulers: *Gerusalemme liberata*, *Orlando Furioso*,[31] *The Faerie Queene*,[32] *Il*

---

[30]This would surprise no Renaissance Englishman familiar with Anthony Nixon's catechism in *The Dignitie of Man* (London, 1612), p. 79:

> Q. What be the effects of *Temperance?*
> A. It is the piller of *Fortitude.*
> The Helmet against luxuriousness.
> The Guide of the eyes.
> It preserveth good-will.
> It represseth ill thoughts.
> It tameth desires.
> It hindereth dishonest actions.
> It mollifies mens hearts, And giveth
> reason for a rule.

Compare Michael's catechism on "The rule of *Not too much*, by temperance taught" in *Paradise Lost*, 11.530ff.

[31]In his "morall" note to Ariosto's 42nd Canto, John Harington has occasion to draw attention to another *locus classicus* on the temperate ruler, Cicero:

> *Tully* in his Oration *pro Marcello* hath many excellent sayings to this effect to praise *Caesar* and all such as being able to revenge yet rather choose to forgive, as in one place he saith . . . . To overcome

pastor fido,[33] *La vida es sueño*,[34] as well as numerous court

---

the passions of the minde, to bridell ones anger, to moderate the victorie, &c. who doth these things I compare not him to the best sort of men, but I liken him to God himselfe.

(p. 490)

[32]Similar to Prospero's speech is this crux from book 2, which is devoted to temperance. Indeed, this stanza is crucial to the entire poem:

But in a body, which doth freely yield
    His partes to reasons rule obedient,
    And letteth her that ought the scepter wield,
    All happy peace and goodly government
    Is setled there in sure establishment;
    There *Alma* like a virgin Queene most bright,
    Doth florish in all beautie excellent:
    And to her guestes doth bounteous banket dight,
Attempred goodly well for health and for delight.

(2.11.2)

[33]In act 5, scene 5 of Guarini's play, as its denouement begins to unfold, the authorial figure Carino offers this advice:

Anger was never in a noble mind
A furious tempest: but a gentle wind
Of Passion onely, which but stirs the soul,
(Where Reason still doth keep her due comptroll)
Lest it should grow a standing pool, unfit
For vertuous action.

(ll.4747–52, Fanshawe trans.)

Guarini adds this note to these lines in his 1602 edition: "From this passage we see clearly that it is possible for anger to be good and evil; one is not obedient to reason, the other is. One is furious, and the other is very complaisant to the rational appetite" (p. 224ʳ, my trans.).

[34]Another important play featuring a fifth-act turnabout like Prospero's is Calderón's *La vida es sueño,* ed. Albert Sloman (Manchester, 1961). In this play Segismundo voices commonplaces with which we have already become familiar:

He who hopes to master his fate
Should act with temperance and prudence.

(ll. 3216–17)

    Today I aim
At the highest triumph,
That over myself!

(ll. 3257–59)

The forgiving heart is noble.

(l. 3318)

93

masques.[35] The common import of these works is unambiguous: every man must be his own moderator and must obey the royal and divine moderators; every man must acquire and beget a temperance from the tempest of his passions and ambitions and from the tempest of social disorder.

When temperance is practiced by the ruler, political harmony results. So it is natural to find James praised for just the unifying social feats Prospero performs in act 5. And he is praised in imagery that leads us back to the "sounds and sweet airs" of the enchanted island:

> Behold, how . . . he draweth to the true knowledge of God, very salvage Beasts . . . by the sweet Harmony of his harp: the most fierce, and wilde, the most stupid and insenced, the most brutish and voluptuous, are changed and civilized by the delectable sound of his Musicke. The which may transport and ravish our eares, at his mellodious touchinges and concordes, and not tickle them with any delicate noise, tending unto voluptuous and sensuall pleasure: but rather such, as (by well tempered proportions) are able to reduce all extravagant rudenesse, and cir-

[35]The masque presented the perfect occasion for flattering the monarch or lecturing him. I have chosen one passage from Jonson's *Haddington* masque (1608) because it is based upon James's chosen motto from Virgil, as well as because it mirrors the action of Prospero in act 5. Hymen is speaking to Aeneas's mother, Venus:

> Thinke on thy lov'd Aeneas, and what name,
> Maro, the golden trumpet of his fame,
> Gave him, read thou in this. A Prince, that drawes
> By'example more, then others doe by lawes:
> That is so just to his great act, and thought,
> To doe, not what Kings may, but what Kings ought.
> Who, out of pietie, unto Peace, is vow'd;
> To spare his subjects, yet to quell the proud,
> And dares esteeme it the first fortitude,
> To have his passions, foes at home, subdued.
> (VII, 256)

cuites of our soules, though they had wandered from
the right way, to the true path of dutie, and settle all
thoughts in . . . harmony.[36]

Prospero is precisely such a civilizing and harmonizing
character—Shakespeare's ideal peacetime ruler who must
be placed alongside his ideal prototype of the warrior king,
Prince Hal.

Deliverance and Reconciliation

Literature and art of the courtly aesthetic naturally show
the popularity of the themes of deliverance and reconciliation,
two common focuses of royal praise. Writers of both episodic
and epic romances relied for their denouements on these two
themes and so these genres proved a rich quarry for masque
inventors, court painters, and politically shrewd poets.[37] The
theme of deliverance is the central conceit of the triumphal
arches that inaugurated the reign of James, and throughout his
time the related conceits of peace and union were also a staple
of Jacobean propaganda. Court masques were consistently
based upon themes involving the King's heroic virtue, the
power of his reason, and the mercy and justice of his rule.
Hence the frequent comparison of James with the various epic
heroes of deliverance, especially Aeneas. The courtly aesthetic
was preoccupied with virtuous rulership, the scenic result of
which must be a form of deliverance.

[36]George Marcelline, *The Triumphs of King James the First* (London,
1610), p. 35.

[37] "The romance theme *par excellence:* the theme of liberation, which
accommodates well the political intentions of the masque inventor. It requires
a liberator—a role which suits the king admirably when one wishes to throw
his glory into relief" (Margaret McGowan, *L'Art du Ballet de Cour en France,
1581–1643* [Paris, 1963], p. 72, my translation). Bruce Smith describes a
number of progress entertainments for Elizabeth in which the Queen appears
as a liberator; see his "Landscape with Figures: The Three Realms of Queen
Elizabeth's Country-house Revels," *Renaissance Drama,* new series, 8 (1977):
57–115.

The "book" Prospero drowns at the end of the play contains the wisdom of political reconciliation. It is like the hero's book in *Orlando Furioso*. Translator Harington explains Ariosto's allegory thus: "Astolfo is a praise of learning, who with his sounding horne, by which is ment eloquence, and with his booke (betokening wisedome) both the gifts of Logestilla [i.e. virtue], becommeth a tamer of monsters, as well as a conqueror of men, and accomplisheth greater matters alone, then all the rest doe with their force and arms" (p. 414). Prospero is such a hero: he accomplishes the great matters of the play, not through violence, but through the wisdom of his books and of his "virtue." Through his reason—and the eloquence of his ideas—he achieves the reconciliation of the last act. His wisdom enables him finally to tame the monstrous characters Caliban and Antonio. The play ends with the final words of reconciliation: "Please you, draw near." This is the tone of the conclusion of many romance episodes and court masques. The end of the play is one of multiple deliverance: the members of the royal party from their sinful greed and ambition; the entire *dramatis personae* (excepting Caliban) from the barren island; Ariel from his apprenticeship; Milan from the tyranny of Alonso and Antonio.

Of course, figures of deliverance appear outside the courtly aesthetic, but one might generalize that the great studies and elaborations upon such figures are largely found in works associated with a courtly audience or readership. *Philaster* can again serve as an example for comparison with *The Tempest*. The structure of the Beaumont and Fletcher play is comparable in many ways to that of *The Tempest*: Philaster, the victim of a usurping tyrant, is suppressed for four acts, but in the last regains power and finds himself in a position to return vengeance for the wrongs committed against him. Philaster, too, chooses the rarer action of clemency. One of the play's villains asks for mercy:

Sir, there is some humanity in you,
You have a noble soul. Forget my name
And know my misery, set me safe aboard.

(5.4.99–101)

To which Philaster replies: "I do pity you. Friends, discharge your fears." The theme of taming beasts is made explicit when the reformed Pharamond is "exhibited" to the citizenry:

Look you, friends, how gently he leads. Upon my
                                                    word
He's tame enough, he needs no further watching.
Good my friends, go to your houses,
And by me have your pardons and my love,
And know there shall be nothing in my power
You may deserve but you shall have your wishes.

(5.4.121–26)

Philaster is then confronted by the man who usurped his throne:

       Streams of grief
That I have wronged thee and as much of joy
That I repent it issue from mine eyes.
Let them appease thee. Take thy right, take her;
She is thy right too; and forget to urge
My vexed soul with that I did before.

(5.5.12–17)

Philaster's answer is like Prospero's to Alonso ("I here could pluck his highness' frown upon you"):

Sir, it is blotted from my memory,
Past and forgotten.

(5.5.18–19)

As in the last act of *The Tempest,* the evil characters have very little to say: eloquence is power and speechlessness is impotence.

The final benediction of the suddenly reformed usurper in
Philaster reminds me of Prospero's last speeches:

> Last, join your hands in one. Enjoy, Philaster,
> This kingdom, which is yours, and after me
> Whatever I call mine. My blessing on you;
> All happy hours be at your marriage-joys
> That you may grow yourselves over all lands
> And live to see your plenteous branches spring
> Wherever there is sun. Let Princes learn
> By this to rule the passions of their blood,
> For what heaven wills can never be withstood.
>
> (5.5.217–25)

As a recent editor of the play has observed, "the world of
Philaster is as much a golden one as in the masques, where evil
is an intrusion, to be isolated and in the end banished from the
scene."[38] The method of *The Tempest* is very similar.

[38]Andrew Gurr, in the introduction to his edition of Beaumont and
Fletcher's *Philaster* (London, 1969), p. lxviii.

· IV ·

THE COURTLY AESTHETIC: FORM AND EXPRESSION

The age of a great prince whose delight is
in the encouragement of all beautiful things
is the age for men of talent.
BENVENUTO CELLINI

*J*AMES'S EARLY YEARS as King of England represent the period of the Continentalization of English art. During this time, which followed a long tutelary preparation by English humanists, greatly increased expenditures for entertainments at Whitehall made possible the exploitation of new French and Italian fashions. The success of these fashions was the result of royal extravagance. James accepted—as did, even more vigorously, his wife and sons—Drayton's early admonition to support the arts:

> Renowned Prince, when all these tumults cease,
> Even in the calme, and Musick of thy peace,
> If in thy grace thou deigne to favour us,
> And to the Muses be propitious,
> *Caesar* himselfe, Romes glorious wits among,
> Was not so highly, nor divinely sung.[1]

While Elizabeth was content to display royal pomp by covering herself with jewels and rich clothing and to allow her subjects to pay for her royal perquisites, the wealth of James's

[1]Michael Drayton, "To the Majestie of King James" (1603), *Works,* ed. J. W. Hebel (Oxford, 1961), I, p. 475.

exchequer was spread prodigiously in many directions and settled upon many whom the King delighted to honor. The fine arts indirectly benefited from this munificence: fittingly, the Stuart court gathered to see the epitomic courtly art form, the masque, in a banquet hall designed by England's first great courtly architect. The ceiling of that hall came to be graced with the most important courtly painting ever commissioned by an English monarch, Rubens's *Whitehall Ceiling*.

Shakespeare, a servant of the King and most likely a participant in the King's revels, could not have remained untouched by the Jacobean artistic efflorescence. My purpose in the following pages is to suggest ways the playwright might have been affected by the new fashions, and to observe the influence of what might be called the new Jacobean royalism in the arts upon Shakespeare's working environment and, hence, upon his Late Plays.

This chapter focuses upon an important watershed in the history of English art extending approximately one decade backward and forward from the year of James's accession, 1603. The contrasting aesthetics set forth below are, in short, those of the Late Elizabethan and Early Jacobean reigns, though I shall be drawn now and then outside these arbitrary boundaries. Also, though this chapter addresses the contrast between a traditional and a revolutionary aesthetic, their intrinsic similarities are also examined at some length. Courtly aesthetics did not spring full-fledged from the brow of the reigning monarch; indeed, their lines of continuity are breached perhaps less often than are the dynastic lines of kings. The five sections of this chapter touch upon both the continuities ("Aesthetic Elitism," "Comic Structure") and the innovative characteristics ("The Virtuoso Artist," "Illusion," "Spectacles of State") that significantly affected the courtly art of Shakespeare's last years in London.

Courtly art under Elizabeth and James tended naturally to

be flattering, optimistic, insulating, illusionistic, and magnificent. These qualities, related and overlapping, had distinct effects on the forms of artistic expression favored at court, as well as on the sophistication of supporting technologies. Just as certain themes proved very popular, so did certain forms and genres find an especially congenial reception among royalty and their surrounding aristocracies. Artists found the masque, the tragicomic romance, the oversized, full-length or equestrian portrait, the allegorical panorama—to name just a few genres—apt for creating experiences that an early seventeenth-century courtly audience expected. To appreciate how a courtly artist dealt with obligatory forms and themes in the reign of James, we must look briefly at the general state of the arts near the turn of the century. At that time revolutionary methods of achieving richly flattering effects finally reached England from France and Italy. The introduction of Continental methods of designing movable scenery, stage perspectives, lavish costumes, and lighting effects for *theatralia spectacula* at court radically changed the artistic environment surrounding the English court of the early 1600s. Only a few months after Elizabeth died, an observer noted that "neither the memory nor the name of Queen Elizabeth is nowadays mentioned at Court,"[2] and a similar remark could be made about the art associated with her reign: in the English court, Elizabethan art ended nearly as abruptly as did the life of Gloriana herself. A new aesthetic heavily influenced by European fashions replaced the older, more primitive, more insular modes of expression, broadening English artistic horizons in the first decade of the century. These changes might be characterized as causing a progression toward the elaborate architectonic, moving or flowing textures, and the complex spatial organization of the great seventeenth-century Baroque courts—a move from the localized charms and intricate

[2]G. B. Harrison, *A Jacobean Journal* (London, 1941), p. 38.

detail-work of the Renaissance arras to the sweeping momentum of the enormous canvases that dominated the Baroque period.

In 1586 John Case expressed the Elizabethan bias in music: "Yet antiquitie the mother of simplicitie and singlenesse . . . contented her selfe with meaner choice, & incombred her selfe with smaller busines."[3] The only native English musical form of the period seems to have been the ayre for solo voice and lute— "smaller busines" indeed.[4] But with James came the complex musical programs that were part of the masque, the development of the large consort, and in 1617 the first masque performed throughout in *stilo recitativo,* Jonson's *Lovers Made Men,* the first English equivalent of the *dramma per musica* or opera.

In painting, Elizabeth's court was dominated by the miniaturists Isaac Oliver and Nicholas Hilliard, both praised for "the countenance in small."[5] Even the larger portraits of the period (like Hilliard's of Elizabeth: "The Queen and the Pelican" or "Elizabeth and the Phoenix") show in their scrupulous details of jewellery and embroidery a miniaturist at heart. But the painters the Stuarts patronized—Rubens, Van Somer, Mytens, and Honthorst—were more at home following Alberti's advice to "get used to making large pictures."[6] The very ceiling over the Stuart throne in the Banqueting House was painted by an artist who admitted he was "by a natural instinct more suited to creating quite large works than little curiosities."[7] From the flat, static, half-length or miniature portraits of Elizabeth's reign, painters moved

[3]John Case, *The Praise of Musicke* (London, 1586), p. 12.

[4]See John Buxton, *Elizabethan Taste* (London, 1963), p. 203.

[5]Henry Peacham, the Younger, *The Gentlemans Exercise* (London, 1612), p. 7.

[6] Leone Battista Alberti, *On Painting* (circa 1435, trans. Cecil Grayson, London, 1972), p. 101.

[7]Peter Paul Rubens, quoted in Per Palme, *The Triumph of Peace* (Stockholm, 1956), p. 251 (my translation).

under the Stuarts toward larger-than-life reflections of the pomp of the royal Presence, massive allegories, finer perspectives, greater scope, and more adroit treatment of the moving form. Though Ortega y Gasset's terms are different (primitive/neoclassical instead of Elizabethan/Jacobean), he also finds in painting a move from casual or sprawling forms to architectonic construction. What he says of the earlier methods of painting is relevant to the "visual" structuring of *The Faerie Queene* and other Elizabethan artworks:

> The primitive picture is, in a certain sense, the addition of many small pictures, each of which is independent and painted from a close viewpoint. The painter has directed an exclusive and analytical gaze at each one of the objects. Hence comes the fascinating richness of these fifteenth-century panels. We can never run out of things to see in them. We are always discovering some new little interior picture which we had failed to notice. On the other hand, they exclude contemplation as a whole. Our eyes have to wander step by step over the painted surface, lingering at the same viewpoints which the painter himself had taken.[8]

Ortega y Gasset sets in contrast the painter of the new neoclassical school: "In place of ingenuously limiting himself, like the primitive painter, to painting what he sees as he sees it, he subjects everything to an alien power: the geometric idea of unity" (p. 26). Such was the explicit artistic intention of the new aesthetic's two great Jacobean protagonists, Inigo Jones and Ben Jonson.

[8]José Ortega y Gasset, "On the Artist's Viewpoint" (1924), in *Velázquez, Goya, and the Dehumanization of Art*, trans. Alexis Brown (New York, 1972), p. 26. On the "visual" structure of *The Faerie Queene*, see John Bender's *Spenser and Literary Pictorialism* (Princeton, 1972). Madeleine Doran makes a dichotomy similar to Ortega y Gasset's in a discussion of drama and painting in *Endeavors of Art: A Study of Form in Elizabethan Drama* (Madison, Wisconsin, 1954), p. 373.

In architecture the Elizabethan period could hardly be described as one of particular stylistic integrity or large, well-integrated compositional ideas. Only with James did the first brilliant native English architect, Inigo Jones, a deep-dyed Palladian in the Italian mold, receive the royal patronage necessary to create his unified and classically proportioned edifices. Although many of Jones's most stupendous plans were never realized, his extant drawings show that a new architectural vanguard had arrived in England. As both architect and stage designer, Jones singlehandedly introduced England to neoclassical traditions.[9] The changes wrought by Jones can be seen, for instance, by a comparison of the fabulous grotesquerie of Henry's and Elizabeth's beloved Nonesuch Palace (it is a shame we have no satisfactory pictorial record of it) with the refined, classically ordered residence Jones built for Queen Anne at Greenwich.

Finally, under James, and for the first time in English history, enormously expensive and complex staged events became a recurring medium for monarchical propaganda. To be sure, staged entertainments were presented for Elizabeth's enjoyment; some were lavish by any standards, though the Queen rarely bore the expense of them herself. Nevertheless, these presentations do not compare with the extravaganzas invented for her successor.[10] I refer to such events as the triumphal arch and procession, the fireworks display, the masque, the Lord Mayor's shows, and investiture and marriage entertainments. What Samuel Daniel said of the first masque under James applies to many of these lavish affairs:

[9]Until recently Jones was one of the unsung great men of English art. The work of Stephen Orgel and Roy Strong has now redressed this injustice. The Puritans seem to have been the first to blame for the quick evanescence of his reputation: "When the Long Parliament proposed to impeach Inigo Jones (for destroying property without a court order to rebuild a church), D'Ewes the antiquarian had to stand up and ask who he was" (Conrad Russell, *The Crisis of Parliaments* [London, 1971], p. 179).

[10]For general information on this point, see David Bergeron's *English Civic Pageantry 1558–1642* (Columbia, South Carolina, 1971).

"These ornaments and delights of peace are in their season, as fit to entertaine the world, and deserve to be made memorable as well as the graver actions—both of them concurring to the decking and furnishing of glory and Majestie."[11] With the influx of neoclassical Vitruvianism and Palladianism came a new imperial deployment of the arts in self-congratulatory, awe-inspiring spectacle. Art became larger than life. *Colossi,* or over-life-size representations of rulers, succeeded upon the more modest, human dimensions of earlier sculpture (most of this in the form of funeral effigies).[12] The humanists' neoclassicism led inevitably to the growth of art beyond human proportions, for, as Pierio Valeriano explained in his *Hiero-glyphica,* the heroes of antiquity were honored in dimensions that matched their merit, not their physical stature. Hence the extraordinary disparity between the real-life James and the James of Rubens's *Whitehall Ceiling.* This disparity between myth and reality becomes clear if one compares the enormously forceful and muscular figure of James in the upper and lower central panels in the Banqueting Hall with the more realistic Mytens portrait of James—small-boned, lifeless hands, forlorn and sunken eyes, smothered in finery (Plates 3 and 1).

The monumental Roman aesthetic of *imperium* lent itself easily and naturally to the aesthetic of Stuart absolutism. In fact, Henry Wotton's comment on the art of imperial Rome is

[11]Samuel Daniel, *The Complete Works,* ed. Alexander Grosart (London, 1885), III, pp. 187–88.

[12]Two paintings particularly show the new artistic trend. An equestrian portrait of Prince Henry (90 × 86 inches, attributed to Isaac Oliver, circa 1610; in the Parham Park Collection) is the earliest of its kind in England. Roy Strong finds Paul Van Somer's portrait of Anne (104 1/2 × 82 inches, 1617; in the Collection of H.M. The Queen, Windsor Castle) an epitome of the new style: "Van Somer's portrait of her *à la chasse,* her dogs jumping up at her skirts, her palace of Oatlands in the distance with Inigo Jones's new classical doorway, represents a court aesthetic revolution" (*The English Icon: Elizabethan and Jacobean Portraiture* [New York, 1969], pp. 26–27; both pictures discussed here are reproduced in this volume). Van Somer's influence was succeeded by that of Mytens, Rubens, and finally Van Dyke.

3. *James I*, portrait by Daniel Mytens (1621).
The National Portrait Gallery, London.

at the same time a comment on the art of Jacobean England:

> And true it is indeed that the Marble *Monuments &*
> *Memories* of well deserving Men, wherewith the very
> high wayes were *strewed* on each side was not a bare
> and transitory entertainement of the *Eye,* or onely a
> gentle deception of *Time,* to the *Travailer:* But had
> also a secret and strong *Influence,* even into the ad-
> vancement of the *Monarchie,* by continuall representa-
> tion of vertuous examples; so as in that point *ART*
> became a piece of *State.* [13]

Wotton (1568–1639), a prominent courtier of his time, must
have observed the development of English art into a "piece of
State." Much courtly art of James's early reign may seem to
modern readers "bare and transitory" and merely a gentle de-
ception of time for an idle, profligate court. We are ad-
monished by Wotton, however, to look more closely at art
intended for courtly consumption to find its significance as
spectacle of state.

AESTHETIC ELITISM

> To sluggards, niggards, & dizzards, the
> secrets of nature are never opened.
> REGINALD SCOT

A harsh literary and artistic aristocracy dominated Shakespeare's time. It assumed that true art concealed the essence of
its meaning from the view of the shallow, the lazy, and the

[13]Henry Wotton, *The Elements of Architecture* (1624; rpt. ed. Frederick
Hard, Charlottesville, Virginia, 1968), pp. 106–7. Refer also to Jonson's
well-known description of masques as "Spectacles of State" in his "Expostulation with Inigo Jones." Jonson most succinctly expressed the concept of
artistic royalism in the *Discoveries:* "Learning needs rest: Sovraignty gives it.
Sovraignty needs counsell: Learning affords it. There is such a Consociation
of offices, betweene the *Prince,* and whom his favour breeds, that they may
helpe to sustaine his power, as hee their knowledge" (VIII, 565).

107

ignorant. All who have eyes may behold superficial reality, but there is also an inner significance that only the initiated can appreciate. George Chapman (echoing, for instance, Boccaccio's famous pronouncements in the fourteenth book of his *Genealogy of the Pagan Gods*) expressed this elitism when he wrote:

> As *Learning,* hath delighted from her Cradle, to hide her selfe from the base and prophane *Vulgare,* her ancient Enemy, under divers vailes of *Hieroglyphickes,* Fables, and the like; So hath she pleased her selfe with no disguise more, then in mysteries and allegorical fictions of *Poesie.* [14]

The same theorem—"Art hath a world of secrets in her powers"[15]—and its corollary—"Art hath an enemy called ignorance"[16] were stated by two of England's courtly poets.

[14]George Chapman, *Poems,* ed. Phyllis Bartlett (New York, 1962), p. 327. In *Symbolic Images* (London, 1972), Ernst Gombrich quotes the eloquent elitism in Giarda's *Bibliothecae Alexandrinae Icones Symbolicae* of 1626: "The Symbolic Images, however, present themselves to contemplation, they leap to the eyes of their beholders and through the eyes they penetrate into their mind, declaring their nature before they are scrutinized and so prudently temper their humanity that they appear to the unlearned as masked, to the others however, if they are at least tolerably learned, undisguised and without any mask. How pleasantly they perform this, Sweetness herself, if she could speak, could hardly describe" (pp. 145–46). Compare Boccaccio, in his fourteenth book of *The Genealogy of the Pagan Gods* (a defense of poetry): "Surely no one can believe that poets invidiously veil the truth with fiction, either to deprive the reader of the hidden sense, or to appear the more clever; but rather to make truths which would otherwise cheapen by exposure the object of strong intellectual efforts and various interpretation, [so] that in ultimate discovery they shall be more precious" (*Boccaccio on Poetry,* trans. Charles Osgood [Princeton, 1930], p. 60). See John Steadman's *The Lamb and the Elephant: Ideal Imitation and the Context of Renaissance Allegory* (San Marino, Calif., 1974), which treats at length the philosophy that would produce such aesthetic elitism; see also the earlier *Veil of Allegory* (Chicago, 1969) by Michael Murrin, especially pp. 11–18.

[15]Michael Drayton, quoted in *Englands Parnassus* (1600; ed. Charles Crawford, Oxford, 1913), p. 9.

[16]Ben Jonson, quoted in *Englands Parnassus,* p. 9. Note also Jonson's assertion (VIII, 588) that ignorance is a "pernicious *evill*" to the arts and sciences.

Caliban, Shakespeare's most pristinely ignorant creation, proves (albeit unwittingly) to be such an enemy to art when his conspiracy causes the premature dissolution of Prospero's masque.

Sophisticated art glorified the allusive, the cleverly "shadowed," the "rare" at the expense of the direct and literal.[17] Spenser was making this point in a literary context when he wrote to Raleigh about *The Faerie Queene:* "To some I know this Methode will seeme displeasaunt, which had rather have good discipline delivered plainly in way of precepts, or sermoned at large, as they use, then thus clowdily enwrapped in Allegoricall devises" (I, 168). Spenser's cloud image reveals the pervasive feeling of the courtly elitist that the riches of art ought to be hidden and mysterious. Thus Jonson writes of the masque's "more removed mysteries," Peacham explains that emblems express themselves "mystically and doubtfully," John Harington adds notes on the "hidden mysteries of cullers" in *Orlando Furioso,* Henry Wotton admires the "secret Harmony in the Proportion" of a beautiful church, Du Jon praises the "hidden force" of a fine painting, Sidney writes of the "sweet mysteries of poetry," and Tasso warns that "only understanders of the nature of things" will be able to comprehend the "notes mysticall" in his *Gerusalemme*

[17]A wonderful evocation of this bias is found in the Nineteenth Expostulation from John Donne's *Devotions upon Emergent Occasions* (1624; ed. John Sparrow, Cambridge, England, 1923), p. 113:

> My *God,* my *God, Thou* art a *direct God,* may I not say a *literall God,* a *God* that wouldest bee understood *literally,* and according to the *plaine sense* of all that thou sayest? But thou art also (*Lord* I intend it to thy *glory,* and let no *prophane misinterpreter* abuse it to thy *diminution*) thou art a *figurative,* a *metaphoricall God too:* A *God* in whose words there is such a height of *figures,* such *voyages,* such *peregrinations* to fetch remote and precious *metaphors,* such *extentions,* such *spreadings,* such *Curtaines* of *Allegories,* such *third Heavens* of *Hyperboles,* so *harmonious eloquutions,* so *retired* and so *reserved expressions,* so *commanding perswasions,* so *perswading commandements* . . . O, what words but thine, can express the inexpressible *texture,* and *composition* of thy *word.*

109

liberata. Allegorical methods were the pillars of the courtly aesthetic; Puttenham, indeed, refers in his *Arte of English Poesie* to the "Courtly figure Allegoria."[18] Reason was the means of approaching the sublime beauties and moral truths that art concealed. Rational energy separated the elite from those who were helpless when presented with cloudily enwrapped precepts. This sophisticated art was not for those in whom nurture cannot stick.

This observation of an aesthetic elitism would be unnecessary—so general was its presence—except that in James's early years as king spectacular royal entertainments like Lord Mayor's shows, fireworks displays, and processional structures were first made available for the public to view, if not to understand. Little from Elizabeth's reign could match them. Never before in England had been created such elaborate compositions involving poet, emblemist, artisan, and all manner of builders for royalty, nobility, and the general public alike. These spectacular new art forms were based upon the theories of Vitruvius and Palladio; their matter was drawn from ancient commentaries as well as Renaissance iconologies; their attention to decorum was conscientious. They exuded rich artifice but were also superficially magnificent. They were "spectacles of state" for all concerned, the learned and the ignorant.

The construction of seven triumphal arches in the streets of London in 1604 must be seen as a crucial event in the chronicle of English courtly art. These arches represent the first public appearance on a truly stupendous scale of courtly "théâtres des rues"—the first great Jacobean artistic pieces of "state" (see Plate 2, p. 37).[19] They mark the first flowering in

[18]George Puttenham, *The Arte of English Poesie* (1589), ed. Gladys Willcock and Alice Walker (1936; rpt. London, 1970), p. 196.

[19]David Bergeron's *English Civic Pageantry* offers an excellent opportunity to compare Elizabeth's triumphal progress in 1559 (pp. 13–23) with that of James (pp. 65–91, plus plates). Bergeron summarizes: "The somewhat rigid, static form and structural simplicity in 1559 give way to more complex

England of pompous Baroque, royalist art and architecture; they were the London public's first palpable hint of how courtly entertainment would develop in the following decade. While he would have missed the masque's unique use of stage perspective, the viewer who followed the King's progress through London on 15 March 1604 would have gained a good idea of the visual splendor of the court masques: these gorgeous palaces and solemn temples built in the streets were soon to appear in the Banqueting House on scene-cloth magically arranged by perspectivists.

The assumptions underlying these arches are expressed at length in Ben Jonson's description of the arch he designed in Fenchurch Street. This statement is redolent of that elitism which suffused courtly art:

> The nature and propertie of these Devices being, to present always some one entire bodie, or figure, consisting of distinct members, and each of those expressing it selfe, in the[ir] owne active spheare, yet all, with that generall harmonie so connexed, and disposed, as no one little part can be missing to the illustration of the whole: where also is to be noted, that the *Symboles* used, are not, neither ought to be, simply *Hieroglyphickes, Emblemes,* or *Impreses,* but a mixed character, partaking somewhat of all, and peculiarly apted to these more magnificent Inventions: wherein, the garments and ensignes deliver the nature of the person, and the word the present office. Neither was it becomming, or could it stand with the dignity of these shewes (after the most miserable and

and ornate architecture, dramatic action, and dramatic speech in the 1604 royal entry" (p. 23). To catch a taste of "what passion wonder wrought" for the viewers of the 1604 arches, see Drayton's "Paean Triumphall" (1604), *Works,* I, pp. 481–84. An interesting recent article on "triumphal dramatists" is Gordon Kipling's "Triumphal Drama: Form in English Civic Pageantry," *Renaissance Drama,* new series, 8 (1977): 37–56. In the same volume see Paula Johnson's "Jacobean Ephemera and the Immortal Word," pp. 151–71.

desperate shift of the Puppits) to require a Truch-
man, or (with the ignorant Painter) one to write, *This
is a Dog;* or, *This is a Hare;* but so to be presented, as
upon the view, they might, without cloud, or
obscuritie, declare themselves to the sharpe and
learned: And for the multitude, no doubt but their
grounded judgements did gaze, said it was fine, and
were satisfied.

(VII, 90–91)

Profoundly neoclassical, this aesthetic in time produced the
great court masques, the future Lord Mayor's shows, and
other processional pageants. And, though obliquely, it affected the stages for which Shakespeare was to write.

The influence of the arches was directly felt in the annual
Lord Mayor's shows, and in reports of these we find frequent
indications of the appeal they had to all capacities. Thomas
Heywood, writing of a show from the 1630s, put the elitism
of the event in certain terms:

The third Pageant or Show meerly consisteth of
Anticke gesticulations, dances, and other Mimicke
postures, devised onely for the vulgar, who are better
delighted with that which pleaseth the eye, than con-
tenteth the eare, in which we imitate *Custome,* which
alwayes carrieth with it excuse: neither are they altogether to be vilified by the most supercilious, and
censorious, especially in such a confluence where all
Degrees, Ages, and Sexes are assembled, every of
them looking to bee presented with some fancy or
other, according to their expectations and humours.[20]

Heywood's remarks are interesting because they might ap-
proximate the situation (and artistic psychology) of a playwright, like Shakespeare, who found himself concerned to

[20]Thomas Heywood, *The Dramatic Works* (1874; rpt. London, 1964), IV,
p. 312.

write for both public and courtly audiences. Lord Mayor's show inventors felt the pressure to keep vulgar auditors at ease. Anthony Munday, writing about his *Sidero-thriambos* (1618), explained the situation: "For better understanding the true morality of this devise, the personages have all Emblemes and Properties in their hands, & so neere them, that the weakest capacity may take knowledge of them; which course in such solemne Triumphes hath alwayes beene allowed of best observation: both for avoiding trouble to the Magistrate, by tedious and impertinent speeches, and devouring the time" (sig. C^v). Perhaps because Jonson so aggressively resisted this kind of acquiescence, he never offered or was never asked to prepare a show.

As I have hypothesized, in his later career Shakespeare was pulled between two extremes. One was the public stage with its focus on language (and, hence, its great rhetorical demands), vigorous characterization, and a certain amount of low humor. The other lay in the court masque, where the arrogance not only of power but of learning was enormous. Unsophisticated tastes eventually caused what many critics, and certainly Jonson himself, considered the decay of the masque. The antimasque, carefully controlled by its inventor Jonson in the early years, came to encroach upon the stately masque proper. Featuring a variety of ridiculous gestures ("mocks and mows"), the antimasque eventually included much ribald, colloquial dialogue. After the death of Henry in 1612 and of Anne in 1618 (both were patrons of notable sophistication), the antimasque gained ascendancy. This deterioration of the elitists' pride and joy, however, took place after Shakespeare's time. When Shakespeare was feeling the masque's influence, it was still primarily a genre involving harmonious visions, richly allusive poetry, scenic marvels, and romance panoply. As Shakespeare in his Late Plays moved more and more into the sophisticated and demanding courtly realm, he was increasingly obliged to cast for more

113

removed mysteries and to distance himself from the require-
ments of Hamlet's "barren spectators."

This removal is chronicled in the change of Shakespeare's
style from the romance chaos of *Pericles* to the classical unity
of *The Tempest*. To judge from its crude characterization and
often poor poetry, *Pericles* must have been intended for the
delight of what Jonson called "grounded judgments." In a
commendatory verse to Brome's *A Joviall Crew* (1641), in
fact, John Tatham refers to "*Shakespeare* the *Plebean* Driller"
in connection with *Pericles*. In tone and artistry *Pericles* reminds us of the popular romances of Greene—not the more
elegant productions like Sidney's *Arcadia*, Montemayor's *Di-
ana*, or D'Urfé's *L'Astrée*. This may well be because *Pericles*
suffered, in preparation for the public stage, much as "Hero
and Leander" suffered in the *Bartholomew Fair* puppet show;
Leatherhead rightly observes that "the printed book" is "too
learned and poetical for our audience." He therefore entreats
Littlewit to "take a little pains to reduce it to a more familiar
strain." This process of filtering out the more sophisticated
artifice seems evident in Heywood's *Rape of Lucrece*, his *Foure
Prentises*, the anonymous *Mucedorus*, and in the rustics' version
of Pyramus and Thisby in *A Midsummer Night's Dream*. And I
believe it lies behind the strange nature of *Pericles*.

But as we progress from this play to *Cymbeline* and *The
Winter's Tale*, poetic artifice begins to assert its presence more
strongly. The climax of this artificiality may be found in plays
like *The Tempest*, *Henry VIII*, and *The Two Noble Kinsmen*.
This is the kind of play, praised by Jonson, which was

offered, as a *Rite*,
To Schollers, that can judge, and faire report
The sense they heare, above the vulgar sort
Of Nut-crackers, that onely come for sight.
("Prologue for the Court,"
The Staple of News, Works, VI, 283)

Even *The Tempest's* main plebeian remnant—the scenes
for Stephano and Trinculo—has an importance in the structure of the play that cannot be brushed off merely as stock
Elizabethan clowning. Their buffoonery not only satisfied a
taste for "anticke gesticulations" and "mimicke postures"
but also offered a highbrow parody of the tastes of the *profanum vulgus.*[21] On a political level, Stephano and Trinculo
represent the many-headed monster, all too easily disposed to
that monster's most notable sin, rebellion. But where taste is
concerned these two are also potential stalwarts of Jonson's
"many-headed Bench," who bring no intellect and only their
senses to a theatrical performance. Perhaps the experience of a
dramatist who had long coped with the tastes of the "unskill-
ful" is behind Prospero's ploy to catch Stephano and Trinculo:
would not the appeal of "glistering apparel" in act 4 imply the
sort of taste most apt for spectators who "onely come for
sight"? And the taste for which *Pericles* was probably designed?

The Two Noble Kinsmen (1613) completes this progression
from a public to a courtly aesthetic—Shakespeare's return to
an intrinsically elitist style. Here is a stately, polished, allusive
world reminiscent, but for more sophisticated stage spectacle,
of the plays of Lyly, *Love's Labour's Lost,* and *A Midsummer
Night's Dream.*[22] Here is the ironic return to a high aesthetic
vantage-point from which (as with Holofernes' presentation

---

[21]A classic expression of the enmity of the *profanum vulgus* to art occurs
in Boccaccio's *Genealogy:* "Let such men [who condemn poetry] go . . . and
gabble their applause to innkeepers, trainers, fishmongers, and queans: and
sodden with wine and sleep, bestow praises upon such as these, but leave the
wise to labor in their own light. For there is nought so ugly as an ignoramus"
(p. 19). Such is the world of Caliban, Stephano, and Trinculo.

[22]Shakespeare's career began on an elitist note. To the dedication of his
first publication, "Venus and Adonis," he added this epigraph from Ovid's
Amores (1.15.35–36):

Vilia miretur vulgus: mihi flavus Apollo
Pocula Castalia plena ministret aqua.

of the Nine Worthies and the mechanics' Pyramus and Thisby) the lowbrow's version of highbrow art becomes the subject of mirth:

> Here stand I; here the Duke comes; there are you,
> Close in the thicket. The Duke appears, I meet him
> And unto him I utter learned things,
> And many figures; he hears, and nods, and hums,
> And then cries, "Rare!" and I go forward. At length
> I fling my cap up; mark there! Then do you,
> As once did Meleager and the boar,
> Break comely out before him; like true lovers.
>
> *(The Two Noble Kinsmen,* 3.5.12–19)

The theme of the courtly aesthetic as "understood" by plebeians is, I think, an indication that a learned audience is intended by the author. The case of *The Knight of the Burning Pestle* supports this notion, for it failed on the public stage, possibly, as its eventual publisher guessed, because the audience did not catch the "privy marke of *Ironie* about it (which shewed it was no off-spring of any vulgar braine)" (*Dramatic Works of Beaumont and Fletcher* I, p. 7). The publisher adds that the public was only capable of "meerely literall interpretation, or illiterate misprision" and hence found it unfunny. The play is a burlesque of the taste for such plays as Heywood's *Foure Prentises*—a taste not far from that which would have found *Pericles* delightful. Also pertinent to this point are Jonson's *Tale of a Tub* and the puppet-show scenes in *Bartholomew Fair.*

The Tempest, then, lies near the end of this movement toward an increasing artificiality. The difficulty the Late Plays

---

Marlowe's translation is: "Let base-conceited wits admire vile things, / Fair Phoebus lead me to the Muses' springs." It is pregnant for my present point that the only works of Shakespeare read between the years of 1606 and 1614 by Drummond of Hawthornden are his court-oriented *Romeo and Juliet, Love's Labour's Lost, A Midsummer Night's Dream,* "The Rape of Lucrece," and "Venus and Adonis" (John Munro, *Shakespeare Allusion Book* [1909; rpt. London, 1932], I, p. 164).

have presented to critics may be in part due to this Shakespearean move toward an aesthetic that addressed the initiated, contained possible hidden courtly references, and relied
more upon sheer pleasure in poetic elegance—an aesthetic in
which the medium was an important part of the message. The
result was art that, "being with a little endevour serched, ads a
kinde of majestie to Poesie; [it] is better then that which every
Cobler may sing to his patch."[23]

In defense of such obscurity Jonson wrote (much as he did
for the Fenchurch Street arch) about *The Masque of Queenes:*

> For, to have made themselves [the hags] their owne
> decipherers, and each one to have told, upon their en-
> trance, *what they were, and whither they would,* had
> bene a most piteous hearing, and utterly unworthy
> any quality of a *Poeme:* wherein a *Writer* should al-
> wayes trust somewhat to the capacity of the *Spectator,*
> especially at these *Spectacles;* Where Men, beside in-
> quiring eyes, are understood to bring quick eares, and
> not those sluggish ones of Porters, and Mechanicks,
> that must be bor'd through, at every act, with Narra-
> tions.
>
> (VII, 287)

Happily, we have Jonson's own lavishly footnoted editions of
the masques to explain his characters and "whither they
would." Otherwise, we should be pitifully ignorant of their
author's intentions. Unfortunately, we have nothing comparable for Shakespeare's Late Plays. Inquiring though their
eyes have been, modern scholars have not been notably successful at explaining many of the characters in these plays.
One reason I wish to suggest for this difficulty is the failure to
recognize that Shakespeare was beginning to "trust somewhat the capacity" of a more sophisticated audience. The

[23]George Chapman, "Dedication," *Ovids Banquet of Sence* (1595), *The
Poems,* ed. Phyllis Bartlett (New York, 1962), p. 49.

"subtleties o' the isle" are a product of this renewed trust in a courtly aesthetic.

THE VIRTUOSO ARTIST

Late Elizabethan art is often poised, articulate, graceful, and happily complacent. It rarely makes us blush, seldom disturbs. It is the rare Elizabethan portrait that catches its sitter without a mask of decorous impassivity. The concept of the artist as agonist had not yet arrived in England.[24] We have in Nicholas Hilliard's *Treatise concerning the arte of limning* a fine expression of the painterly attitude behind Elizabethan art. Hilliard is not encumbered by theory (he finds Alberti's rules "hard to be remembered, and tedious to be followed by painters"[25]), and in true elitist fashion allows painting only to gentlemen of leisure who are free from cares and able to destroy "unworthy" works. Hilliard's description of the paint-

[24]It is not surprising that Michelangelo, one of the first Renaissance agonists, was criticized for "raising up his muscles a little too much" (Paolo Lomazzo, *A tracte containing the artes of curious paintinge* . . . [London, 1598], p. 20). Heinrich Wölfflin's discussion in *Renaissance and Baroque* tells us something of the aesthetic that produced the art of Elizabeth's last golden decade: "Renaissance art is the art of calm and beauty . . . . Its creations are perfect: they reveal nothing forced or inhibited, uneasy or agitated . . . . Everything breathes satisfaction" ([1888; trans. Kathrin Simon, London, 1964], p. 38). Wölfflin's ideas figure in Madeleine Doran's *Endeavors of Art*, pp. 3–6 and 247–48. On the virtuoso artist, see Angus Fletcher's discussion in *The Transcendental Masque: An Essay on Milton's Comus* (Ithaca, New York, 1971), pp. 1–39.

[25]All quotations are from the edition by Philip Norman, Volume I of the Walpole Society (London, 1911). Hilliard wrote this treatise, which is more autobiographical than theoretical, at the request of Lomazzo's English translator, Richard Haydocke. Incidentally, Alan R. Young has recently suggested that Shakespeare found the name for his protagonist in *The Tempest* in a reference to "Vicont *Prospero* a Knight of Millan and a great Scholler" in Haydocke's translation of Lomazzo, *A tracte containing the artes of curious paintinge* (sig. Hh5ᵛ). See "Prospero's Table: The Name of Shakespeare's Duke of Milan," *Shakespeare Quarterly* 30 (1979): 408–10.

er's working conditions (extreme cleanliness), ideal character ("a good painter hath tender sences, quiet and apt"), his proper diversions ("discrete talke or reading, quiet merth or musicke offendeth not"), and his self-effacing artistry ("to shadowe as if it were not at all shadowed is best shadowed") reminds us of England's great Renaissance man, Sir Philip Sidney. No wonder that Hilliard praises Sidney extravagantly in his treatise. Indeed, the art of Elizabeth's late years embodied that great expression of the Renaissance courtly aesthetic, Castiglione's *Book of the Courtier,* which is so close in ambience to the work of Sidney. Castiglione's aesthetic "drift" was to "cover arte" and achieve a "pure and amiable simplicity."[26] For the courtiers of his Urbino, the greatest disgrace was "curiositie"—affectation that called attention to itself, or skill displayed without the masking effect of gentle self-abnegation. The greatest English expression of this masked virtuosity is in the writing of Sidney and Spenser.

But Elizabeth's was the last English court for which Castiglione's aesthetic was pertinent. Under James new approaches to art conceived upon a magnificent scale took its place. The encouragement of artistic vanity and the appearance of the virtuoso artist followed in turn. As this more ambitious aesthetic increased its influence, the complex work of art developed, coordinated and contrived by an inventor or architect and realized by various craftsmen. (This relation between inventor and craftsman is reflected in Prospero's relationship with Ariel and his "meaner fellows" [4.1.35] who help create the magic effects on the island.) "Order is the balanced adjustment of the details of the work separately, and, as to the whole, the arrangement of the proportion with a view to a symmetrical result": this Vitruvian concept influenced many art forms gaining prominence in Shakespeare's later

[26]Baldassare Castiglione, *The Book of the Courtier,* translated by Sir Thomas Hoby (1561; reprint, London, 1928), pp. 46, 47.

years.[27] Jonson's statement of procedure for the Fenchurch Street arch (quoted above, p. 117) may be taken as a typical paraphrase. Behind his formulation lies the Vitruvian idea that a good architect should be all things—"a man of letters, a skilful draughtsman, a mathematician, familiar with scientific inquiries, a diligent student of philosophy, acquainted with music, not ignorant of medicine, learned in the responses of jurisconsults, familiar with astronomy."[28] Toward the end of Shakespeare's career this idea appears to have become entrenched in the art sponsored by the Office of the Revels: in 1612, Master of the Revels George Buck ended his description of the "University of London" with this note: "I might hereunto adde for a *Corollary* of this discourse, the Art of *Revels,* which requireth knowledge in Grammar, Rhetorike, Logicke, Philosophie, Historie, Musick, Mathematikes, & in other Arts (& all more then I understand, I confesse) & hath a setled place within this Cittie."[29] Vitruvius was also at the heart of the bitter enmity of two collaborators in courtly art, each desiring to be *the* architect in charge, Ben Jonson and Inigo Jones.[30]

[27]Vitruvius, *Vitruvius on Architecture,* translated by F. Granger (New York, 1931–34), I, p. 25.

[28]*Ibid.,* I, p. 9.

[29]From Buck's essay "The Third Universitie of England," appended to the 1615 edition of John Stow's *Annales, or Generall Chronicle of England* (London), p. 988.

[30]Note these opening lines from Jonson's "Expostulation with Inigo Jones":

> Mr. Surveyor, you that first begann
> From thirty pound in pipkins, to the Man
> You are; from them leapt forth an Architect,
> Able to talk of Euclide, and correct
> Both him & Archimede; damne Architas
> The noblest Inginere that ever was!
> Controll Ctesibius: overbearing us
> With mistooke Names out of Vitruvius!
> (VIII, 402)

Jonson and Jones contended so sharply because the final power was seen to lie in the hands of the creative artist in charge, and each saw himself in this

In his treatise on architecture Leone Battista Alberti—
Wotton calls Alberti "the first learned Architect" and
Panofsky calls him the prophet of the "new, grand style"—
illustrates this new concept of the all-knowing virtuoso artist
carefully constructing his work: "We can in our Thought and
Imagination contrive perfect Forms of Buildings entirely
separate from Matter, by settling and regulation in a certain
Order . . . we shall call the Design a firm and graceful pre-
ordering . . . conceived in the Mind, and contrived by an ingenious Artist."[31] This concept of the clever and demonstra-
tive artist behind the art work was new to England under
James, and Prospero alludes at least on one level to this new
dimension in artistic creation. In his asides to Ariel and in his
"overseeing," Prospero keeps alive the sense of a creative
"project" developing.[32] He has control over all aspects of the

<hr />

position. Wotton makes this Vitruvian point in *The Elements of Architecture:*

> [Artisans are] expressly distinguished, from the *Architect,* whose
> glory doth more consist, in the Designement and *Idea* of the whole
> *Worke,* and his truest ambition should be to make the *Forme,* which
> is the nobler Part (as it were) triumph over the *Matter.*
>
> (pp. 11–12)

For an expression of the Vitruvian, or neoclassical aesthetic, see Jonson's *Discoveries* (VIII, 645–49). See also D. J. Gordon, "Poet and Architect: The Intellectual Setting of the Quarrel Between Ben Jonson and Inigo Jones," in *The
Renaissance Imagination,* ed. Stephen Orgel (Berkeley, 1975), pp. 77–101.

[31]Leone Battista Alberti, *Ten Books on Architecture,* translated by James
Leoni (1755; rpt. ed. Joseph Rykwert, London, 1955), pp. 1–2. Lomazzo's
treatise on art, which had circulated in England since 1598 in Haydocke's
translation, paraphrases Alberti's Vitruvianism. Lomazzo defines proportion
as "a correspondencie and agreement of the measures of the partes betweene
themselves, and with the whole, in every worke. This correspondencie is by
Vitruvius called *Commodulation* . . . To conclude then it is impossible, to make
any decent or well proportioned thing, without this symmetricall measure of
the partes orderly united" (*A tracte,* pp. 27–28). See, in this regard, Erwin
Panofsky's chapter on "The History of Human Proportions" in *Meaning and
the Visual Arts* (Garden City, New York, 1955).

[32]Note the references in *The Tempest* indicating unified creative purpose:
"project" (2.1.294; 4.1.175; 5.1.1; Epilogue); "mine end" (5.1.53); "purpose"
and "drift" (5.1.29).

theatrical event; he ravishes the eye of the beholder with his majestic vision. He is, in short, Alberti's ingenious artist.

This new virtuosic exponent of the courtly aesthetic, with his pride and skills, became a worker of wonders, a theatrical magician of sorts. Such an artist, Alberti felt, "should also have an Ambition to produce something admirable, which may be entirely of his own Invention . . . like an Artist that in only seemingly working a common Quarry of Stone, should cut it out into a Labyrinth, a Temple, or some other useful Structure, to the Surprise of all Mankind."[33] Alberti is following that dictum of Vitruvius which is so close to the core of the courtly aesthetic: "Imagination rests upon the attention directed with minute and observant fervour to the charming effect proposed."[34] A demand for "charming effects," orchestrated by a unifying artistic intelligence, is felt throughout the art, architecture, and literature of the court, and the result was an unceasing search for the marvelous, the intoxicating, and the ecstatic.

In the reign of James the concept of the self-conscious virtuoso became more prominent in artistic creations themselves—an inevitable consequence of a belief in the necessity of an elaborate architectonic. This was an age of artistic pride and self-projection, the inclusion of the artist's

---

[33] Alberti, *Ten Books on Architecture,* p. 206. Alberti elsewhere describes the ravishing power of art that he wanted to exploit:

> In short, let every thing be measured, and put together with the greatest Exactness of Lines and Angles, that the Beholder's Eye may have a clear and distinct View along the Cornices, between the Columnes on the Inside and without, receiving every Moment fresh Delight from the Variety he meets with, insomuch, that after the most careful and even repeated Views, he shall not be able to depart without once more turning back to take another Look.
>
> (p. 204)

[34] Vitruvius, *Vitruvius on Architecture,* I, p. 27.

countenance in pictures. The artist, according to Alberti, felt himself to be "almost like the Creator."[35]

Such pride of artistry is frequently noticeable in the plays and masques of Jonson, as well as the masques designed by Jones. On the title page of Chapman's *Memorable Maske* (1613) we find:

> Invented, and fashioned, with the ground, and
> speciall structure of the whole worke,
> By our Kingdomes most Artfull and Ingenious
> *Architect* Innigo Jones.

Jones's pride symbolizes the new ethos in which *artificial, curious, witty,* and *rare* were terms of high praise. Dürer was celebrated as a "most painful and wittie Painter," Michelangelo's *Last Judgment* as a "most artificiall and admirable picture,"[36] and Prospero as "so rare a wonder'd father and a wise" (4.1.123). With the Stuarts we become more aware of artistic hauteur, for the artist has conquered mere matter (the marble, the clapboard, the scenecloth, the flat and empty quadrature, or whatever) with the form, the artistic *idea,* of his invention. At the same time we are witnessing the disappearance of artistic anonymity. Our cluster of sophisticated English plays shows the emergence of the self-conscious artist.[37] As Arthur Kirsch has observed, the basic impulse of the new highbrow drama was "to make the dramatist's art a subject of his art,"[38] and this self-displaying contrivance is man-

---

[35]Alberti, *On Painting,* par. 26. This surrogate divinity of the artist is a part of Prospero's characterization considered in chapter seven.

[36]Lomazzo, *A tracte containing the artes of curious paintinge,* pp. 186, 15.

[37]That is, the mirror is held up to art rather than to nature: "I do not know how it is that paintings that are without fault look beautiful in a mirror" (Alberti, *On Painting,* par. 46).

[38]Arthur Kirsch, "*Cymbeline* and Coterie Dramaturgy," *English Literary History* 34 (1967): 303. Frank Kermode approached *Cymbeline* similarly, finding Shakespeare "somehow *playing* with the play," and he felt that *The*

ifest in most of the plays I have associated with courtly tastes.

Insofar as *The Tempest* is a conscious and elaborate attempt to treat dramatically the dramaturgical process—that is, to play with the different segments of the theatrical continuum that stretches from the author to his figures who act as presenters or *metteurs en scène,* to the actual figures in the play, and thence to the audience—the play is an example of the virtuosity of the courtly aesthetic. It shows the sophisticated development of the delicate and exhilarating ambivalence between reality and art and an increasing interest in the enticing, problematical space between art work and beholder. Alberti shows this interest when he advises, "I like there to be someone in the 'historia' who tells the spectators what is going on, and either beckons them with his hand to look, or with ferocious expression and forbidding glance challenges them not to come near . . . or points to some danger or remarkable thing in the picture."[39] Alberti is in effect describing the presenter Guarini employed in *Il pastor fido,* Jonson's Cordatus in *Every Man out of His Humour* ("The Authors friend; A man inly acquainted with the scope and drift of his Plot: of a discreet, and understanding judgement; and has the place of a Moderator"), the flamboyantly theatrical

---

Tempest "deals in illusions—not in theatrical illusions of reality, but in the reality of theatrical illusions." *Shakespeare, Spenser, Donne* (London, 1971), pp. 232, 255.

In his splendid reading of *The Tempest* (*Shakespeare Studies* 5 [1969]: 253–283), Harry Berger sees Prospero as "the impresario busily pouring wonders, surprises and re-unions out of his baroque bag of tricks." And are we not brought back to Alberti's eagerness to be admired as a surrogate Creator when Berger asserts that Prospero is placed above the action "so that we can watch him enjoy a god's-eye view as he sees his work performed and observes the audience's reaction"?

[39] Alberti, *On Painting,* par. 42. A last chapter on the Late Plays in Anne Barton's *Shakespeare and the Idea of the Play* (London, 1962) is relevant to the present discussion.

magician Alcandre in Corneille's *L'Illusion comique,* and of course Prospero.

When Granville-Barker observed in *Cymbeline* an "art which deliberately displays its art," he was pointing not merely to the recurrence of Shakespeare's early courtly style, but to a far more complex attitude toward the work of art itself. The character of Prospero and *The Tempest* in general are the most moving and pregnant indication of this new self-consciousness.

ILLUSION AND THE NEW PERSPECTIVE

Oh what a sweet thing this perspective is.
PAOLO UCCELLO

In his later years Shakespeare began to feel the pressures of an aesthetic that served to insulate a court from reality; its means were the poetic and artistic license to go "beyond the life" and create imaginary worlds of illusion. Hamlet's plea to hold the mirror up to nature, we too easily forget, has a limited application to Shakespeare's plays. In the Late Plays we find miraculous events, strange distortions and discontinuities—all the result, it might be said, of holding up to nature, not Hamlet's ordinary mirror but what Elizabethans called "perspective glasses" or trick mirrors.

Behind illusion lies the concept of perspective, the knowledge of which gives one the power to organize experience. In his "Mathematicall Praeface" to Euclid's *Geometry* (1570), John Dee stressed the importance of understanding the laws of perspective: "Perspective is an Art Mathematicall, which demonstrateth the maner, and properties, of all Radiations Direct, Broken, and Reflected. This Description . . . is brief: but it reacheth so farre, as the world is wide. It concerneth all Creatures, all Actions, and passions. . . . By this Art . . . we

125

may use our eyes, and the light, with greater pleasure: and perfecter Judgement" (sig. bʳ). Long before Dee made this observation, artists had recognized that perspective is vital to the artistic translation of experience. Following the first modern theorist of perspective, Alberti, Leonardo da Vinci could speak of it as "the first thing in painting" and as "the guide and gateway; without this nothing can be done well in the matter of drawing."[40] The "Arte Opticke, or Perspective" is one of the few arts wholly praised by Agrippa: "it giveth a very greate Ornamente to Painters crafte, and to forginge of Glasses."[41] Henry Peacham speaks of the "rules and infallible principles of perspective."[42] And Castiglione, offering up his "purtraict in peinetinge of the Court of Urbin," adds this telling *sprezzatura* warning: "this booke . . . [is] not of the handiwoorke of Raphael, or Michael Angelo, but of an unknowen peincter, and that can do no more but draw the principall lines, without setting furth the truth with beawtilfull coulours, or makinge it appeere by the art of Prospective that it is not."[43]

The "subtill and ingenious Arte of Perspective" (Serlio's phrase), however, was only sporadically evident in England before the reign of James.[44] Even in 1591, John Harington could proudly advert to the engravings he imported from Italy to accompany his translation of Ariosto's *Orlando Furioso*. His explanation suggests that perspective was something new on the English scene:

[40]Leonardo da Vinci, *The Literary Works of Leonardo da Vinci*, ed. J. P. Richter (London, 1970), I, pp. 118–19.

[41]Cornelius Agrippa, *Of the Vanitie and uncertaintie of Artes and Sciences* (1569 English translation; rpt. Northridge, Calif., 1974), p. 78.

[42]Henry Peacham, the Younger, *The Gentlemans Exercise* (London, 1612), p. 30. Lomazzo observed that "when a thing is expressed by the Perspectives . . . the eye is very well pleased therewith" (*A tracte . . .*, p. 185).

[43]Baldassare Castiglione, "Epistle of the Author . . . ," *The Book of the Courtier* (Thomas Hoby translation, rpt. London, 1928), p. 10.

[44]The "Dedication to Prince Henry" of the 1611 edition of Sebastiano Serlio's *Ten Books on Architecture* (trans. Robert Peake, fac. rpt. New York,

The use of the picture is evident, which is that (having read over the booke) you may reade it (as it were againe) in the very picture, and one thing is to be noted which every one (haply) will not observe, namely the perspective in every figure. For the personages of men, the shapes of horses, and such like, are made large at the bottome and lesser upward, as if you were to behold all the same in a plaine, that which is nearest seemes greatest and the fardest shewes smallest, which is the chiefe art in picture.

(p. 17)

Comparing an engraving from *Orlando* (Plate 4) with, for instance, the Sir Henry Unton portrait (Plate 5), one sees that the perspective of the engraving has made its chronology apparent, while the Unton picture's elaborate biographical chronology, perspectiveless, is left in an orderless jumble. The Harington engraving is organized perspectively and represents the new foundation upon which the visual arts of the next century were to be raised; in the seventeenth century optical illusion became a basic artistic tool.[45]

According to Ménestrier, Vitruvius thought the decoration of the theatrical scene was the occasion for the discovery of perspective. Whether true or not (Serlio declines to "dispute Philosophically what Perspective is, or from whence it hath the originall"), it is fairly certain that the process was reversed in England. Theatrical presentations grew in com-

---

1970) states that English artists had long suffered from inability to deal with "right Symmetry." Nicholas Hilliard, whose specialty was miniatures requiring no perspective, admitted that Alberti's rules of painting were "hard to be remembered." Peacham noted among the "absurdities that our Painters ordinarily commit" the fault of "Landtskip, or Locall distance [i.e., skewed perspective]" (*The Gentlemans Exercise*, p. 58).

[45]See Ernest Gilman's splendid comparatist study *The Curious Perspective: Literary and Pictorial Wit in the Seventeenth Century* (New Haven, Conn., 1978). Also relevant is Per Bjürstrom, *Giacomo Torelli and Baroque Stage Design* (Stockholm, 1961).

4. Engraving by an unknown artist for the
first canto of *Orlando Furioso,* by Ludovico
Ariosto.
From the English translation by John Harington
(London, 1591).
Reproduced by permission of the Huntington
Library,
San Marino, California.

5. *Sir Henry Unton*

portrait by an unknown artist, circa 1596.

plexity only after a knowledge of perspective was introduced. Perspectively oriented entertainments began to thrive in the presence of James; the royal point-of-view from the State or Throne (positioned in the audience at exact stage center) was the basis of stage mathematics.[46] The new knowledge of perspective made visual effects more intriguing to the audience and created a thirst for purely technical innovations. This new mode of filling a stage (which made its first stunning appearance in the masque) influenced theatrical tastes of the time.[47]

The way the art of perspective was viewed has a further, metaphorical significance for our understanding of Prospero as a magician and as a creator of theatrical illusion. Men of this period called the power of perspective magical and considered it miraculously deceptive. Jonson alludes to this illusionistic power in his *Discoveries:* "From the Opticks it [painting] drew reasons; by which it considered how things plac'd at distance, and a farre off, should appeare lesse: how above, or beneath the head, should deceive the eye" (VIII, 611). Reginald Scot

[46]See generally *Inigo Jones: The Theatre of the Stuart Court* by Strong and Orgel, and Angus Fletcher's passage on "the politics of the vanishing point" in *The Transcendental Masque* (Ithaca, New York, 1971), pp. 79–85. Roy Strong asserts ("Inigo Jones and the Stuart Court," the London *Times,* 7 July 1973, p. 7) that perspective staging was a solely and specifically courtly phenomenon, however. Of perspective and the King, Strong writes, "Perspective made the ruler the emblematic and ethical centre of all court productions and emphasized the hierarchical gradations of court life. All the lines of perspective met in the eyes of James I or Charles I, and the more important one was, the nearer one was to the King, and the nearer one was to reading the unfolding spectacle with his eyes."

[47]Glynne Wickham considers this influence to have been debasing: "The decadence which is generally deemed to have entered into late Jacobean and Caroline drama springs, in my opinion, as much from specifically theatrical causes as from any serious shortage or weakening of literary ability . . . . Perhaps the most inhibiting factor of all upon the writing of plays was the growing interest in stage spectacle of the landscape artists; for this provided a threat to all the emblematic conventions which had governed dramatic art up to that time" (*The Early English Stages, 1300–1660* [London, 1957–72], Part 1, II, p. 43).

observed that "the woonderous devises, and miraculous sights and conceipts made and contened in glasse, doo farre exceed all other; whereto the art perspective is verie necessarie."[48] And Elizabeth's personal adviser in magic, John Dee, asserted "this Art of *Perspective* is of that excellency, and may be led, to the certifying and executing of such thinges, as no man would easily believe, without Actuall profe perceived."[49] All these statements might describe metaphorically the way a purveyor of the new aesthetic thought of himself, and we do find in aesthetic treatises of the time definitions of perspective that associated it with the magical and that make it necessary to the creation of theatrical miracles. The very title of Jean Niceron's *La Perspective curieuse ou Magie Artificiele des effets merveilleux* (Paris, 1638) suggests the awe in which this knowledge was held. Niceron writes:

> We have every right to call Artificial Magic that which produces for us the most admirable effects of mankind's ingenuity . . . True Magic, or the perfection of science, is found in Perspective, which lets us know and discern more perfectly the great works of nature and of art. ($e_5{}^v$ + $e_6{}^r$, my translation)

Niceron is defending the "magic" created by artists; his *summum bonum* is in effect the same as Guarini's in *Il pastor fido*—to create the most beautiful and admirable effects. In all the arts, this aesthetic sought after illusionistic miracles. At courts this was an era of the artist as mage.

In this period, then, the science and art of perspective were refined. The ocular proofs and geometric underpinnings of perspective were explored and explained. With the rise of the virtuoso artist came a desire not only to organize experience, but to play with it as well. With the achievement of a

[48]Reginald Scot, *The Discoverie of Witchcraft* (1584; rpt. Carbondale, Illinois, 1964), p. 316.

[49]John Dee, "Mathematicall Praeface" for *The Elements of Geometrie of Euclid of Megara* (1570; ed. Allen Debus, New York, 1975), sig. $b_1{}^v$.

sense of theatrical space and the marvelous effects created within it came the desire to manipulate space cunningly. Perspective made this possible.

Prospero's magic must have had its greatest resonance when *The Tempest* was performed in the Banqueting House, where a full consort, stage machinery, and the efforts of numerous meaner ministers were a commonplace—and where expectations for special effects were high. To be sure, it is inconceivable that *The Tempest* was actually performed at Whitehall with the scenic trappings of the masque; unlike Inigo Jones, Prospero did not wield the literal power of perspective. Rather, Shakespeare sought to clothe his play, not in the realities of courtly theatrical magic but in its essential ambience. By the time Shakespeare came to write the play he must have become acutely aware of the visual limitations of the stages for which he had mainly written during his career, and we may therefore discern a late and increasing unwillingness to acquiesce to those limitations. Finding himself concerned to express the two-edged nature of magnificent illusion (a common *topos* in courtly art, as we shall see in chapter seven), Shakespeare naturally sought to shift from the weakness of the relatively bare stage to its strengths, which were gestural and rhetorical. The magical transformations wrought by the masque perspectivists become metaphorical in *The Tempest*. The ultimate purpose, however, remains the same: to create and comment upon illusion. What Inigo Jones achieved with sightlines Shakespeare had to achieve through poetic lines.

Prospero is a creator of theatrical illusion, and in order to make this illusion "work" in the context of the larger plot, the real author of the illusion—Shakespeare—must play with theatrical perspectives. Illusions, whether of a storm or a wedding masque, that serve more than one purpose must necessarily be observed from more than one point of view. It is nearly impossible, in fact, to discuss this play without speaking of planes, perspectives, viewpoints, depth, and space.[50]

The author of *The Tempest* has complicated the distance between the actor and the spectator—what might be called the normal theatrical perspective. He has made his presence felt as did Alberti, who liked to put a figure in his paintings who points further "into" the action represented. In *The Tempest* Shakespeare explores *en profondeur* the theatrical experience itself and makes us aware that a single plane of reality cannot offer the full "form" of the work.

By allowing us to observe a masque *and* play producer at work, by making the time of the action coincide with the length of the play, by the strong dramaturgical references of the Revels Speech and the Epilogue, Shakespeare has marked out with considerable (though ultimately and intentionally incomplete) clarity the planes or realms of the actor, audience, and creator. In doing so he has drawn attention to that barrier,

---

[50]At least four critics have hinted at the possibility of viewing the Late Plays in terms of perspective. In the final part of his long essay *Shakespeare's Last Plays* (rpt. London, 1964), E. M. W. Tillyard discusses briefly the topic of "Planes of Reality." In an article titled "Word and Picture in the Final Plays," *Stratford-upon-Avon Studies* 8 (1966): 81–101, Francis Berry attempts to see structural parallels to "planes in pictorial art according to the laws of perspective." In "*Trompe-l'Oeil* in Shakespeare and Keats," from *Strains of Discord: Studies in Literary Openness* (New York, 1958), Robert Adams finds "five levels of reality in *The Tempest*." They are "(1) the revels, (2) *The Tempest*, (3) the audience in London at Whitehall, (4) Milan identified with Stratford and the kingdom of Shakespeare's mind, and (5) eternity" (p. 61). See also S. L. Bethell's chapter, "Planes of Reality," in *Shakespeare and the Popular Tradition* (London, 1944), pp. 31–41.

A recent book that treats the concept of perspective and its relation to dramatic structure is Jackson Cope's *The Theater and the Dream* (Baltimore, 1973); see also Claudio Guillén's article "On the Concept and Metaphor of Perspective," in *Comparatists at Work*, ed. Stephen Nichols, Jr. (Waltham, Mass., 1968). Ernst Gombrich's studies in the history and perception of art lie behind this entire discussion. An important recent study of relevance is Joan Girgus, *Seeing is Deceiving: The Psychology of Visual Illusions* (Hillsdale, New Jersey, 1978).

illusion, separating them. Sometimes he removes the barrier partially, sometimes, one feels, completely. We can never be certain, though, and this ambiguity is one glory of the play. The perfect perspective of truth, once found, is fixed.

The "fixing" of perspective never happens in *The Tempest*. If any single effect in the play is intended, it is surely one of ambivalence. We leave the play with the same dizzying sense of the equivocal nature of the human condition and of artistic expression that Romeo felt of love:

> O heavy lightness, serious vanity,
> Misshapen chaos of well-seeming forms,
> Feather of lead, bright smoke, cold fire, sick health,
> Still-waking sleep, that is not what it is!
>
> (1.1.178–81)

Perspective—"that is and is not" (*Twelfth Night,* 5.1.217)—is a clue to this profound and intentional confusion of realms in *The Tempest*. Perhaps because we take the knowledge and effects of perspective for granted now, we have little of the Renaissance sense of its magic. Because we do not have a lively awareness of perspective's philosophical and metaphorical significances, *The Tempest* may seem to us a more difficult *tableau à secret* or *Vexierbild* than it did to those who first saw it, especially those in its first courtly audiences. Through the illusionistic aesthetic not only the act 4 masque but the play as a whole becomes a "serious vanity" of the playwright's art.

SPECTACLES OF STATE:
MAGNIFICENCE AND VARIETY

> It is amongst the greatest and most difficult
> Mysteries of Government to bring People
> together for Recreations and Spectacles. . . .
> For this reason wise Princes have frequently
> exposed themselves (which is the most be-
> loved Object) in Splendid Shews of Tri-

umph, to the View of the Subjects, and
contrived Occasions and Opportunities in
that Manner to entertain them; and next that
Prospect of their real Sovereign, and his
graceful Exercises in Masques, and Dancing,
and Riding, the View of imaginary Courts
and Princes upon the Theatre . . . yield great
Pleasure and Profit to the Spectator.

LORD CLARENDON

James was the first English monarch to practice consistently
the "wise Deliberation" of exposing himself and his court at
spectacular "Shews of Triumph." His court's taste for imaginary, idealized monarchies encouraged the vogue of the masque
and romantic tragicomedy, forms peculiarly apt for such flattering themes. Having touched upon some of the theory behind
the courtly aesthetic, its effect upon artists and their self-image,
we can now see the actual visual effects it produced by turning
attention to the period's most intriguing, astonishing, and innovative art form, the masque.

Ben Jonson's *Vision of Delight* (1617) typifies the kinds of
courtly pleasure the masque offered. The opening scene presents the figure of Delight, accompanied by Grace, Love,
Harmony, Revel, Sport, Laughter, and Wonder. In the
masque, as in the courtly aesthetic as a whole, Wonder is the
key figure: "How better then they are, are all things made /By
WONDER!" (VII, 468). We learn from Delight that the purpose
of the masque is to create amazement through magnificence
and variety:

Let us play, and dance, and sing,
   let us now turne every sort
O' the pleasures of the Spring,
   to the graces of a Court.

From aire, from cloud, from dreams, from toyes,
   to sounds, to sence, to love, to joyes;

Let your shewes be new, as strange,
   let them oft and sweetly varie;
Let them haste so to their change,
   as the Seers may not tarrie;
Too long t'expect the pleasing'st sight
   doth take away from the delight.
                              (VII, 463–64)

Measured against the masque, mere drama as it was played on the stages of the Globe or even the private theaters must have seemed quite pale—even to those who only read the numerous printed descriptions of the masques or heard about them through word of mouth. Not surprisingly, playwrights were eager to draw what they could from the masque to grace their plays and to indulge the new infatuation with spectacle, music, and dance.

The masque audience came expecting something new under the sun. In 1613 Sir Francis Bacon had charge of a wedding masque in honor of the Princess and the Elector of Palatine. James, weary of all the festivities, had "no edge to it," and he cancelled the performance. Chamberlain wrote afterward in a letter of both the novelty and ephemerality of the masque: "But the grace of the Mask is quite gone, when their apparel hath been already showed, and their devises vented, so that how it will fall out God knows; for they [the producers] are much discouraged and out of countenance."[51] Masques were for one time only.

The masque was a self-study in magnificence—a mirror in which the court saw itself reflected. The sight of the assembled courtiers basking in pleasure at the 1613 festivities captures exactly the effect masque designers wanted on their stage: "For the whole Court so gloriously shined with embroidered abilliaments, that it made even a smiling cheerefulness sit upon the countenances of many thousand beholders."[52]

[51]Nichols, *The Progresses,* II, p. 590.
[52]*Ibid.,* p. 549.

Smiling cheerfulness—such was the effect of a successful masque on its audience.

Because the masque was a self-congratulatory event usually tied to weddings, Twelfth Night, or other days of celebration, it was necessarily topical. Jonson tried to transcend this limitation, but even he worked within the occasional demands of the masque: "Though their *voice* be taught to sound to present occasions, their *sense*, or doth, or should alwayes lay hold on more remov'd *mysteries*" (*Hymenaei*, VII, 209). In sterner terms, Chapman expressed the topical center of the masque in his dedication to his *Masque of the Middle Temple* (1613): "There is no Poem nor Oration so generall, but hath his one perticular proposition, nor no river so extravagantly ample, but hath his never-so-narrow fountaine, worthy to be nam'd: so all these courtly and honoring inventions . . . should expressively arise out of the places and persons, for and by whome they are presented; without which limits they are luxurious and vaine."[53]

Glorification of the King and court was the *raison d'être* of the masque. It was an elaborate, pompous compliment to a social elite. The audience was a necessary part of the performance, and the decorum observed in the audience was scrupulously followed by the masque designers. As for instance in Daniel's *Tethys' Festival* of 1610: "In all these shewes, this is to be noted, that there were none of inferiour sort mixed among these great personages of state and honour . . . but all was performed by themselves with a due reservation of their dignity."[54] When the need arose for personators of the boisterous antimasques, players like the King's Men were hired. The Revels office paid £15 for "Players" on two occasions chronologically significant to a discussion of *The Tempest*: 6 January 1610 (for Henry's *Barriers*) and 1 January 1611 (Jonson's masque *Oberon*). Shakespeare was plausibly among these players.

[53]*Ibid.*, p. 572.   [54]*Ibid.*, pp. 357–58.

A final hallmark of the masque I will mention is its sheer splendor—its power to create wonderful, eye-stealing effects. Of countless contemporary expressions of this appeal, Jonson's description of his *Hymenaei* (1606) may suffice here: "Such was the exquisit performance, as (beside the *pompe, splendor,* or what we may call *apparelling* of such *Presentments*) that alone (had all else beene absent) was of power to surprize with delight, and steale away the *spectators* from themselves. Nor was there wanting . . . *riches,* or strangenesse of the *habites,* delicacie of *daunces,* magnificence of *scene,* or divine rapture of *musique.*" And Jonson then adds wistfully—in the spirit of Prospero's Revels Speech: "Onely the envie was, that it lasted not still, or (now it is past) cannot by imagination, much lesse description, be recovered to a part of that *spirit* it had in the gliding by."[55] During these years spectacular courtly entertainments like the Jonson masques began to influence related arts throughout Europe.

An example from Italy can show the unenviable position in which dramatists found themselves as audiences were exposed to, or simply became aware of through hearsay or printed accounts, new stage technologies. This example is also pertinent because it captures the excitement of the new techniques, shows the great extent to which the vogue was con-

[55]Ben Jonson, *Hymenaei* (VII, 229). As is well known, these masques were an important part of Jacobean diplomacy. The scheduling of masques was often affected by squabbles over precedence at them. The letter of at least one ambassador, upon whom the masque had the wished-for, awe-inspiring effect, is worth quoting here (from Jonson's *Works,* ed. Herford and Simpson, X, 457):

> I must just touch on the splendour of the spectacle, which was worthy of her Majesty's greatness. The apparatus and the cunning of the stage machinery was a miracle, the abundance and beauty of the lights immense, the music and the dance most sumptuous. But what beggared all else and possibly exceeded the public expectation was the wealth of pearls and jewels that adorned the Queen and her ladies, so abundant and splendid that in everyone's opinion no other court could have displayed such pomp and riches.

This Venetian was referring to *The Masque of Beauty* (1608).

tinent-wide, and shows the striking similarities of subject matter from court to court. Between 18 October and 19 November 1608 festivities took place in Florence celebrating the marriage of Cosimo de Medici and Maria Magdalena, Archduchess of Austria. These included a triumphal procession with arches, banquets, equestrian ballets, mock battles on land and water, fireworks, and theatrical performances—the entire gamut of courtly revels. The highlight of these events was a performance of the pastoral *Il giudizio di Paride,* with spectacular *intermezzi* inserted between the scenes of this "favola." In a contemporary account of this performance, the play itself is scarcely mentioned. For the audience and for the readers of the printed descriptions, the main attraction was clearly the extravagant interludes: "Because the action of the story did not use machine marvels, the entr'actes were added in order to make the spectacle more admirable in every thing and every way."[56] The magnificence of these six interludes is astonishing. Praise is expressed for "the grandeur" of the evening, "the novelty of the subject," and the "great admiration of all the spectators." The narrator's concluding remark is very much like the statement of Guarini's poetic purpose (quoted in note 42 for chapter two, page 159): "With these words the curtain fell and the scene vanished, and the delights of the senses came to an end, for the night was far advanced."

The themes of the six interludes recur in countless English and French masques of the time:

[56]*Descrizione delle Feste fatte nelle reali nozze . . . di Cosimo de' Medici* (Florence, 1608), p. 34 (my translation). See also A. M. Nagler, *Theatre Festivals of the Medici* (New Haven, Conn., 1964). The 1608 *intermezzi* were largely copied from those presented with Girolamo Bargagli's play *La Pellegrina* in the Uffizi Palace on 2 May 1589. These preceding spectacles Roy Strong rightly calls "one of the great landmarks of artistic creation in late sixteenth-century Europe" (*Splendour at Court: Renaissance Spectacle and the Theatre of Power* [Boston, 1973], p. 194). For a brief description of the 1589 and 1608 entertainments, with illustrations, see Strong's chapter, "A Medici Maecenas."

1. The Palace of Fame (scene of majestic buildings, temples, palaces, and arches). Compare Jonson's *Time Vindicated,* and *The Masque of Queenes.*
2. The Return of Astraea (allegorical figures of Golden Age, Innocence, and Purity). Compare Greene's *Descensus Astraeae,* Jonson's triumphal arch in Fleet Street, and his *Golden Age Restored.*
3. The Garden of Calypso (formal garden, Jupiter, and Mercury descending). Compare the *Balet comique de la Royne, The Maske of Flowers, Circe and Ulysses, Luminalia.*
4. Amerigo Vespucci (marine scene). Compare *The Masque of Blacknesse, The Masque of Beautie,* and *Neptune's Triumph.*
5. Vulcan's Forge (labyrinthine cave). Compare *The Masque of Beautie, The Masque of Blacknesse, Neptune's Triumph.*
6. The Temple of Peace (a golden temple). Compare *The Masque of Queenes, Oberon, Salmacida Spolia.*

The poor pastoral comedy must have elicited little interest amid these visual feasts with their nine stage machines and over three hundred performers. This disparity is worth contemplating when the influence of the Jacobean masque on other arts is doubted.

A new aesthetic intent upon ravishing the senses was sweeping Europe and, with the Jones–Jonson masques, had finally made its way to England. The object became, as Jonson phrased it, "to surprize with delight." This desire led to the creation of new stage technologies that could produce visual panoply and striking effects. The opening of Serlio's chapter "A Treatise of Scenes; or places to play in" from the 1611 translation of his *De perspectiva* suggests the serious challenge presented to the bare Elizabethan stage by the new scenic styles. This passage is relevant both to the masque fashions and the theatrical uses that Shakespeare attempted to make of them in *The Tempest*. It is also an archetypal expression of the courtly aesthetic's stage form in its emphasis on the crafted and "made" artificiality of the performance; reiteration of "admiration" (not searching or conflict) as the prime artistic effect; suggestion that the whole enterprise thrives on "fantasies"; "cunning" of the virtuoso artist; and concatenation of the resources of perspective, music, dance, and artificial light.

Among all the things that may bee made by mens hands, thereby to yield admiration, pleasure to sight, and to content the fantasies of men; I thinke it is placing of a Scene, as it is shewed to your sight, where a man in a small place may see built by Carpenters or Masons, skilfull in Perspective worke, great Palaces, large Temples, and divers Houses, both neere and farre off . . . triumphant Arches, high Pillars or Columnes, Pyramides, Obeliscens, and a thousand faire things and buildings, adorned with innumerable lights, great, middle sort, and small . . . which are so cunningly set out, that they shew foorth and represent a number of the brightest stones. . . . And when occasion serveth, you shall by Arte see a God descending downe from Heaven; you shall also see some Comets and Stars shoot in the skies: then you see divers personages come upon the Stage, richly adorned with divers strange formes and manners of Apparell both to daunce Moriscoes and play Musicke. Sometimes you see strange beasts, wherein are men and children, leaping, running, & Tumbling, as those kind of beasts use to doe, not without admiration of the beholders: which things, as occasion serveth, are so pleasant to mens eyes, that a man could not see fairer made with mens hands.[57]

[57]Serlio, *The First Booke of Architecture,* Book II, "Of Perspective," chap. 3, fol. 24. Serlio's work, originally printed in 1569 (rpt. New York, 1970), was one of the most used and annotated in Inigo Jones's library. The 1611 English edition was dedicated to Prince Henry.

Here is art dominated by the *trompe l'œil* and the "special effect," the moving eye searching for the ingenious deceptions of the artist, the eye capturing the spectator's senses.

The courtly aesthetic was dominated not only by the royal person but also by what Henry Wotton called "the *Royaltie of Sight.*"[58] This art (which is essentially Baroque) depends upon the delight of the eye moving through an illusionistic perspective. The reports of masques are full of references to the use of perspective, and in Jonson's *Oberon* (dating roughly from the year of *The Tempest*) we are once again in the world Serlio describes: "There the whole palace open'd, and the nation of *Faies* were discover'd, some with instruments, some bearing lights; others singing; and within a farre off in perspective, the knights masquers sitting in their severall sieges" (VII, 351). The courtly aesthetic was based, as Stephen Orgel has so vigorously argued, upon the creation of illusion, and this illusion was only possible after the stage technicians had acquired the knowledge to organize and fill the space at their disposal (a point Serlio emphasizes). Only then could they create on stage the "cose impossibile" that Guarini so favored in his *Il pastor fido.*

In the fall and winter of 1610–11—when it is my guess Shakespeare was writing *The Tempest*—preparations were under way for the presentation of two masques: *Oberon,* given on 1 January 1611, and *Love Freed from Ignorance and Folly,* performed on 3 February 1611. We know that for the former the Revels office paid £15 for "Players imployed in the Maske" and that the latter required the services of twelve "fools." Shakespeare, or boys and younger actors familiar to him, could well have been among them. At any rate, the rich and dazzling illusions of Jones's extant designs for these two masques (Plates 6 and 7) can help us appreciate the imagery of Prospero's Revels Speech. The purpose of the speech is to

[58]Wotton, *The Elements of Architecture,* p. 4.

6. "Oberon's Palace," set design by Inigo Jones
for the court masque *Oberon, the Fairy Prince*
(performed 1 January 1611). Devonshire
Collection, Chatsworth.
Reproduced by permission of the Trustees of the
Chatsworth Settlement.

7. "The Release of the Daughters of the Morn,"
set design by Inigo Jones for the court masque
Love Freed from Ignorance and Folly (performed 3
February 1611).
Devonshire Collection, Chatsworth. Reproduced
by permission
of the Trustees of the Chatsworth Settlement.

separate the realm of illusion from the realm of reality, and Prospero does this by reference to the kinds of majestic visions that Serlio, and so often Jonson, had occasion to describe: cloud-capped towers, gorgeous palaces, and solemn temples.

COMIC STRUCTURE

Turbulenta prima, tranquilla ultima

Post tenebras spero lucem

Owen Feltham cynically observed in his *Resolves* (1628) that "for *Flatterie,* no man will take *Poetrie literall:* since in commendations, it rather shewes what men *should bee,* then what they *are.*"[59] Feltham's point could well stand as a theorem of the courtly aesthetic. Especially under James, art was obliged to present a courtly picture far more enchanting than the truth justified. It had to praise the monarch and the benefits of his government energetically (the wisest courtly art, as Stephen Orgel has argued, instructed through praise). To do this, fiction, artifice, and illusion were necessary, for James was a far from ideal king.

Because courtly art was obliged to reach happy conclusions, it was essentially comic. History and tragedy tend to center on the process of dissolution and disease, and so their usefulness in the atmosphere of a pleasure-loving court would obviously be limited.[60] For an understanding of courtly theat-

[59]Owen Feltham, *Resolves, or Excogitations: A Second Century* (London, 1628), p. 201. Jonathan Goldberg persuasively argues for a far more complex and manipulative mode of royal praise (on the part of Ben Jonson) in "James I and the Theater of Conscience," *ELH* 46 (1979): 379–398.

[60]Histories were attractive in the popular theaters, and comedies dominated the repertory of the select theaters. See "The Rival Repertories" in Alfred Harbage's *Shakespeare and the Rival Traditions* (rpt. Bloomington, Indiana, 1952). "In the public theatres, the plays, exclusive of three moral interludes, are in round numbers 49 per cent comedies, 30 per cent tragedies, and

rical tastes we must turn rather to the genres of comic fiction, the genres based upon the Donatan comic formula *turbulenta prima, tranquilla ultima*. In other words, we must focus on art of the first two phases of the myth of time and existence that Northrop Frye outlines:

> 1. The dawn, spring and birth phase. Myths of the birth of the hero, of revival and resurrection, of creation and (because the four phases are a cycle) of the defeat of the powers of darkness, winter and death. Subordinate characters: the father and the mother. The archetype of romance and of most dithyrambic and rhapsodic poetry.
> 2. The zenith, summer, and marriage or triumph phase. Myths of apotheosis, of the sacred marriage, and of entering into Paradise. Subordinate characters: the companion and the bride. The archetype of comedy, pastoral and idyll.[61]

Works produced in the courtly environment generally conclude in the mood of Frye's second phase. This is the phase for which Puttenham would have recommended "the forme of Poeticall rejoysings."[62] Romances, pastorals, pastoral com-

---

21 per cent histories. . . . In the select theatres, the plays, exclusive of one moral interlude, are 85 per cent comedies and 15 per cent tragedies. In view of the prominence of history plays in our conception of the Elizabethan drama, it is notable that, so far as we know, none ever appeared in the coterie theatres" (p. 85). These statistics refer to the years 1599–1613.

[61] "My Credo," *Kenyon Review* 13 (1951): 104. Frye's ideas, concisely expressed in this article, are elaborated in his *Anatomy of Criticism*. Compare Frye's characterizations with the quotation from *The Vision of Delight*, pages 135–36 above.

John Bender explores in illuminating detail the implications of the fact that *The Tempest* was first performed at court on All Saints' or Hallowmas, the first feast of winter. He views the play as becoming "a conjuration against winter, a miniature reenactment of the annual endeavor to countermand the cold, dark, fearful out-of-doors through indoor revels." See "The Day of *The Tempest*," *ELH* 47 (1980): 235–58.

[62]Puttenham, *The Arte of English Poesie*, pp. 45–46. In his chapter so titled Puttenham lists the kinds of courtly events that provided the basis for

edies, and tragicomedies—all what might be called constructive or reconstructive genres—were not only themselves the staples of royal entertainment in Shakespeare's time but also the primary sources for the quintessentially courtly masque.

The structure implied by the formula of Donatus is the usual one for romance. "Fortune ending frownes with favours, did thus absolve the catastrophe of this royal Comedy"—so ends John Dickinson's short but otherwise typical romance *Arisbas* (1594). This structure is also the basis for the tragicomedy that became so popular in most European courts. "Alla fine vince il migliore," wrote Guarini of the fifth act of *Il pastor fido*, and its last lines are: "Quello è vero gioire, / Che nasce da virtù dopo il soffrire" (p. 258^r). Ferdinand's thoughts upon his ordeal by woodpile are a proximate translation of Guarini's lines:

> Some kinds of baseness
> Are nobly undergone; and most poor matters
> Point to rich ends.

(3.1.2–4)

The Donatan formula is most clearly apparent in the court masques, which Ménestrier happily described as "comedies muettes."[63] The masques were specifically designed to trumpet the final achievement of tranquillity; they celebrated real-life events of the kind we typically find concluding romance episodes and romance-comedies. This song from

---

an optimistic aesthetic: "nature and civility have ordained . . . publike rejoysings for the comfort and recreation of many. And they be of diverse sorts and upon diverse occasions growne: one and the chiefe was for the publike peace of a countrie the greatest of any other civill good. . . . An other is for just & honourable victory atchieved against the forraine enemy. A third at solemne feasts and pompes of coronations and enstallments of honourable orders. An other for jollity at weddings and marriages. An other at the births of Princes children. An other for private entertainements in Court, or other secret disports in chamber, and such solitary places."

[63]Claude-François Ménestrier, Preface to *Des Ballets anciennes et modernes selon les règles du Théâtre* (1682: rpt. Geneva, 1972), sig. e$_2^v$.

Thomas Campion's *Lord Hay's Mask* (1607) is a typical mixture of political statement and wish-fulfillment; the song also captures the mood and idealizing momentum of act 5 in *The Tempest*:

> Shewes and nightly revels, signes of joy and peace,
> Fill royall Britaines court while cruell warre farre off
>   doth rage, for ever hence exiled.
> Faire and princely branches with strong arms
>   encrease
> From that deepe rooted tree whose sacred strength
>   and glory forren malice hath beguiled.
> Our devided kingdomes now in frendly kindred
>   meet
> And old debate to love and kindnes turns.[64]

With the development by Jonson in 1608–9 of the antimasque (*turbulenta prima*) as an antithesis to the masque (*tranquilla ultima*), the themes of deliverance from dissolution and the entry into an earthly paradise became a fixed part of the form. In *The Masque of Queenes,* a bevy of witches bent on obstructing a renewed Golden Age is overwhelmed by the figure of Heroic Virtue (symbolic of James). The imagery is of tempestuous, warring elements transformed by the king into calm order.

A companion metaphor for the Donatan formula is *post tenebras spero lucem.* Purveyors of the courtly ethos, which relied so much upon figures like Apollo and Astraea who shine the light of benevolence on the darkness of evil, resorted frequently to this metaphor. The idea of light banishing darkness had its most stupendous effect in the masque, where techniques of lighting—by candle of course—were developing rapidly. The visual climax of Jonson's first masque, *The Masque of Blacknesse* (1605), is a lighting effect:

[64]Thomas Campion, *Works,* ed. Walter Davis (Garden City, New York, 1967), p. 229. The "princely branches" refer to Henry and Charles (Ferdinand is their counterpart in the play).

> At this, the *Moone* was discovered in the upper part of the house, triumphant in a *Silver* throne, made in figure of a *Pyramis.* Her garments *White,* and *Silver,* the dressing of her head antique; & crown'd with a *Luminarie,* or *Sphere* of light: which striking on the clouds, and heightned with *Silver,* reflected as naturall clouds doe by the splendor of the *Moone.* The heaven, about her, was vaulted with blue silke, and set with starres of *Silver* which had in them their severall lights burning.
>
> (VII, 175–76)

Spectacular lighting accompanies the climactic moments of *The Masque of Beautie* (1608), *Hymenaei* (1606), and *The Haddington Masque* (1608).[65] But the most brilliant realizations of the *post tenebras* theme occur in the two Jonsonian masques most proximate to the time Shakespeare was writing his Late Plays. In *The Masque of Queenes* (1609), a vision of the House of Fame replaces a witches' Hell:

> The whole face of the *Scene* alterd; scarse suffring the memory of any such thing: But, in the place of it appear'd a glorious and magnificent Building, figuring the *House of Fame,* in the upper part of which were discovered the twelve *Masquers* sitting upon a Throne triumphall, erected in forme of a *Pyramide,* and circled with all store of light.
>
> (VII, 301–2)

A similar change takes place in Jonson's *Oberon* (1611) when a dark habitat for satyrs gives way to Oberon's palace: "There the whole *Scene* opened, and within was discover'd the *Frontispice* of a bright and glorious *Palace,* whose gates and walls were transparent" (VII, 346). William Trumbull attended this performance and recorded that "the rock opened discovering a great throne with countless lights and colours all shifting, a lovely thing to see" (X, 522).

[65]Jonson, *Works,* VII, pp. 186, 232, 258, respectively.

149

All these climactic moments in the masque were miraculous in design and symbolic effect. The success of the action was signaled by a *fiat lux*. There was nothing so unseemly as a struggle between the clearly defined forces of good and evil. Rather, the forces of darkness and disorder were suddenly and completely banished, as Jonson wrote, "scarse suffring the memory of any such thing." Evil was displayed only for the more sweet delectation of the moment when benevolent powers banished it.

There is little suspense in literature of the courtly aesthetic because its end is predetermined: this is a literature of delayed gratification, not the conflict of unpredictable or motiveless forces. The hellish hags of *The Masque of Queenes,* after carrying on for half its length, are overthrown by the nondramatic means of "loud Musique," a vanishing scene, and bright light. In *The Golden Age Restored* (1615), Iron Age and his cohorts are overwhelmed by Pallas with these expeditious words: "So change, and perish, scarcely knowing how, / That 'gainst the gods doe take so vaine a vow" (VII, 423). The Banqueting House was no place for true conflict between the forces of good and evil. The world of the masques and of the court that supported them could not be completely at ease with the slightest suspicion that evil forces are potent. Just such a suspicion brings the masque in *The Tempest* to a hasty end: "Prospero starts suddenly, and speaks; after which, to a strange, hollow, and confused noise, they [the dancers] heavily vanish" (s.d. 4.1.138). This is in essence a reversal of the customary antimasque-to-masque progression, for here the forces of evil subvert the wedding masque's majestic vision: Caliban's "foul conspiracy" is still afoot. The stage direction requiring "strange, hollow, and confused noise" might be compared with the "confused noise" made by the Hags in *The Masque of Queenes,* also their "strange and sodayne musique," the "strange musique of wilde Instruments" from *Love Freed from Ignorance,* and the "contentious Musique" of

Hymenaei—all accompaniment for subversive antimasque figures.

The Tempest exhibits these prominent themes and structure of courtly fiction. Its action, stretching from a sea "mounting to th' welkin's cheek" to Prospero's promised "calm seas, auspicious gales," is *turbulenta prima, tranquilla ultima*. The denouement is achieved through miraculous means and, as it always does in court-oriented fictions, takes place amid general rejoicing, hymeneal celebrations, the passing of an old order to a promising younger one, the union of contentious forces, the subjugation of undermining figures, and strong emphasis upon the acts of a delivering and clement ruler. This formula is also reflected in the action of *The Winter's Tale*—the movement there being from "th' fearful usage / (At least ungentle) of the dreadful Neptune" to the "prosperous south-wind friendly" that helps make the reunions of act 5 possible.

The careful orchestration of good and evil in *The Tempest* parallels the methods of masque inventors. As in the masque, in Shakespeare's play the interest lies not in the conflict of antagonistic forces but in the cumulative certainty that the evils will in fact be purged. Or in simplified terms, the play builds the expectancy of a masque rather than the suspense of a drama, and this is due largely to the masque (and romance) technique of contrasting and "pointing" good and evil. Like all masques, *The Tempest* presents a world of absolutes— something we first learn from the tendentious epithets in the *dramatis personae*. The balance between "good" Prospero and his "false," "evil," and "perfidious" brother is a main axis of the play. All the public vices Jonson has Iron Age call forth in *The Golden Age Restored*—ambition, avarice, pride, force, rapine, treachery—are practiced by Antonio and his plot-double Caliban. Arrayed on the side of Prospero are the public virtues of compassion, magnanimity born of noble reason, friendship, and obedience. The world of the island lends itself

151

to absolute judgments, as Miranda's respective views of Caliban and Ferdinand suggest:

> Abhorred slave,
> Which any print of goodness wilt not take,
> Being capable of all ill!
>
> (1.2.353–55)
>
> There's nothing ill can dwell in such a temple.
>
> (1.2.460)

Great virtues and vices meet but never collide in the play. *The Tempest*'s is a theatrical world of carefully controlled and buffered confrontations, and of profound polarities (three of which are discussed in the following chapter).

What is more, for the audience the threat of evil is not serious. Prospero's potent art foils Antonio's plot, and Caliban's conspiracy is doomed from the outset by sack and low mentality. These plots are dwarfed by Prospero's grand project arching over the entire play. The scene in which he walks among the immobilized, reasonless malefactors in act 5 (lines 58–87), confronting each with his wrongs, is merely the most striking example of the way a magic shield separates good and evil in *The Tempest*.

The theme *post tenebras spero lucem,* too, is completed in act 5. Like all idealized rulers, Prospero brings light to men. Alonso, Antonio, Sebastian, and Trinculo have given themselves over to their lusts and ambitions. Having renounced the rational power that controls their actions, they are, like Caliban, things of darkness. When Prospero comes to pronounce their return from sensual slavery to rational dominion, the imagery is of darkness giving way to light:

> The charm dissolves apace;
> And as the morning steals upon the night,
> Melting the darkness, so their rising senses

Begin to chase the ignorant fumes that mantle
Their clearer reason.

(5.1.64–68)

In the foregoing chapters some of *The Tempest*'s various associations with the courtly aesthetic have been sketched, giving color and sharper outline to the artistic environment against which it and Shakespeare's other Late Plays should be viewed. Because the courtly aesthetic is a nebulous and complex phenomenon—and especially because too little critical attention has heretofore been directed by literary scholars toward the influence of the Stuarts upon English art—the assertions in these chapters have frequently been speculative and suggestive. More remains to be learned of the limitations and exigencies that applied to works exclusively or eventually seen at court. My strategy has been to make both general and specific observations about the courtly aesthetic—to combine the advantages of a formulative and a specific approach. Having explored the chronological setting, certain central *topoi*, and formal aspects of courtly art in James's early reign, I will now examine *The Tempest* in greater detail.

· V ·

THE POLARITIES
OF COURTLY ART

Just as in music of harps and flutes or in the
voices of singers a certain harmony of the
different tones must be preserved, the inter-
ruption or violation of which is intolerable
to trained ears, and as this perfect agreement and harmony is produced by the
proportionate blending of unlike tones, so
also is a State made harmonious by agreement among dissimilar elements, brought
about by a fair and reasonable blending together.

CICERO

As Cicero's words in *De re publica* suggest, the "sounds
and sweet airs" of the island help Prospero to
achieve, and Shakespeare to symbolize, the harmonizing
momentum that is virtually the structural principle of the
play. This harmony represents a political *summum bonum*.
Shakespeare's masterpiece is a statement about *homo civilis*—
about the "fair and reasonable blending together" of men into
a society, about the renovation of a political structure, and
about the self-education of its fallen ruler in the skills and
magnanimity of an ideal governor.

Christopher Morris has speculated, "It may not be entirely fanciful to suppose that, among all the layers and levels
of his last play *The Tempest*, there lies concealed Shakespeare's

political testament."[1] I am convinced he is right. The themes, structure, imagery, characters, and various levels of meaning of the play all draw us into its political thought. I have already observed the growing importance of art as a "piece of state" and associated *The Tempest* with this increasingly dexterous use of art for political purposes. The central themes in the play are eminently political, and I hope to suggest in the succeeding pages other important "civilizing" themes: the nature of the ideal courtier, of the good (Ariel) and the bad (Caliban) apprentice or servant, and of the many-headed monster. The morality of *The Tempest* is preoccupied with the relationship between rulers and subjects and with the "use [and abuse] of service" that Gonzalo jestingly forsakes in his utopia. The noblest virtue (civic *pietas*) and the most infamous vice (civic *furor*) identified on the island are both political, and the *dramatis personae* divide with stark clarity along the axis of political morality and immorality. The characters Prospero and Caliban are complex political archetypes. The elaborate polarities that make *The Tempest* such a taut fiction also have a political foundation, as we shall see, and even the magic that brings Prospero's plans to consummation is Shakespeare's fictional surrogate for the royal Presence and its semi-mystical protocols. We shall also find in the Revels Speech a political lesson and perhaps an ironic Shakespearean comment on the political dangers of courtly spectacle. Shakespeare's dramatic vision in *The Tempest* is "harmonious charmingly," and the level of its meaning that most fully opens to view its various and integrated charms is the political one.

To view *The Tempest* as concerned with man in the *polis* helps place the play in a new perspective within the canon. We can, for instance, see a new dimension in the stage-managed morality of *Measure for Measure* and *Pericles* (the romance *moralisé* where the theme of noble-virtue-will-out dominates),

[1]Christopher Morris, *Political Thought in England: Tyndale to Hooker* (London, 1953), p. 107.

and in Shakespeare's most powerful identification of moral evil with a consequent destruction of civilization, *Macbeth*. Macbeth is arguably the playwright's greatest tragic lord of misrule; Prospero is certainly his greatest lord of rule. In *The Tempest* lie all the seeds of civilizing thought—the yearning for peace, dynastic continuity, union, social concord, and "use of service"—that were to dominate the final, visionary *Henry VIII*. As a character study in peacetime governmental error (too much trust in subordinates) and the acquisition of prescience, Prospero very much parallels Henry VIII, with Antonio and Wolsey playing the respective villains.

We have contemplated some of *The Tempest*'s historical, thematic, and formal aspects that suggest the influence of the courtly aesthetic; we are now in a position to draw back and look at some general polarities that show Shakespeare's intention to write a play about man as a political and social animal. These polarities were common features of the courtly aesthetic and offered writers frequent occasion to express the view that a healthy and humane courtly life is society's greatest good. The polarities that are the subject of the present chapter show not only one crucial and conscious political concern of the play (as opposed to the subconscious "meanings" over which all authors have less control) but also its courtly character. After examining them we shall be able to consider in more detail, in the next two chapters, the play's two figures who represent the polarity of good and evil in courtly fiction.

STORM AND CALM

> After great storms the calm returns,
> And pleasanter it is thereby.
> SIR THOMAS WYATT

In the Renaissance the effect of the ideal ruler on his or her realm was often expressed meteorologically in the movement from tempestuous passion to temperate reason. Between intemperance and temperance—storm and calm—lies much of the political science of the Renaissance, if indeed political ideas that depended so heavily upon metaphor and argument by correspondence should be called science at all.[2] The praise of monarchs was often couched in the fundamental and obviously attractive belief that the right ruler, wielding his scepter like Neptune's "dread trident," could pacify the destructive winds of Aeolus, calm the swollen seas, and bring back the sun. This analogy greeted Elizabeth:

> After all the stormie, tempestuous, and blustering windie weather of queene Marie was overblowne, the darkesome clouds of discomfort dispersed, the palpable fogs and mists of most intollerable miserie consumed, and the dashing showers of persecution overpast: it pleased God to send England a calme and quiet season, a cleare and lovely sunshine, a quitsett from former broiles of a turbulent estate, and a world of blessings by good queene Elizabeth.[3]

It greeted James as well:

> For whereas it was the expectation of many, who wished not well unto our Sion, that upon the setting of that bright *Occidentall Starre Queene Elizabeth* of most happy memory, some thicke and palpable cloudes of darkenesse would so have overshadowed this land, that men should have beene in doubt which way they were to walke, and that it should hardly be

[2] "In one sense the sixteenth-century Englishmen had no political theory whatsoever, for they had no theory of what we call the State. The theories they had were theories of Society" (Morris, *Political Thought in England*, p. 1). An important study of Renaissance political thought has just appeared: Quentin Skinner, *The Foundations of Modern Political Thought* (Cambridge, England, 1978). See especially Skinner's discussion of "The Northern Renaissance" (I, pp. 193–262).

[3] Raphael Holinshed, *Holinshed's Chronicles of England, Scotland, and Ireland* (London, 1586), III, p. 1170.

knowen, who was to direct the unsetled State: the appearance of your *Majestie*, as of the *Sunne* in his strength, instantly dispelled those supposed and surmised mists, and gave unto all that were well affected, exceeding cause of comfort.[4]

And it ushered out Charles I: in 1640 when fatal clouds were in fact gathering, the king viewed a masque whose thematic crux was that "his Majesty, out of his mercy and clemency . . . seeks by all means to reduce tempestuous and turbulent natures into a sweet calm of civil concord."[5] This imagery is finely incorporated in the Ditchley portrait of Elizabeth (Plate 8). This imagery, applied so often to real monarchs, was naturally important in the "civil acts" of fictional rulers like Prospero. Previous discussion of temperance in Prospero's characterization and of the literary formula *turbulenta prima, tranquilla ultima* prepares us for a look at Shakespeare's final, highly artificial storm.

There has been a lack of sensitivity to the storm that opens *The Tempest*, an unwillingness to see in it anything more than a pretext for the display of newly discovered theatrical possibilities of sound effects or a landsman's brief nautical tour de force. Though the title is unique in the Shakespearean canon (no other refers to so specific an event or, for that matter, to a natural event), critics have shown a remarkable lack of interest in the storm scene and its relation to the "fable" of the play. Jonson notwithstanding, the first scene is no mere drollery but an essential part of the drama.

---

[4] "To the most high and mightie Prince, James," *Holy Bible* (London, 1611), sig. A₂ʳ.

[5] Inigo Jones and William Davenant, *Salmacida Spolia* (1640), in *A Book of Masques in Honour of Allardyce Nicoll*, ed. T. J. B. Spencer (Cambridge, Mass., 1967), p. 349. The same idea occurs in Milton's *Paradise Lost*, where God speaks: " 'Silence, ye troubled waves, and thou deep, peace,' / Said then th'omnific Word, 'your discord end' " (7.216–17). Compare Donne: "It was only Christ Jesus himself that could say to the Tempest, *Tace, obtumesce*, be still, not a blast, not a sob more" (*Sermons*, III, p. 184).

8. *Elizabeth I* (The "Ditchley" Portrait),
by Marcus Gheeraerts the Younger, circa 1592.
Reproduced by courtesy of the Trustees, the
National Portrait Gallery, London.

This portrait is traditionally thought to have been painted to
commemorate an entertainment given for Elizabeth in Sep-
tember 1592 by Sir Henry Lee, Master of the Queen's Armory,
at his Oxfordshire seat, Ditchley.

Men have long contemplated the analogy of the land and the sea with the known and the unknown, and with the palpable present and the unfathomable future. They have been immemorially moved by the symbolism of the tempestuous upheavals in nature and the inner man.[6] The clash of the inner and the outer tempest finds its greatest expression in act 3 of *King Lear;* man struggling with what Lear calls "the tempest in my mind" has proved to be one of the archetypal agons of Western literature. Not surprisingly, Shakespeare's greatest expression of the personal storm, staged on that desolate heath, came toward the end of the period in which his interest focused upon solitary man.

To see fully the symbolism of the storm in the first scene of *The Tempest,* we must look to the various levels of experience it draws attention to. We can start with the meaning of the word *tempest* in the Renaissance. A canvassing of contemporary Latin-English dictionaries (an English one, of course, had not yet appeared) shows that the word connoted social and political behavior, as well as that of nature. A typical entry is made by Thomas Thomas, a lexicographer who first published his dictionary in 1588:

> *Tempestas, atis* . . . Time: a seasonable time and faire weather: a faire or good season: a tempest or storme . . . a boisterous or troublous weather, be it winde, haile, or raine: commonly it signifieth a tempest, or storme of raine and haile togither: also great trouble,

6 "We with the vessel of mortalitie fleing away, go one after another through the tempestuous sea, that swalloweth up and devoureth all thinges, neither is it graunted us at any time to come on shore againe, but alwayes beaten with contrary windes, at the end wee breake our vessell at some rocke" (Baldassare Castiglione, *The Book of the Courtier* [trans. Thomas Hoby, rpt. London, 1928], p. 87). See La Primaudaye's chapter 64 in book 3 of *The French Academy,* "That the world is like a sea." Donne preached a brilliant sermon on the theme *mundus mare* at The Hague on 19 December 1619 (*Sermons,* III, pp. 306–7).

business, or ruffling in a common weale: a storme or
trouble of adversities.[7]

The word *tempest* potentially referred to the political system,
and I believe Shakespeare draws on this political connotation
in the first scene. The boatswain's imperious question—
"What cares these roarers for the name of King?"—sets the
political overtones of the event reverberating; Kermode notes
in his edition that "'roaring boys' was a slang expression . . .
for young men whose pride it was to break the peace" (p. 5).
The unleashed forces of the storm have overturned decorum,
making it necessary for the king and the royal party to "keep
below." The boatswain further makes clear that in these desperate circumstances no king or counselor shall be able to
"work the peace of the presence." Normal authority is use-
less. From the very beginning, the dichotomies storm/calm
and political upheaval/order are associated. Shakespeare's
storm is, in Thomas's formulation, both a "boisterous and
troublous weather" and a symbol of the "great trouble, business, or ruffling in a common weale" that took place years
earlier in Milan.

The storm scene performs an elaborate proleptic function:
it points ahead to the plotting by figures who care not for the
name of king, Antonio and Caliban; it sets up the tension between human motives and the motives of Destiny or Provi-
dence; it establishes a basis for the metaphorical deepening
and imagistic continuities so well described by Reuben
Brower;[8] it is the "direful spectacle" that balances the joyful
spectacle of act 5. Finally, it reminds us of the *distance* the play

[7]Thomas Thomas, *Dictionarium linguae Latinae et Anglicanae* (London,
1606). This definition follows nearly verbatim the entries for *tempestas* made
by Elyot in 1548 and Cooper in 1584. Florio's entry for a later dictionary of
1598 is the same also.
    [8]See Reuben Brower, "The Mirror of Analogy: *The Tempest,*" in *The
Fields of Light: An Experiment in Critical Reading* (New York, 1951).

has moved, the distance between the "roaring war" of "mutinous winds" to the promised "calm seas, auspicious gales," between political chaos and order. What passes in the storm scene is indeed prologue.

Frequently in his career Shakespeare provided tempest imagery for moments embodying bellicose and anticivilizing demonism. In *Richard II*, Scroop reports that the imminent civil strife will come "like an unseasonable stormy day" (3.2.106). The meteorological eruption of Northumberland in *2 Henry IV* is more terrific. Here is a Shakespearean Até figure if ever there was one:

> Let heaven kiss earth! now let not Nature's hand
> Keep the wild flood confin'd! let order die!
> And let this world no longer be a stage
> To feed contention in a ling'ring act;
> But let one spirit of the first-born Cain
> Reign in all bosoms, that each heart being set
> On bloody courses, the rude scene may end,
> And darkness be the burier of the dead!
>
> (1.1.153–60)

The tempests of war, rebellion, and greed—raised through passion and ambition—shake civilization to its foundations, rend the civic oak, and drown the peace. *Macbeth* is founded upon this idea, as are *Pericles* and *King Lear*. When the natural order is upset, as in *Macbeth*, men are made to "float upon a wild and violent sea."

Prospero's tempest, however, is a storm with a difference. Though it typifies the Renaissance use of tempests as symbols of political chaos, on another level it is a *means* of re-establishing order. This storm is unique because Prospero has the power to calm it himself, unlike other figures in Shakespeare who raise tempests in their societies or in themselves. His potent art makes him superior to Aeolus in the *Aeneid*, who can release the winds but then is helpless to control them. Prospero's storm is something "performed," a spectacle that is part of a larger project. He is beyond the dilemma that Hamlet (like so many other tragic heroes) faces—

> Whether 'tis nobler in the mind to suffer
> The slings and arrows of outrageous fortune,
> Or to take arms against a sea of troubles,
> And by opposing, end them.
>
> (3.1.56–59)

—for he has already suffered, armed himself against misfortune, and acquired the power to produce the happy outcome of act 5. The tempest is the greatest evidence of his power over the elements of sedition and self-destruction.

We need only place Lear next to Prospero to see the difference between man and superman—between the real monarch of a Montaigne and the idealized monarch of courtly artists. When Lear issues his imperious commands in act 2,

> Blow, winds, and crack your cheeks! rage, blow!
> You cataracts and hurricanoes, spout
> Till you have drench'd our steeples, drown'd the
>   cocks!
> You sulph'rous and thought-executing fires,
> Vaunt-couriers of oak-cleaving thunderbolts,
> Singe my white head! And thou, all-shaking thunder,
> Strike flat the thick rotundity o' th' world!
>
> (3.2.1–7)

he displays the ultimate hubris, the fine impotence of a man who is contending with elements beyond his control. He is by his own admission "A poor infirm, weak, and despis'd old man." Lear's vain demands upon the elements are repeated by Prospero in the benediction upon his magic art. There is no air of impotence or hubris here, though. The speech is one of achieved mastery and command:

> I have bedimm'd
> The noontide sun, call'd forth the mutinous winds,
> And 'twixt the green sea and the azur'd vault

Set roaring war: to the dread rattling thunder
Have I given fire, and rifted Jove's stout oak
With his own bolt; the strong-bas'd promontory
Have I made shake, and by the spurs pluck'd up
The pine and cedar: graves at my command
Have wak'd their sleepers, op'd, and let 'em forth
By my so potent Art.

(5.1.41–50)

The storm Lear suffers within and without strips him of civilization and leaves him "unaccommodated man . . . no more but such a poor, bare, fork'd animal" (3.4.106). The over-riding tone is of revulsion, nakedness, helplessness, and despair. The storm of *The Tempest* is one over which a man has control; its forces are leashed, its energies directed to a constructive end. The storm on the heath is an individual one and all the more terrible therefore; the storm a few leagues off the island is an emphatically social event. The storm in *Lear* exposes the vanity of human nature; the storm of *The Tempest* celebrates the vanity of art—Prospero's political art and Shakespeare's theatrical art. The storm in *Lear* does not give the protagonist "leave to ponder"; the storm Prospero creates is specifically designed to give the "men of sin" the occasion to consider their misdeeds. That the storm has a rehabilitative purpose is suggested by Ferdinand's absence from the scene, for his character, as it is later developed, sets him apart from the others, who are tainted by the storm's symbolism of human error.

Through his potent knowledge and the "rarer action" of substituting clemency for vengeance, Prospero achieves civilizing effects for which James himself was often praised. Sun-like, Prospero melts the "darkness" and "ignorant fumes" from the minds of the erring royal party, just as James dispelled the "supposed mists" enveloping the fearful subjects of a dying queen. He is able, like James, to "reduce all extravagant rudenesse . . . to the true path of dutie." He is, again like James, able to give all that are "well affected, exceeding cause of comfort" by calming the stormy contention of passions, humors, and men.

FUROR AND PIETAS

Since courtly literature focuses on the distinction between actions that foster and those that subvert civilization, it tends to be preoccupied with the maintenance of stability, order, and custom. Virgil's *Aeneid,* the first great example of civilizing literature, is organized upon such a distinction. In this epic, ethical motivation revolves on the great axis of *pietas* and *furor.* To give a sense of this axis, I offer a compilation of its Virgilian manifestations:

PIETAS	FUROR
Foundation of Rome	Fall of Troy
Order	Chaos
Civic virtue	Civic violence
Calm	Storm
Serenitas	*Ira, insania, saeva fraudis*
Peace	War
Hope	Despair
Amor pius	*Amor furor*
Love of country	Love of self
Light	Darkness
Loyalty	Treachery
Life	Death

In its simplest meaning *pietas* implies dutifulness—the subjugation of personal feelings or ambitions that, if pursued, may corrupt civilization.[9] A sense of *pietas* gives Aeneas the power

[9]*Pietas,* according to Viktor Pöschl (*The Art of Vergil: Image and Symbol in the Aeneid* [1950; trans. Gerda Seligson, Ann Arbor, Michigan, 1962], p. 40), is "nothing else but doing [one's] duty to gods, country, ancestors, and descendants." It is necessary to emphasize that the most important level of *pietas* for Virgil is political. Cicero, too, observes in *De re publica* (6.16) that it means primarily the duty of a citizen to his city: *pietas quae cum magna in pa-*

to withstand the harassment of Juno, overcome his emotions and leave Dido, and finally establish the Roman state in Italy. For Aeneas, Italy (and for Virgil, Augustan Rome) is the most important end of moral behavior: *hic amor, haec patria est* (4.347). The *insigniae pietatis vir* is above all a civilizing man.

Furor, on the other hand, is represented by the forces that threaten to destroy the *polis*. *Furor* turns constructive energies into destructive ones: Dido's deep love for Aeneas is turned into the volcanic *amor furor* of a spurned queen (this, Virgil hints, leads to the decay of the Carthaginian state); Juno's love for Dido's people produces the *saeva ira* (1.4) from which the Trojan refugees suffer. In the *Aeneid* the "furious" are invariably at odds with the "pious." The latter have a mission, a straight path to beat, an order to establish; the furious are eager to frustrate this mission and introduce chaos.

The control of *furor* on the political level is a great concern in the Virgilian epic. In *Aeneid* 1, Jupiter concludes his vision of the golden age with these famous words: "The gates of war, grim with iron and close-fitting bars, shall be closed; within, impious Rage [*furor impius*], sitting on savage arms, his hands fast bound behind with a hundred brazen knots, shall roar in the ghastliness of blood-stained lips" (1.293–96). The essence of the evil represented in the courtly aesthetic is mirrored in these lines. Conservative literature of the courtly aesthetic naturally looks forward to a golden age when *furor impius* is rendered impotent. As we shall see, Caliban and Spenser's Blatant Beast ought to be compared to the *Aeneid*'s culminating figure of *furor*, Allecto. This Fury, who incites war between the peoples of Latium and Troy at Juno's behest, is simply the social manifestation of *furor*. Allecto releases the

---

rentibus et propinquis, tum in patria maxima est. The lesson of political *pietas* is the greatest that Aeneas must learn. Thus, he gains spiritual power for the struggle in the *Aeneid* 7–12 in the vision of Anchises. Patriotic *pietas* grows from mere familial *pietas*: *vincet amor patriae laudumque immensa cupido* ("Love of country shall prevail, and boundless passion for renown," 6.823).

social forces of *discordia demens* and *infandum bellum* in the last half of the epic.[10]

Virgil's is a world of political absolutes in which good and evil are easily discerned. On the side of civic decency and harmony is Aeneas. On the other side are Juno and her factors Dido, Turnus, and Allecto. With their "high wrongs" the reader of the *Aeneid* is "struck to the quick." A similarly distinct division of the *dramatis personae* occurs in *The Tempest.* The cast is described in stark defining epithets unusual for Shakespeare: *right, usurping, honest, savage, deformed.* Prospero, Ferdinand, Miranda, Ariel, and Gonzalo represent the forces of *pietas;* Antonio, Sebastian, Caliban, Stephano, and Trinculo those of *furor.*

Both epic and play focus on a protagonist with a mission. Prospero, like Aeneas, sides with destiny—a destiny that promises to a near certainty by the end of act 1 that Naples and Milan will ultimately be united. Prospero's *pietas* gives him "an undergoing stomach, to bear up / Against what should ensue" (1.2.157–58). Virgil desired to create in Aeneas the greatest exemplar of leadership for Augustan Rome, and what was good enough for Romans was good enough for Renaissance Englishmen, who held up Aeneas as the finest

---

[10]The goal Allecto looks forward to is like that Antony prophesies over the body of Caesar:

> Domestic fury and fierce civil strife
> Shall cumber all the parts of Italy;
> Blood and destruction shall be so in use,
> And dreadful objects so familiar,
> That mothers shall but smile when they behold
> Their infants quartered with the hands of war;
> All pity chok'd with custom of fell deeds.
>
> (*Julius Caesar,* 3.1.263–69)

Allecto, whose character is drawn from the Discordia of Ennius's *Annals* and from Lyssa in Euripides's *Mad Heracles,* is an important symbol for political destruction in Virgil's epic, the great concern of which is to establish political order. See Howard Felperin's discussion of Até (i.e. Allecto) figures in the Late Plays in *Shakespearean Romance* (Princeton, N.J., 1972), pp. 20–31.

example of heroic virtue combined with prudent governing powers:

> Only let *Aeneas* bee worne in the Tablet of your memorie, how hee governeth himselfe in the ruine of his Countrey, in the preserving his olde Father, and carrying away his religious Ceremonies, in obeying the Gods Commaunment, to leave *Dido*, though not onelie all passionate kindnesse but even the humane consideration of vertuous gratefulnesse, would have craved other of him: how in stormes, howe in sports . . . how victorious, how besieged, how besieging . . . lastly, how *in his inwarde selfe, and howe in his outward government*, and I thinke in a minde moste prejudiced with a prejudicating humour, Hee will bee founde in excellencie fruitefull.[11]

Prospero's character also evokes the perfect leader described above by Sidney. Prospero dramatizes

> the king-becoming graces,
> As justice, verity, temp'rance, stableness,
> Bounty, perseverence, mercy, lowliness,
> Devotion, patience, courage, fortitude
> (*Macbeth*, 4.3.91–94)

that finally triumph in the political horror story of *Macbeth*.[12]

---

[11]Sir Philip Sidney, *The Defence of Poesie, Prose Works,* ed. Albert Feuillerat (London, 1912), III, p. 25 (emphasis added). For a sense of Aeneas's reputation and how the *Aeneid* was read in Renaissance England, see Reuben Brower, *Hero and Saint: Shakespeare and the Graeco-Roman Heroic Tradition* (New York, 1971), pp. 52–56.

[12]Compare these "graces" with those of Aeneas described by Torquato Tasso in his *Discorsi del poema eroico:* "formò in Enea la pietà, la religione, la continenza, la fortezza, la magnanimità, la giustizia e ciascun'altra virtù di cavaliero" (*Prose,* ed. Ettore Mazzali [Milan, 1959], pp. 608–9). D. C. Allen's discussion of Landino's allegory in *Mysteriously Meant* (Baltimore, 1970) is particularly relevant: "Carthage is on an inlet because no man is a continent but rather an island, separate and torn by the surges of the ocean. Aeneas's experience in Carthage is, consequently, an education in kingship" (p. 151).

Prospero is called "good" by Ariel with the same conviction that Aeneas is called *pius* (T. Phaer in 1558 and T. Twyne in 1573 translated Virgil's *pius* as *good*). Both are tempest-tossed, exiled from their native lands by demonic forces. Prospero, too, would sense the sadness that lies between these two thoughts of Aeneas: "With tears I quit my native shores and harbours, and the plains, where once was Troy. An exile, I fare forth upon the deep" (3.10–11). Prospero has like Aeneas a human side, though we must wait until act 5 to discover it fully. He finally proves he has not lost what Sidney happily calls the "passionate kindnesse" of Aeneas. Prospero does not lose his humanity, though he is privy to omnipotent arts and finds his enemies in his grasp; the triumph of his magnanimity is therefore all the more resplendent.

In addition to their common trait of humane leadership, both Aeneas and Prospero feel the burden of history. The existence of each is suspended between the memory of a ruined past and the vision of a happy destiny. Aeneas is an especially profound figure because, as Sidney points out, his sense of historical mission pervades the inward as well as the outward self. Aeneas possesses great psychological depth because he can see the long view *and* he can see into himself; he must govern himself with regard to both his mission and his humanity. Prospero is subjected to the same tensions, and he resolves them much as Aeneas does, displaying a strong combination of humanity and moral realism. He is thus able to govern his inner self while fulfilling his political responsibilities.

Prospero struggles to nurse a bitter memory and yet retain hope and humanity, confront evil and yet avoid cynicism. This humanizing struggle is the most attractive aspect of both Aeneas and Prospero, and it is no coincidence that the most famous speech uttered by each occurs when the tension between idealism and harsh reality is greatest. In *Aeneid* 1 the hero is encouraging his despondent followers:

169

"O comrades—for ere this we have not been ignorant of evils—O ye who have borne a heavier lot, to
this, too, God will grant an end! Ye drew near to
Scylla's fury and her deep-echoing crags; ye have
known, too, the rocks of the Cyclopes; recall your
courage and put away sad fear. Perchance even this
distress it will some day be a joy to recall. Through
divers mishaps, through so many perilous chances,
we fare towards Latium, where the fates point out a
home of rest. There 'tis granted to Troy's realm to
rise again; endure, and keep yourselves for days of
happiness."

So spake his tongue; while sick with weighty
cares [*curis ingentibus aeger*] he feigns hope on his face,
and deep in his heart stifles the anguish.

(1.198–209)

Here in such glimpses of the "other" side of heroism is one
source of the complexity of Aeneas. Prospero's Revels Speech
provides a similar fleeting look behind the exterior of an
idealized hero of political *renovatio*. Reminded of "that foul
conspiracy" of Caliban, Prospero suddenly calls the masquers
to a halt and they leave sorrowfully. What follows is another
extraordinary view of the inner life of the visionary. Prospero's "Sir, I am vex'd; / Bear with my weakness; my old
brain is troubled" has the same effect as the last Virgilian lines
quoted above. This is the world-weary *dolor* of Aeneas, the
same note of having seen the real presence of evil behind the
baseless fabric of the offered vision. Prospero and Aeneas are
both uneasy with the monstrous cares (*curis ingentibus aeger*) of
achieving a civilized world when the demonic forces of a Juno
or Caliban threaten.

Like Aeneas, Prospero must confront various forces of
furor. Already the victim of treachery and rebellion, he must
cope with the plot of Caliban and the "open-eyed conspiracy"
of Antonio and Sebastian. These three political upheavals set
at issue one central question of *The Tempest:* to obey or not to

obey. Obedience is the centerpiece of Renaissance English political *pietas*, the central concept of any tolerable social existence.[13] The idealized characters Miranda, Ferdinand, and Ariel are scrupulously obedient; the villainous characters are as scrupulously otherwise.

Perhaps because the contemporary political themes of *The Tempest* have not seriously concerned critics (though there has been some eagerness to apply modern political ideas to the action), the central political significance of Caliban has not been fully appreciated. This strange monster is crucial to an understanding of a play eminently concerned with political order because Caliban is the symbolic opposite of order, an embodiment of *furor*. (He is compared in the following chapter with *furor* figures in *The Faerie Queene* and a Jonsonian masque.) Caliban is no mere "servant monster" as Jonson asserted, but also a "civil monster" of the kind Iago warns is quite common "in a populous city." He is not merely noncivilized or noncivilizable but anticivilized.[14] His presence never fails to have political connotations.

[13]During the years of the Late Plays, one might note, both Puritans and an increasingly obstinate Parliament were beginning to subvert the Tudor theory of obedience. See the discussion of Caliban and the *Homilies* in chapter six. Note Edward Dowden's remark (*Shakespeare: A Critical Study of His Mind and Art* [London, 1875], p. 419), "A thought which seems to run through the whole of *The Tempest* . . . is the thought that the true freedom of man consists in service." See also Dean Ebner, "*The Tempest:* Rebellion and the Ideal State," *Shakespeare Quarterly* 16 (1965): 161–73.

[14]The nature of a "civil monster" is analyzed by Thomas Wright in *The Passions of the minde in generalle* (London, 1604). There he lists traits that can bring a "private man" into "contempt and hatred" of his fellow men. Many apply to Caliban:

Ingresse [i.e. birth]
   "If his Parents were base, wicked . . . deformed in body."
   "If the manner of his begetting was unlawfull."
Progresse
   If he shows "irreligion toward God."
   If he conspires "against the Prince or State."
   "If he be of a bloody nature" and conspires "injustice toward
      men."

171

Caliban does not desire the liberty from apprenticeship that Ariel wants, a quite respectable desire in Shakespeare's time. Rather he wants the liberty to be "mine own King." Ariel wishes liberty from an agreed bondage, Caliban a reckless liberty of the will. Like the political misfits confined in the adamant of Virgil's Tartarus, Caliban is confined in "hard rock" (1.2.345, 363) because he lacks the imprint of civilization and is congenitally disobedient. He and his "vile race" are *The Tempest's* equivalent of the Virgilian *ignobile vulgus* (1.149) or, as Elizabethans put it, the beast with many heads.[15] When Stephano first discovers Caliban he has four legs and two heads; the resulting conspiracy is that of a "many-headed monster."

Caliban is a "thing of darkness" like Allecto—a vile conglomerate of execration, lust, malevolence, and uncontrol. He is Shakespeare's distillation of the kind of unthinking that ruins civilization. He is called "salvage" because he is deeply *uncivil.*[16] The "salvage and deformed slave," then, is akin to

---

"If he hath iterated often the same sinne, so that it is rooted in him and become connaturall: and consequently we may despair of emendation."

"If . . . he be addicted to lying, swearing, perjuring, cursing, lust, gluttony, drunkennesse, pride, ambition, envie, detraction, railing, reviling, gaming, &c."

(pp. 265–70)

[15]See Christopher Hill, "The Many-Headed Monster in Late Tudor and Early Stuart Thinking," in *From the Renaissance to the Counter-Reformation: Essays in Honor of Garrett Mattingly* (New York, 1965), pp. 296–324. See also C. A. Patrides, "The Beast with Many Heads: Renaissance Views of the Multitude," *Shakespeare Quarterly* 16 (1965): 241–46.

[16]For Shakespearean uses of *savage* in antonymy to *civil,* see *Antony and Cleopatra,* 3.13.128; *King John,* 5.2.74; *Timon of Athens,* 5.1.168; and *Cymbeline,* 3.6.18. According to Rose Abdelnour Zimbardo in "Form and Disorder in *The Tempest*" (*Shakespeare Quarterly* 14 [1963]: p. 53), Caliban is "the very incarnation of chaos." Her discussion is excellent but does not treat the political themes of the play. See also *The Crown of Life* (London, 1940), where G. Wilson Knight writes that Caliban "symbolizes all brainless revolutions . . . and the absurdities of mob mentality" (p. 211).

the terrifying abstraction of civil violence Jupiter describes in *Aeneid* 1. In the play, however, *impius furor* is never allowed to burst its bonds as it does in the epic. Caliban is crushed by the plot; the final subjugation of his base nature through Prospero's civilizing nurture is a supremely symbolic moment of the play. And this sets Prospero in a literary tradition that began with Aeneas: "Aeneas . . . stands for a new idea in history, the idea that *violentia* and *superbia* can be controlled, that a just *imperium* can be established, that universal peace can be a fact as well as an ideal." [17] Prospero stands for the same principles, and in order for them to have an effect artistically there must be a Caliban to work upon, a character whose violence and ignominy are complete. *The Tempest* is a symbolic chronicle of the ascendancy of *imperium* over *violentia*, just as Shakespeare's histories are a "chronicle of day by day" of this same theme.

THE BEAST AND
THE COURTIER

Having considered a metaphorical and a conceptual polarity, we turn now to a polarity in characterization and to a closer comparison of *The Tempest* with a work of indubitable "courtly" standing, *The Faerie Queene*, book 6. The book "Containing the Legend of Sir Calidore, or Courtesie" stands in relation to Spenser's oeuvre as does *The Tempest* to Shakespeare's, reflecting back and summarizing its author's preceding work. [18] Both works are culminating expressions of ideal

---

[17]Brooks Otis, *Virgil: A Study in Civilized Poetry* (Oxford, 1963), p. 382.

[18]This view of *The Tempest* has been expressed by many, by none more strongly than G. W. Knight in *The Shakespearian Tempest* (London, 1932), pp. 263–65: "*The Tempest* is Shakespeare's instinctive imaginative genius mapped into a universal pattern; not neglecting, but enclosing and transcending, all his past themes of loss and restoration, tempest and music . . . . *The Tempest* reflects the whole Shakespearian universe."

In his study of book 6, *Spenser's Courteous Pastoral* (Oxford, 1972),

courtly life, one Elizabethan and the other Jacobean; both are crucially concerned with social man. Humphrey Tonkin's summary of the central issues of book 6 applies readily to Shakespeare's play: "the emphasis falls time after time on man's obligation to help and respect those around him. Aid to the afflicted, honour to superiors, treatment of inferiors humanely, forgiveness, readiness to learn from the best traditions of society—these are the very basis of courtesy, the orderly running of society."[19] Both works have raised the same critical issues: the uses of pastoral, the conflicts between art and nature and between nature and nurture, the theme of regeneration, and the meaning of grace. Finally, book 6 and *The Tempest* turn inward and reflect upon themselves as works of art—courtly art. (This is one of Isabel MacCaffrey's central points about book 6 in her *Spenser's Allegory*.) In the last stanzas of book 6 we learn that the devastation of the Blatant Beast extends to Spenser's own art:

> Ne spareth he most learned wits to rate,
> Ne spareth he the gentle Poets rime,
> But rends without regard of person or of time.
>
> Ne may this homely verse, of many meanest,
> Hope to escape his venemous despite,
> More then my former writs, all were they
> cleanest
> From blamefull blot, and free from all that wite,

Humphrey Tonkin writes, "it is my contention that a knowledge of Spenser's Legend of Courtesy and its ramifications is in large measure the key to the whole work. Book 6 sums up and re-examines the issues raised by the work as a whole" (p. 1). A recent and extensive discussion of Spenser's book 6 can be found in Isabel MacCaffrey's *Spenser's Allegory: The Anatomy of Imagination* (Princeton, 1976), pp. 343–422. MacCaffrey refers to other readings of book 6—"the most original and unexpected of his imaginings"—in her footnotes.

[19]Tonkin, *Spenser's Courteous Pastoral,* p. 11.

> With which some wicked tongues did it backe-
> bite.
>
> (6.12.40–41)

Spenser's closing sally is significant for the present study: forces that will destroy civility—and courtly civility *is* a focus of book 6—will also attack men like Spenser who write for "mighty peers." These are the enemies who will backbite the richly allusive, complex, and polished art fostered by the courtly aesthetic. The enemies of the courtier's ethic, like Caliban or the Blatant Beast, are also enemies of the courtier's aesthetic.

Three themes shared by the two works are largely responsible for their similar action, which is essentially the conquest of civic monsters by idealized courtiers. The themes of obedience, manners, and pastoral regeneration illustrate the courtly ideal. Obedience is the cementing bond in the hierarchical organization of society, upon which the court and its aesthetic ideal ultimately depend. In a "semi-official" opening stanza Spenser lays his political foundation:

> What vertue is so fitting for a knight,
>> Or for a Ladie, whom a knight should love,
>> As Curtesie, to beare themselves aright
>> To all of each degree, as doth behove?
>> For whether they be placed high above,
>> Or low beneath, yet ought they well to know
>> Their good, that none them rightly may reprove
>> Of rudenesse, for not yeelding what they owe:
> Great skill it is such duties timely to bestow.
>
> (6.2.1)

The "grace" Calidore displays in book 6 is due to his ability to yield what he owes to a hierarchical social system, and one of the overriding intentions of the book is to give more precise meaning through fictional amplification to the "great skill" of bestowing one's social duties in a timely fashion. In politic book 6, *grace* and *obedience* are synonymous.

In the last canto, the Blatant Beast must learn obedience under the hand of Calidore:

> Yet durst he not draw backe; nor once withstand
> The proved powre of noble *Calidore*,
> But trembled underneath his mighty hand,
> And like a fearfull dog him followed through the
> land.
> Him through all Faery land he follow'd so,
> As if he learned had obedience long.
>
> (6.12.36–37)

The disheartening qualifier *if* is poignant, though, for we soon learn that the Beast, unable to learn true obedience, may break his bonds again. His groveling is mere pretense forced upon him by momentary adversity. This might well make us wonder if the obedience of Caliban in act 5 ("I'll be wise hereafter / And seek for grace.") is feigned for similar reasons. I am inclined to think the silence of Antonio and Sebastian as well as Caliban's uncharacteristic promise—a true ignorant has no memory for promises—are ominous. The Spenserian idea that evil may be momentarily overcome but not extinguished still persists in the aura of act 5. Neither Shakespeare nor Spenser could avoid glancing at the "fault of men" (6.12.38). Obedience, then, is one index in establishing the polarity between the courtier and the beast—between the civilized and the uncivilizable. [20]

[20]To Spenser and, I believe, Shakespeare, there was a difference between the uncivilizable and the noncivilized or primitive. This is very clear in book 6, where the Blatant Beast reflects the former and the "salvage man" in canto 4 the latter. We quickly learn this primitive is no Caliban, but rather a proto-Rousseauesque figure for whom there *is* hope:

> O what an easie thing is to descry
> The gentle bloud, how ever it be wrapt
> In sad misfortunes foule deformity,
> And wretched sorrowes, which have often hapt?

A second theme shared by the play and the epic is that the *manners* of men are unerring clues to their nobility or baseness. This is one of the controlling means of characterization for both Spenser and Shakespeare. The idea that manners show the man is clarioned in Spenser's first stanza:

> Of Court it seemes, men Courtesie doe call,
>> For that it there most useth to abound;
>> And well beseemeth that in Princes hall
>> That vertue should be plentifully found,
>> Which of all goodly manners is the ground,
>> And roote of civill conversation.
>
> (6.1.1)

The point is reinforced in canto 3: "For a man by nothing is so well bewrayed / As by his manners." A practiced Spenserian soon gains the ability to tell from the slightest initial hint whether a character is noble or base.

The Tempest is equally clear in its characterization. The positive figures in the play have a knack for ingratiation; the evil ones are just as involuntarily obnoxious. One of the marvels of the first scene, for instance, is how the tiniest speeches of Alonso, Gonzalo, Antonio, and Sebastian prepare us for their subsequent development. The figures of *pietas* like Miranda and Ferdinand show a grace in the Spenserian qualities of "civill conversation" and "goodly manners," while the villains must speak relentlessly execratious, mean-minded lines reminiscent of other Shakespearean social misfits like Thersites, Apemantus, and Cloten.

> For howsoever it may grow mis-shapt,
> Like this wild man, being undisciplind,
> That to all vertue it may seeme unapt,
> Yet will it shew some sparkes of gentle mind,
> And at the last breake forth in his owne proper kind.
>> (6.5.1)

Some figures, though "salvage" and "deformed," may respond to nurture if given the chance. Prospero took such a chance with Caliban, but he proved a hopeless recidivist and hence one of the Blatant Beast's race.

Finally, the pastoral interlude in book 6 (cantos 9–11) helps to answer a question that may trouble many readers: how, in a poem and a play so far removed from the venue of courtly life, can the themes of Tasso's "politicke blessedness" be as centrally important as I suggest? Is it to damn courtly life with faint praise if its regeneration must take place in a kind of pastoral laboratory far from the confines of normal courtly life? The answer is probably yes, perhaps because the Elizabethan and Jacobean courts deserved faint praise in the eyes of Spenser and Shakespeare. The corruption and morally corrosive nature of life at court reflected in book 6 (see especially the speeches of the shepherd Meliboe) are not essentially different from what is depicted in *Timon of Athens*. The realities of courtly life may well have been too sordid, too desperately vile to support an "artist's conception" of an ideal court. One might reasonably compare the three pastoral cantos to the withdrawal to "fair Bohemia" in *The Winter's Tale,* where the power to revitalize the Sicilian dynasty is incubated, and to the removal to the isle for a similar regeneration of the dukedom of Milan and the kingdom of Naples.[21]

The repair to pastoral surroundings has the distinct advantage of offering the perspective, if not of rustic innocence, at least of directness, honesty, and the plain style. For Calidore the sojourn in the meadows near Acidale is a way of avoiding the treacherous machinations of a Turpine and the sugared

[21] "While there is little evidence of courts and cities in the landscape through which Calidore and Calepine pass, we should not forget that the justification for this landscape lies in the very fact that book 6 is a poem *about* courts and cities, even if the redefinition of man's role in society—the practice of courtesy and the knowledge of 'civility'—involves his stepping outside its framework" (Tonkin, *Spenser's Courteous Pastoral,* p. 179). Puttenham makes a similar point when he concludes his list of reasons why courtiers might choose to rusticate: "By sequestring themselves for a time fro the Court [they are] able the freelier and cleerer to discerne the factions and state of the Court and of all the world besides, no lesse then doth the looker on or beholder of a game better see into all points of avauntage, then the player himselfe" (*Arte of English Poesie,* p. 306).

circumlocutions of a Blandina. It is a way of extricating himself from the pain and sorrow of a corrupt courtly existence. "How much more happie," says Calidore to the old shepherd,

> is the state,
> In which ye father here doe dwell at ease,
> Leading a life so free and fortunate,
> From all the tempests of these worldly seas,
> Which tosse the rest in daungerous disease;
> Where warres, and wreckes, and wicked enmitie
> Doe them afflict, which no man can appease.
> That certes I your happinesse envie,
> And wish my lot were plast in such felicitie.
>
> (6.9.19)[22]

And, like so many pastoral withdrawals in courtly literature, what Calidore sees on Mount Acidale is by no means a scene of pastoral naiveté, but rather a most artificially contrived expression of the ideal, harmonious court. In the elaborate precision of the scene, the central figure, the "fourth Maid," represents Elizabeth. The pastoral interlude that begins so unprepossessingly soon metamorphoses into an astonishing set-piece of courtly propaganda. Through it Calidore reacquaints himself with the essential goodness of courtly harmony and the "complements of curtesie" that

> teach us, how to each degree and kinde
> We should our selves demeane, to low, to hie,
> To friends, to foes; which skill men call Civility.
>
> (6.10.23)

Remote from civilization, Calidore learns civility.

The same strategy occurs in *The Tempest*. The royal party, and Ferdinand and Miranda with them, learn the same lesson as Calidore through their experience on the island.

---

[22]The shepherd and his tale of woes experienced at the "royall court" remind me of Belarius's attack upon "the city's usuries," "the toil o' th' war," and the "art o' th' court" in *Cymbeline* (3.3).

They learn to rule their passions, to demean themselves "timely" to their superiors—whether parent, master, or governor. The harmonious action of act 5 is a counterpart to Calidore's vision of the Dance of the Graces,[23] and, while these visions of social harmony may through human frailty prove transitory, they can still be realized if courtiers act as Calidore and Ferdinand do. In neither case should the romance environment or pastoral furniture lead us astray from the fact that Calidore's "high behest" to capture the Beast and Prospero's project to put his enemies in his power will have their ultimate and most important effects in the court of Gloriana and the court of Milan, that is, among "the infinite doings of the world" (*The Winter's Tale*, 1.2.253).

These remarks upon the themes of obedience, manners, and "courtly" pastoral prepare us for a consideration of the polar opposites of the perfect courtier Sir Calidore and the Blatant Beast. In them are shadowed the figures of Ferdinand and Caliban—and the antagonism between courtly beauty and courtly bestiality.

Calidore and Ferdinand are idealized courtly neophytes.[24] The characterization of each young nobleman leaves not the slightest doubt that they are being offered as embodiments of what is praiseworthy in a courtier. Calidore is introduced in the first radiant stanzas with his "gentlenesse of spright," "manners milde," "comely guize," "gracious speach," "fair usage and conditions sound." This is fittingly followed by the description of his antagonist, the Blatant Beast. After eight stanzas the polarity is fully set forth.[25] Calidore's appearance,

[23]Other implications of Calidore's vision on Mount Acidale are discussed in chapter six below, pp. 203–207.

[24] "Calidore, integrated into society, nobly born, nobly educated, is Spenser's ideal courtier. Book 6 tells the story of how even the ideal courtier needs to understand that the roots of courtesy lie outside the court, though their blossom is within the court" (Tonkin, *Spenser's Courteous Pastoral*, p. 225).

[25]As is usual for Spenser, other minor characters participate in the meaning of the Beast. Of his party, for instance, are Turpine, Despetto, Decetto,

it would seem, has the same effect on his fellows that Ferdinand has on Miranda:

> [Praise] well in courteous *Calidore* appeares,
> Whose every act and word, that he did say,
> Was like enchantment, that through both the eares,
> And both the eyes did steale the hart away.
>
> (6.2.3)

Ferdinand is the "noble creature" whose presence upon the foundering ship Miranda guesses at, and after slim acquaintance she correctly concludes, "There's nothing ill can dwell in such a temple." In both of the paragons the theme of virtue-will-out plays an important part: Spenser's dictum that "gentle bloud will gentle manners breed" is reflected in the carriage of Calidore and the Shakespearean prince.

Both exhibit the same modest appetites. Each can "his wrath full wisely guide" (6.1.30), show "goodly patience" (6.1.40), and manifest a promising self-control: "In vaine he seeketh others to suppresse, / Who hath not learnd him selfe first to subdew" (6.1.41). This self-control contrasts with their allegorical opposites. Caliban has, before the play begins, attempted to rape Miranda, and this violent act is paralleled three times in book 6: the Beast's attempt to "spoil" Serena (6.3.24), the savage nation's attempt to take their "beastly pleasure" with her (6.8.35–45), and the thieves' abduction of Pastorella (6.10–11). Spenser's and Shakespeare's point is clear: a continent court is ruined by the libidinous and unrestrained courtier.

Defetto, the "salvage nation," Cormoraunt, and the "lawless brigands." The Beast's identity is filled out by their actions. Thus, the polarity reaches far beyond the two central antagonists. The same is true of *The Tempest:* the polar opposites Caliban and Prospero, or Ferdinand and Caliban, are reflected by others in the play. Note also MacCaffrey's comment: "The fierce Lapiths, the Brigants, the mighty peer whose displeasure makes *The Faerie Queene* end on a dying fall (6.12.41) are all agents of the Blatant Beast" (*Spenser's Allegory,* p. 398).

Most importantly, Ferdinand and Calidore are symbolic of the socializing process itself. Both are conceived as students of social restraint and lore. Two passages emphasize the significance of the learning process. In the first, in canto 4, a hermit instructs Serena and Timias (a Calidore surrogate). The Hermit is, like Prospero, a dispenser of social wisdom:

> through the long experience of his dayes,
> Which had in many fortunes tossed bene,
> And past through many perillous assayes,
> He knew the diverse went of mortall wayes,
> And in the mindes of men had great insight;
> Which with sage counsell, when they went
> astray,
> He could enforme, and them reduce aright,
> And al the passions heale, which wound the weaker
> spright.
> (6.6.3)

The advice the Hermit bestows is a near paraphrase of Prospero's warning to Ferdinand in act 4:

> First learne your outward sences to refraine
> From things, that stirre up fraile affection;
> Your eyes, your eares, your tongue, your talke
> restraine
> From that they most affect, and in due termes
> containe.
>
> For from those outward sences ill affected,
> The seede of all this evill first doth spring,
> Which at the first before it had infected,
> Mote easie be supprest with little thing:
> But being growen strong, it forth doth bring
> Sorrow, and anguish, and impatient paine
> In th'inner parts, and lastly scattering

> Contagious poison close through every vaine,
> It never rests, till it have wrought his finall bane.
> $(6.6.7–8)$[26]

In this advice, as in all prescriptive *sententiae* in *The Faerie Queene*, virtue is manifest in the willingness to accept and be guided by rules of conduct. We may feel that interest of character is sacrificed by the creators of Calidore and Ferdinand to the ideal of self-abnegation, and this may be because we are less enamored of the strictly ordered society envisioned in *The Faerie Queene* and *The Tempest*. Be that as it may, both works are biased in favor of social decorum and the willingness "duties timely to bestow." They identify noble behavior with voluntary obedience and bestial behavior with the grudging servitude of a Caliban.

The central polarity of book 6 is one of attitude. The proper attitude is given dimension by Calidore and his satellites in the Spenserian scheme, but over them hangs the terrible pall of the omnipresent Blatant Beast and his own allegorical entourage. He must be sought "throughout the world" (6.12.13) and hunted down "through every place" (6.12.22).

---

[26]A passage from Chapman's conclusion to *Hero and Leander* (*The Poems,* New York, 1962) is pertinent here. Indeed, the comparison of the Marlowe and Chapman sections is instructive of the general difference between "public" and "courtly" art. Marlowe's lines might be considered representative of all that was best in the realistic Elizabethan drama and in the plays for which Shakespeare will always be best known. These lines are engrossingly dramatic, human, passionate, and personal; the poetry itself is lithe and witty. Chapman's lines are more reminiscent of the courtly aesthetic—they are didactic, conservative, static, ceremonious, impersonal, and somewhat turgid. Chapman's section is less human and more spectacular, something that has often been said of Shakespeare's Late Plays. Not surprisingly, the Chapman addition is the part of the poem that reminds one of *The Tempest* and of Prospero: here is the sound of music, rich apparel, stately verse, and the ritual emphasis upon the values of civility.

Prospero and Spenser's Hermit are relevant to Chapman's description of a dream in which Leander is berated by the figure of Ceremony for his unseemly passions. In this figure—who appears amid the masque-like stage ef-

The threat to the courtly ideal, Spenser implies, is everywhere. Throughout book 6, the part of *The Faerie Queene* most concerned with man as a social being, the polarity of courtier and beast is used to elaborate and define the nature of

---

fects of "musicke so divine" and "rainbow light"—we see someone who functions as do Prospero and the Hermit:

> A rich disparant [diversely colored] Pentackle she weares,
> Drawne full of circles and strange characters:
> Her face was changeable to everie eye;
> One way lookt ill, another graciouslie;
> Which while men viewd, they cheerfull were & holy:
> But looking off, vicious and melancholy:
> The snakie paths to each observed law,
> Did *Policie* in her broad bosome draw:
> One hand a Mathematicque Christall swayes,
> Which gathering in one line a thousand rayes
> From her bright eyes, *Confusion* burnes to death.
> . . . .
>
> Thus she appeard, and sharply did reprove
> *Leanders* bluntnes in his violent love;
> Tolde him how poore was substance without rites,
> Like bils unsignd, desires without delites;
> Like meates unseason'd; like ranke corne that growes
> On Cottages, that none or reapes or sowes:
> Not being with civill forms confirm'd and bounded,
> For humane dignities and comforts founded:
> But loose and secret all their glorie hide,
> Fear fils the chamber, darknes decks the Bride.
>
> *(Poems, p. 137)*

Gender notwithstanding, the Hermit, Prospero, and Ceremony have much in common. Their concern is with the proper ordering of society, with the rules of civility that make it cohere. All of these figures express the orthodox idea that ritual is necessary if confusion is to be banished. And this idea—that "substance without rites" is very poor indeed—is a theorem of the courtly aesthetic. The discussion of "Hero and Leander" in M. C. Bradbrook's *Shakespeare and Elizabethan Poetry* ([London, 1957], pp. 61, 66–70) also emphasizes the radical differences between the styles of Marlowe and Chapman. For an excellent discussion of Chapman the literary elitist, see D. J. Gordon, "The Renaissance Poet as Classicist: Chapman's *Hero and Leander*," in *The Renaissance Imagination,* ed. Stephen Orgel (Berkeley, 1975), pp. 102–33. See also Raymond Waddington, *The Mind's Empire: Myth and Form in George Chapman's Narrative Poems* (Baltimore, Maryland, 1974), on the poet's attempt "to restore the societal context" of the story that Marlowe ignored.

man's social responsibilities. Calidore and the Beast are Spenser's representatives of courtly health and courtly disease.

Shakespeare uses the opposition between Ferdinand and Caliban to the same effect. Ferdinand accepts instruction gracefully, performs "some kinds of baseness" without reluctance, and restrains his passions in the interest of "sanctimonious ceremonies." As we will see in chapter six, Caliban is his carefully wrought opposite. He consistently exerts pressure against restraint and frequently displays what Greville called the "violence of pride" and the "narrow selfness" that are the root diseases of human communities. He wishes ultimately to break the bonds of the social system and make himself king. Caliban cannot learn and therefore has no access to civilization; he is a monster because although he is among the civilized he cannot be one of them. For him there is no hope; he is, as Prospero concludes,

> A devil, a born devil, on whose nature
> Nurture can never stick; on whom my pains,
> Humanely taken, all, all lost, quite lost.
>
> (4.1.188–90)

· VI ·

CHARACTERS OF
THE COURTLY AESTHETIC:
CALIBAN

The sleep of reason produces monsters.
FRANCISCO DE GOYA

HE COURTLY AESTHETIC typically clothes ethical, religious, and political commonplaces in forms that are often extraordinarily complex, allusive, and artificial. This paradox is manifest in Caliban and partly explains the difficulty of interpreting his character. The savage and deformed slave's importance in *The Tempest* has been recognized by many commentators, yet there is no consensus on his precise meaning. The failure of critics to look beyond the superficial strangeness of the monster to the commonplaces allegorized through him has resulted in perplexity. Caliban's uniqueness in the Shakespearean canon has often led to hasty conclusions about him, as a passage from *The Spectator* suggests: "It shews a greater Genius in Shakespear to have drawn his *Calyban,* than his *Hotspur* or *Julius Caesar:* The one was to be supplied out of his Imagination, whereas the other might have been formed upon Tradition, History, and Observation."[1] At least since Addison's time Caliban has struck readers by his originality.

[1] Joseph Addison, *The Spectator,* No. 279 (19 January 1712), ed. Donald Bond (Oxford, 1965), II, pp. 586–87. More recently John Hankins has similarly asserted that Caliban is "Shakespeare's most original character" in "Caliban the Bestial Man," *PMLA* 62 (1947): 801.

I want to suggest in this chapter that, on the contrary, Caliban was very carefully formed on tradition, history, and the observation of moral and political commonplaces, that aspects of his role—and many of his physical features—are distinctly derivative. Shakespeare created in Caliban a grotesque, much like nature's anomalous platypus, caught in a backwater of literary evolution. Vestigial allegorical significations are partially responsible for his exceeding strangeness, even amid the fantastic surroundings of Prospero's isle. To understand Caliban we must focus on those allegorical vestiges, their political meaning, and the symbolic trappings of his literary precursors. In a play by Shakespeare Caliban naturally surprised the sensibilities of Jonson, Addison, and many afterward— just as Johnson was disconcerted by the presence of Sin and Death in *Paradise Lost*. But tucked away in a canto of *The Faerie Queene* Caliban would scarcely raise an eyebrow.

The Tempest is an ambivalent and elusive play. The "uninhabited Island" is notoriously hard to visualize, and the same is true of the servant monster, for he is supported with tightrope finesse between the realms of Spenserian allegory and Shakespearean dramaturgy. Even the simple question, Is Caliban essentially bestial or human?, is hard to answer confidently. His first mention shows how carefully Shakespeare plants the doubt:

> Then was this island—
> Save for the son that she did litter here,
> A freckled whelp hag-born—not honour'd with
> A human shape.
> (1.2.281–84)

A "son" or some creature that was part of a litter? "Human shape" or "freckled whelp hag-born"?—the syntax favors the latter, as does the weight of imagery heaped on Caliban throughout the play (the Folio has parentheses in place of the dashes). To understand Caliban's nature we must compromise: he is a demi-allegorical figure just as he is a "demi-devil" or "half a fish and half a monster." This primary visual ambiguity is of a kind rare in Shakespeare and looks back to Spenser's epic, where it is an important and common poetic device. At the least, the allegorical ambivalence enriches Caliban's role in *The Tempest*, makes him an example of that artificial movement "beyond the life" which is a hallmark of the courtly aesthetic. Caliban is a creature of courtly allegory, and this aspect of his literary ancestry is the subject of the following excursions.

CALIBAN AND THE HOMILIES

Renaissance Englishmen had no organization charts, power-flow concepts, or highly abstract political systems. The modern Impossibility Theory that decrees perfect government mathematically unfeasible would have struck them as dangerously subversive. Their concern was not with system but with act—and one act in particular: obedience. The praise of what Greville called the "justice, necessity, and commodities of obedience" was the core of political thought for both Tudor and Stuart monarchs, just as it is the core of *The Tempest*'s political meanings. If we are to understand Caliban fully we must see in him a creature of the theory of obedience that James and Charles took over with little refinement from the Tudors. Indeed, Caliban's relations with Prospero and the play's other characters generally reflect the "abuse, carnal liberty, enormity, sin, and Babylonical confusion" that result when "right order" is undermined by disobedience.

The last-quoted phrases are taken from the most widely circulated contemporary expressions of Tudor orthodoxy, *Certaine Sermons or Homilies*, an authorized collection of sermons that held official sway in England at least until 1623.[2]

[2]The best edition, by John Griffiths (Oxford, 1859), collates many of the numerous editions and includes a long introduction. However, since it is

According to the preface of the 1562 edition, these sermons were to be read, when no licensed preacher was present, by "all Parsons, Vicars, Curates, and all other having spirituall cure, every Sunday and Holiday of the yeere." These sermons, designed for the "better understanding of the simple people," are the best-known, popular contemporary expression we have of Tudor political science.[3] To see Caliban as an expression of Jacobean establishmentarianism (an assessment by no means new), we may profitably refer to the *Homilies* (an approach that is new).

Two of the sermons throw special light on Caliban: "An Exhortation concerning good Order, and obedience to Rulers and Magistrates," which appeared in 1547; and "An Homilie against disobedience and wilfull rebellion," a long, six-part tract that was the final addition to the *Homilies* in 1571.[4] Alfred Hart has demonstrated the importance of these two sermons for Shakespeare, but he confines his attention to the

more readily available, I will quote in the following discussion from the facsimile reprint of the 1623 version, edited by Mary Rickey (Gainesville, Florida, 1968). The first book of homilies (Latimer said in a sermon to Edward VI in 1549 that "they may be well called, for they are homely handled") was published under Cranmer's direction five months after the death of Henry VIII in 1547. It was reprinted at least twenty times, until a second and much larger set appeared in 1563. It is an irony perhaps worth noting that the version of political order contained in Cranmer's homilies was to be reaffirmed by the dramatic Cranmer in Shakespeare's *Henry VIII*.

[3]Nor did they fall into oblivion when Elizabeth died. James sponsored an edition in 1623 (the first, incidentally, combining both books of homilies in one folio volume and also the last to be printed at royal expense). Three more editions appeared during the reign of Charles, and five more after the Restoration.

[4]The history of this homily is unique, being occasioned apparently by the rebellion that broke out under the earls Northumberland and Westmoreland in November 1569. At least five separate editions of this sermon from the year 1570 are extant. At least two other homilies from this collection bear on *The Tempest*. One is the "Sermon against Contention and Brawling." The description there of the "evilfavouredness and deformity of this most destestable vice" is part of the aura surrounding Caliban, Antonio, Sebastian, Stephano, and Trinculo. "An Homily against Idleness" is also significant background to the play. An article that indirectly makes this point is William

histories and tragedies.[5] He does not mention *The Tempest*—another indication that Caliban's political significance and the political concerns of the play have not been sufficently appreciated. Yet Caliban lives in these two sermons, and the sermons in Caliban.

The Exhortation (1547) and the Homily (1571) represent a homely version of Hooker's *Laws of Ecclesiastical Polity*. Their periods may be less magniloquent, but their vision of a "profitable, necessary, and pleasant order" in human society is hardly less forceful. The homilist presents a Hookerian view of man as inextricably part of a social organism: "Some are in high degree, some in low, some Kings and Princes, some inferiours and subjects, Priests and lay men, masters and servants, fathers and children, husbands and wives, rich and poore, and every one have neede of other" (p. 69). As in *The Tempest*, the ideal of the Homily is "quietnesse, joy, and felicitie, which doe follow blessed peace & due obedience" (p. 296). The effects of social evil, on the other hand, are

> to bring in all trouble, sorrow, disquietnes of minds & bodies & all mischiefe & calamitie, to turne all good order upside downe, to bring all good lawes in contempt, and to treade them under feete, to oppresse all vertue and honestie, and all vertuous and honest persons, and to set all vice and wickednesse, and all vicious and wicked men at libertie, to work their wicked willes.
>
> (p. 296)

The homilist consistently asserts the ties of "due and bounden obedience" as the source of felicity in the commonwealth: these are just the ties—"use of service"—blithely forsaken in Gonzalo's intentionally satiric utopia.

Rockett's "Labor and Virtue in *The Tempest*," *Shakespeare Quarterly* 24 (1973): 77–84. He writes, "The ethics of discipline and industry occupies [a] central place in the dramatic framework of *The Tempest*" (p. 83).

[5]Alfred Hart, *Shakespeare and the Homilies* (Melbourne, 1934), pp. 9–76.

What the homilist says about obedience illuminates our understanding of Shakespeare's politic monster Caliban. Perhaps most importantly, the sermons clarify Caliban's relation to Prospero and the efficacy of the power the latter exerts over him. The strategy of the constant bestial references is mirrored in the assumption that, "as GOD would have man to be his obedient subject, so did he make all earthly creatures subject unto man" (p. 275). Prospero's powers rise to the angelic, while Caliban's are deteriorated, animalistic, of the earth and earthy. He is "filth," "earth," a "thing of darkness," and thus is "deservedly confin'd into this rock." The obedience Caliban owes to Prospero is then like that of man to God, man to king, and beasts to man. Within this descending hierarchy, the right of Prospero to rule Caliban is no less than his right to rule in Milan. Prospero is truly a "god of power."

Caliban, we learn, has ruined what potential there was for an edenic island existence. In the micro-society on the island he performs the luciferian function:

> But as all felicitie and blessednesse should have continued with the continuance of obedience, so with the breach of obedience, and breaking in of rebellion, all vices and miseries did withall breake in, and overwhelme the world. The first authour of which rebellion, the root of all vices, and mother of all mischiefes, was *Lucifer,* first GODS most excellent creature, and most bounden subject, who by rebelling against the Majestie of GOD, of the brightest and most glorious Angel, is become the blackest.
>
> (p. 276)

The diabolism of the rebel is a theme of the homilies, and much of their imagery— "wicked impes of the devill" and "blackest and most foulest fiend"—I applied to Caliban. He is variously a "hag-seed," "demi-devil," and "a devil, a born devil." Even beyond this we see in many of his speeches

(2.2.1.–14, for example) the luciferian rage of the fallen and impotent.[6]

The relationship between Prospero and Caliban as we first experience it mirrors the attitude in the homilies toward rebels who "doe onely but inwardly grudge, mutter, and murmure against their governours" (p. 299). The animosity between the two is a reflection of the divine wrath against Satan, and of a Renaissance king against his rebellious subject. The Biblical text that lies behind this tense situation is a *locus classicus* for political obedience, Paul's letter to the Romans: "For rulers are not fearefull to them that doe good, but to them that doe evill. Wilt thou bee without feare of that power? Doe well then, and so shalt thou be praised of the same, for he is the minister of God, for thy wealth. But and if thou doe that which is evil, then feare, for he beareth not the sword for naught" (quoted in the *Homilies,* p. 71). The respective reactions of Ariel and Caliban to Prospero's rule, and the praise and criticism he metes out accordingly, dramatize this Biblical crux of Renaissance political theory.

The exordium of the Homily indicates most clearly that Caliban is meant to figure forth the evil of rebellion:

> Let us therefore awake from the sleepe and darke-
> nesse of ignorance, and open our eyes that wee may
> see the light, let us rise from the workes of darknesse,
> that we may escape eternall darkenesse, the due re-
> ward thereof, and let us walke in the light of GODS
> word, whiles we have light, as becommeth the chil-
> dren of light.
>
> (pp. 318–19)

[6]As a rebel against the benevolent and humane rule of Prospero, Caliban clearly suffers the force of the Biblical warning in Romans, "they that resist shall receive to themselves damnation." In more direct fashion, the rebellious "English monsters" Cambridge and Scroop receive their "damnation" in the King's sentencing speech in *Henry V* (2.2.79–144). The King's vilification ("cruel, / Ingrateful, savage, and inhumane creature," "yoke-devils," "'gainst all proportion") is very similar to that which is heaped on Caliban.

I have already noted the association of darkness and ignorance and may now add to this connection disobedience. Shakespeare's "thing of darkness" is a disobedient and willful rebel, as well as an embodiment of primal human ignorance. The sleep and darkness out of which Prospero draws the royal party in act 5 symbolize their movement into the light of obedience—the rediscovery of their true political roles. The political lesson of *The Tempest* resembles that of the Exhortation: "It is an intolerable ignorance, madnesse, and wickednesse for subjects to make any murmuring, rebellion, resistance, or withstanding, commotion, or insurrection against their most deare and most dread Soveraigne Lord and King, ordeined and appointed of GODS goodnes for their commodity, peace and quietnesse" (p. 74).

Passages from the two sermons tell us something more about other aspects of the rebellions in *The Tempest*. First, the homilist identifies two "principal and most usual causes" of rebellion: ignorance and ambition. These are reflected in the plots of Caliban and Antonio, respectively. Caliban's conspiracy is one of the "ignorant multitude," while Antonio's is of the "ambitious and malicious."[7] Describing the victims of such rebels, the homilist touches very nearly upon the actual facts of Prospero's fall:

> The naughtiest subjects . . . soonest . . . rebell against the best Princes, specially if they be yong in age, women in sexe, or gentle and curteous in government, as trusting by their wicked boldnesse, easily to overthrow their weakenesse and gentlenesse, or at the least so to feare the mindes of such Princes, that they may have impunitie of their mischievous doings.
>
> (p. 279)

[7]*Homilies*, p. 307. Compare Richard Brathwaite's definition of ambition in *The Prodigals Teares* (London, 1614): "Ambition, the great mans passion, who builds imaginary kingdomes in the aire, and climbing, for most part, breaks his owne neck. . . . This is an hereditary evill to great persons" (p. 91).

Gentle and courteous in government—such was Prospero's self-declared nature as the duke of Milan, and such was the evil nature of his brother (what better phrase for him than "wicked boldnesse"?). Antonio's vile outburst after Sebastian's mention of "conscience" (2.1.271–85) might well have reminded a Renaissance audience of the verse from Romans they had so often heard from the pulpit: "Wherefore ye must needes obey, not onely for feare of vengeance, but also, because of conscience" (quoted, p. 71).

Antonio and Caliban are evil in their actions, execratious speeches, and sheer mean-mindedness; this evil culminates in treachery of a political nature. This sequence would not surprise any one familiar with the Homily:

> How horrible a sinne against GOD and man rebellion is, cannot possibly bee expressed according unto the greatnesse thereof. For he that nameth rebellion, nameth not a singular or one onely sinne, as is theft, robbery, murder, and such like, but he nameth the whole puddle and sinke of all sinnes against GOD and man, against his Prince, his country, his countrymen, his parents, his children, his kin folkes, his friends, and against all men universally.
>
> (p. 292)

Rebellion was seen as the logical and ultimate result of antisocial behavior, and the homilist's phrases for the rebellious are just those that come to mind for Antonio and Caliban— unkind, wicked, unnatural, grudging, mischievous, heinous, cruel.[8]

[8]The two plots might well have sparked memory of the story of Saul and David recounted in the first book of Samuel—a passage that is very prominent in the homily:

> Another time also *David* entring by night with one *Abisai,* a valiant and fierce man, into the tent where King *Saul* did lie a sleepe, where also he might yet more easily have slaine him, yet would he neither hurt him himselfe, nor suffer *Abisai* (who was willing and ready to slay King *Saul*) once to touch him. Thus did *David* deale

The political moral of the homilies and *The Tempest* is that those who attempt rebellion are bound to fail, if only under the ultimate vengeance of God:

> Let no man thinke that hee can escape unpunished, that committeth treason, conspiracy, or rebellion against his soveraigne Lord the King, though hee commit the same never so secretly, either in thought, word, or deede, never so privily, in his privie chamber by himself, or openly communicating, and consulting with others. For treason will not bee hid, treason will out at length.
>
> (p. 75, mispaginated 69)

Treason does come out at length in Shakespeare's play, as Ariel predicts in his speech warning of "powers, delaying, not forgetting." Prospero's bird of air is his means of insuring that treason will out at length. The nature of Prospero's "chick," the stage directions "like a Harpy; claps his wings upon the table," and the denunciatory tone of the "men of sin" speech all make Ariel, in effect, the harbinger of doom promised to rebels in the Bible: "For it is notably written of the wise man in Scripture, in the booke called *Ecclesiastes:* Wish the King no evill in thy thought, nor speake no hurt of him in thy privie chamber: for the bird of the aire shall betray thy voice, and with her feathers shall betray thy words."[9]

---

with *Saul* his Prince, notwithstanding that King *Saul* continually sought his death and destruction.

(285)

The story of David and Saul was intended to show that resistance to "evil and unkind" rulers was forbidden, but it applied only with more force to "good and gracious governours" like Prospero. The dialogue over the sleeping King of Naples and Caliban's promise to yield Prospero asleep in order to "batter his skull, or paunch him with a stake" may have reminded some who first saw *The Tempest* of the fierce Abisai.

[9]*Homilies,* p. 75. Ariel's primary role in the play is to act as the idealized foil to the disobedient Caliban. Ariel's first words ("All hail, great master! grave sir, hail! I come / To answer thy best pleasure," 1.2.189–90) are a

195

SALVAGE AND DEFORMED SLAVE

Caliban dramatizes the effect on man of uncontrolled sensual gratification: *homines voluptatis transformantur.* Suspended between Renaissance allegory and stage realism, he represents the idea that men are made beasts by their lusts and ambitions. A letter written by Pico della Mirandola and translated by Sir Thomas More expresses this idea in an archetypal Circean formulation:

> There was sometime in [Aeaea] a woman called Circe, which by enchauntement (as Virgil maketh mencion) used with a drinke to turne as many men as received it, into divers likenes & figures of sondry beastes: some in to liones, some into beares, some into swine, some into wolves, which afterward walked ever tame about her house and waited upon her in such use or service as she list to put unto them. In likewise the flesh . . . chaungeth us from the figure of reasonable men in to the likenes of unreasonable be[a]stes. [10]

Caliban is such a tamed and servile beast; on his nature the nurture of reason will not stick. His likeness is frequently met in literature and entertainments of the time. In Beaujoyeulx's influential French masque of 1581, the *Balet comique de la royne,*

---

pointed contrast to Caliban's recalcitrant first entry ("There is wood enough within," 1.2.316). References to Ariel's worthy service are, of course, frequent in the play.

[10]Thomas More, *The English Works,* ed. W. E. Campbell (New York, 1931), I, p. 10. Giovanni Gelli worked out the story in his famous *Circe* (five Italian editions between 1549 and 1600; an English translation by Henry Iden in 1557). Compare this passage from the dedication to Cosimo de Medici: "In the power of man there hath bene frely put an abilitie to chose a way wherin he mought lede his life moste at his owne pleasure. And almost like a newe Prometheus, to transforme him selfe into what he most willed, takinge like a Cameleont the colour of al those thinges unto the which thaffecte he is most nighe" (p. iii).

the action is based on the Circean story. The sorceress's effect on men is typical:

> Mais le plaisir passé luy devient odieux,
> Les hommes elle rend d'eux mesmes oublieux,
> Qui avec la raison perdent la forme humaine.[11]

These men are deformed by their "captivité et servitude des delices" and suffer the consequent "servitude bestiale du vice." Only when Mercury brings moly ("qui signifie la raison & estincelle divine de nos ames") from Jupiter are the men released. Caliban's circumstance is similar, but his refusal to accept reason from Prospero leaves him a monster.

Or consider the "hoggish forme" of Grill in *The Faerie Queene*. Of him

> Said *Guyon*, See the mind of beastly man,
> That hath so soone forgot the excellence
> Of his creation, when he life began,
> That now he chooseth, with vile difference,
> To be a beast, and lacke intelligence.
> To whom the Palmer thus, The donghill kind
> Delights in filth and foule incontinence:
> Let *Grill* be *Grill,* and have his hoggish mind,
> But let us hence depart, whilest wether serves and
> wind.
>
> (2.12.87)

The hopeless Grill and the recidivist Caliban ("lost, quite lost") are both in the tradition of figures who adamantly refuse "intelligence." Caliban is one of the dunghill kind ("thou earth,"

---

[11]Baltasar de Beaujoyeulx, *Balet comique de la royne,* facs. rpt. ed. Giacomo Caula (Torino, 1965), p. 24ʳ. Compare the similarly based masque *Tempe Restored* (1631) by Aurelian Townshend (*Poems and Masks,* ed. E. K. Chambers [Oxford, 1912]). Townshend appends an "Allegory" to his masque that is essentially in accord with Mirandola and Gelli. See also Ménestrier's analysis of *Orlando Furioso,* quoted here in note 2 of chapter seven.

"filth as thou art"). Prospero and Miranda at last take the Palmer's view of him: let Caliban be Caliban. Though endowed with a human shape, Caliban's body deteriorates, and his mind cankers accordingly through his failure to follow his nobler reason. At play's end he is still a "misshapen knave." Pertinent here is Holofernes' imperious apostrophe on Constable Dull in *Love's Labour's Lost* (4.2.23): "O thou monster Ignorance, how deformed dost thou look!"

That Caliban is also called "this thing of darkness" further suggests his status as a true ignorant. Thomas Walkington makes this connection when he writes of "the inveloped and deformed night of ignorance. . . . For he that is incanoped and intrenched in this darkesome misty cloud of ignorance . . . hath no true lampe of discretion."[12] Ben Jonson voices this common correlation of darkness and ignorance when he defines the latter in his *Discoveries* as "the darkner of mans life: the disturber of his *Reason,* and common Confounder of *Truth:* with which a man goes groping in the darke, no otherwise, then if hee were blind" (VIII, 588).

Caliban, we are told, is deservedly confined "into" a rock by Prospero (1.2.363), another connection with outcast figures (Satan and the infernal hordes being the ultimate types). There is the "wilde and salvage man" of book 4 of *The Faerie Queene* who lives in a "cave," a "dolefull" den. The infernal connection is made explicit by Spenser:

> Thenceforth she [Belphebe] past into his dreadfull
> > den,
> Where nought but darkesome drerinesse she
> > found,
> Ne creature saw, but hearkned now and then
> Some litle whispering, and soft groning sound.

[12]Thomas Walkington, *Optick Glasse of Humors* (London, 1607), p. 1ᴿ⁺ᵛ.

With that she askt, what ghosts there under
ground
Lay hid in horrour of eternall night?
(4.7.33)

And there is the figure of Guyle who "wonned in a rocke" or "den."[13] In Jonson's *Masque of Queenes*, the invocation of the witches and hags from hell places them in dark and subterranean places:

Quickly come, we all are met.
From the lakes, and from the fennes,
From the rockes, and from the dennes,
From the woods, and from the caves,
From the Church-yards, from the graves,
From the dungeon, from the tree,
That they die on, here are wee.

(VII, 284)

Jonson helpfully adds a note to these lines: "These places in their owne nature dire, & dismall, are reckoned up, as the fittest, from whence such persons should come."[14] Such appears to be the nature of Caliban's domicile.

Like the witches of *The Masque of Queenes*, Guyle, and so many symbols of Circean transformation, Caliban is a repul-

---

[13]See book 5, canto 9. Compare Oenene's plaint from Heywood's "Oenene and Paris" (stanza 126):

You Hagges & Goblings, leave your darkesome dennes,
And unfrequented pathes where no man treades.
    Leave your sad caves, & haunt these hatefull grounds,
    And hand in hand hoppe out your divelish roundes.

[14]VII, 284. There are reflections of Caliban in other misanthropic Shakespearean characters. Compare Jacques leaving for his "abandoned cave" in *As You Like It* and Timon's overall characterization in *Timon of Athens*. It is also worth noting that most of Shakespeare's uses of *cave* connote evil: see *Twelfth Night*, 4.1.48; *2 Henry VI*, 3.2.315; *Titus Andronicus*, 3.1.270 and 5.2.35, 52; *Julius Caesar*, 2.1.80; and "Rape of Lucrece," l. 1250.

sive sight. As Miranda says, "'Tis a villain, sir, / I do not love
to look on." Caliban's deformity is another common characteristic of fictional representations of ignorance and sensuality. In Ariosto's *Orlando Furioso*, Rogero is attacked by an
evil-favored band:

> A foule deformd, a brutish cursed crew,
> In bodie like to antike worke devised,
> Of monstrous shape and of an ugly hew
> Like masking Machachinas all disguised.
>
> (canto 6, stanza 61)

The English translator Harington explains the event: "The
monstrous crew that stoppeth *Rogero,* signif[ies] the base conceits of men and foule desires that assaile them."[15] Such mis-
shapen creatures are frequently met in antimasques of the
time, where—like Caliban—they are set up in opposition to
the forces of order and civilization.[16]

　　Finally, Caliban's description plays upon the significant
Renaissance distinction between erect virtue and supine vice.

---

[15]A similar crew is met in *The Faerie Queene* (6.10.39ff.). Compare also
the ten men, "mervailous ugly and evill-favoured to behold, and no lesse
dreadfull," who attack the heroes of Ortuñez's *Mirror of Knighthood* (trans.
Robert Parry, 1585), sig. 3ʳ.

[16]A few can be noted here:

　　The "imperfect creatures" in Jonson's *Mercurie Vindicated*
(1616).

　　The "shapes" in the first antimasque of *Circe and Ulysses* (1614)
by William Browne, including figures "with partes, heades and
bodies as Acteon pictured, baboons" and one Grillus "in the shape
of a hogge."

　　The "monstres plaisans et difformes" of the French masque
La Delivrance de Persée (1617).

　　The "Indians and Barbarians, who naturally are bestiall, and
others which are voluntaries, but half transformed into beasts," in
Aurelian Townshend's *Tempe Restored* (1631).

　　The antimasque of "monsters, and mis-shapen formes" in
Thomas Carew's *Coelum Britannicum* (1634).

Erect figures were associated with the powerful, the self-controlled, the reasoning:

> Onely man, whose bodie is framed erect, with his eyes still looking on that perspicuous and thought-amazing composition of the heavens, is forcibly constrained to believe, that there hath been some one of eternall and infinit command, that hath had that unspeakable wisdom, and inexcogitable care, as first to compose, then to governe and dispose this so rare and miraculous wonderment.[17]

Caliban is an earth-crawling creature unwilling to follow Prospero's commands, let alone the "eternall and infinit command" of Cartari's higher order. Because of his moral retrogression, Caliban has become what both Donne and Milton associated with immorality—a groveler. This helps to distinguish Caliban's and Ariel's relationship with Prospero. We

---

[17]Vincenzo Cartari, *The Fountaine of Ancient Fiction* (trans. R. Linche, 1599), sig. B^{r+v}. Donne expressed the idea in the third meditation of his *Devotions upon Emergent Occasions* (Cambridge, England, 1923): "Wee attribute but one priviledge and advantage to Mans body, above other moving creatures, that he is not as others, groveling, but of an erect, of an upright form, naturally built, and disposed to the contemplation of *Heaven*" (p. 10). Of the supine posture Donne wrote powerfully: "Miserable and (though common to all) inhuman *posture,* where I must practise my lying in the *grave,* by lying still, and not practise my *Resurrection,* by rising any more" (p. 11). The idea is common in Milton. The Attendant Spirit asks in *Comus:*

> Who knows not *Circe*
> The daughter of the Sun? whose charmed cup
> Whoever tasted lost his upright shape
> And downward fell into a groveling swine.
>
> (ll. 50–53)

The idea is most brilliantly worked out in the climactic lines of *Paradise Regained,* 4.550–81; see *Paradise Lost,* 4.289 and 9.501. Note also the supine posture of Detraction and Oblivion in Plate 2.

instinctively feel Ariel's services are respectable; Caliban's are born of fear and grudging.

The "salvage and deformed slave," then, is a composite figure drawn according to various traditional means of describing morally evil forces, particularly forces subversive of society. The traits just mentioned, among others, frequently occur in Até figures who attempt to unleash chaos on men and their societies. Such figures were an important part of the courtly aesthetic, so preoccupied with conservation of order and the status quo. Caliban's monstrosity is rich in traditional resonances.

FIGURES OF *FUROR*

The Blatant Beast

The greatest work of the Elizabethan courtly aesthetic is *The Faerie Queene*—the closest poetic approximation of Castiglione's *Book of the Courtier* ever written in England. I have already noticed the focus on the perfect courtier in book 6 of Spenser's poem. The main action of the "Legend of Courtesy" is Calidore's pursuit of that book's *furor* figure, the Blatant Beast.[18] *The Tempest* dramatizes a similarly focused action. The end of Prospero's "project" is to subjugate the figures of *furor*, Antonio and Caliban.

Spenser's Beast anticipates the monster in Shakespeare's play in many intriguing ways. Calidore is the idealized court-

[18]Furor himself makes a predictable appearance in Spenser's discourse on the virtue of temperance in book 2 of *The Faerie Queene*. Though he has the form of a man, he is described as a "monster" who is full of "beastly brutish rage" (2.4.6, 10). It is Guyon's task to "calme the tempest of his passion wood" (2.4.11), and the method he borrows from Virgil is not unlike the method Calidore applies to the Beast:

> With hundred iron chaines he did him bind,
> And hundred knots that did him sore constraine:
> Yet his great iron teeth he still did grind,
> And grimly gnash, threatning revenge in vaine.
> (2.4.15)

ier, and the Beast is his opposite, representing the aberration of normal social behavior at court. He is

> A wicked Monster, that his tongue doth whet
> Gainst all, both good and bad, both most and
> least,
> And pours his poisnous gall forth to infest
> The noblest wights with notable defame:
> Ne ever Knight that bore so lofty creast,
> Ne ever Lady of so honest name,
> But he them spotted with reproch, or secrete shame.
>
> (6.6.12)

Though Spenser's monster has lost all human physical traits in an allegorical metamorphosis while Caliban still possesses a marginally human shape, both were designed for similar symbolic purposes. The Beast is an "ugly Monster" who is "bred of hellish race." He is, like Caliban, harassed by a large cluster of derogatory epithets—hellish dog, wicked monster, and so on. Like Caliban, too, he is "all spight and malice," and his ancestry is quite as disreputable as Caliban's:

> Of *Cerberus* whilome he was begot,
> And fell *Chimaera* in her darkesome den,
> Through fowle commixture of his filthy blot;
> Where he was fostred long in *Stygian* fen,
> Till he to perfect ripenesse grew.
>
> (6.1.8)

In canto 3 he attempts to rape a figure (Serena) who is cast in the same mold as Miranda.

The Blatant Beast's threat to the courtly life is best symbolized in the pastoral episode of cantos 9 and 10, where Calidore's pastoral idyll interrupts his severe pursuit of the Beast:

> So sharply he the Monster did pursew,
> That day nor night he suffred him to rest,
> Ne rested he himselfe but natures dew,
> For dread of daunger, not to be redrest,

> If he for slouth forslackt so famous quest,
> Him first from court he to the citties coursed,
> And from the citties to the townes him prest,
> And from the townes into the countrie forsed,
> And from the country back to private farmes he
> > scorsed.
>
> (6.9.3)

Weary from his efforts, Calidore is all the more vulnerable to the innocent pleasures of Mount Acidale and the beauty of Pastorella. He naturally finds attractive this life "so free and fortunate / From all the tempests of these worldly seas." Meliboe makes clear (6.9.20–25) that this idyll is one of escape from the "vainenesse" of life in the city and in the "royall court." The richly artificial episode represents an escape from the realities of courtly corruption and is thus much like the Renaissance masques whose flattery disguised courtly vices.

In fact, canto 10 provides a scenic event reminiscent of an elaborate courtly entertainment—full of delightful visions, sensual pleasure, and ravishing beauty. This "masquing" begins with a gorgeously artificial "scene":

> A place, whose pleasaunce did appere
> To passe all others, on the earth which were:
> For all that ever was by natures skill
> Devized to worke delight, was gathered there,
> And there by her were poured forth at fill,
> As if this to adorne, she all the rest did pill.
>
> (6.10.5)

The picture is one of unnatural perfection—the stream is "unmard with ragged mosse or filthy mud"—and is peopled as were so many masques with nymphs and fairies. The setting is fit for royalty:

> They say that *Venus*, when she did dispose
> Her selfe to pleasaunce, used to resort
> Unto this place, and therein to repose

> And rest her selfe, as in a gladsome port,
> Or with the Graces there to play and sport;
> That even her owne Cytheron, though in it
> She used most to keepe her royall court,
> And in her soveraine Majesty to sit,
> She in regard hereof refusde and thought unfit.
>
> (6.10.9)

As in the court masques, music abounds and the focus is on the dance: "There he a troupe of Ladies dauncing found / Full merrily, and making gladfull glee."

The climax of this masque-like event is the appearance of the Three Graces, surrounding a "fourth Maid" of surpassing grace and beauty (Elizabeth). The effect of this on Calidore is suggestive of the pleasure Ferdinand takes in the wedding masque of *The Tempest*, and the ends of Spenser's vision of the Graces and the masque are also similar:

> Much wondred *Calidore* at this straunge sight,
> Whose like before his eye had never seene,
> And standing long astonished in spright,
> And rapt with pleasaunce, wist not what to
>   weene;
> Whether it were the traine of beauties Queene,
> Or Nymphes, or Faeries, or enchaunted show,
> With which his eyes mote have deluded beene.
> Therefore resolving, what it was, to know,
> Out of the wood he rose, and toward them did go.
>
> (6.10.17)

At this point occurs the breaking of the spell. The shepherd's sentiment reflects Prospero's attitude just after the "strange, hollow, and confused noise" brings his own artistic vanity to an end:

> But soone as he [Calidore] appeared to their vew,
> They vanisht all away out of his sight,
> And cleane were gone, which way he never
>   knew;

All save the shepheard, who for fell despight
Of that displeasure, broke his bag-pipe quight,
And made great mone for that unhappy turne.
(6.10.18)

The highly contrived episode in which Calidore is vouchsafed
a glimpse of Acidale's pleasant harmony and exquisite decorum is brought by Spenser to a carefully prepared and shat-
tering conclusion. Taking the scene too seriously, the knight
attempts to move within it and, in a sense, cross the barrier of
illusion that makes it possible (and at the same time limits the
vanity of Colin's art). I do not want to push the parallel too far
but will note that Prospero and the shepherd Colin are authorial *personae* and that there is a connection between the
breaking of the bagpipe and the breaking of Prospero's staff.
Both actions are signs of the artist's frustration and the artist's
sense of the limitations of his art and of human nature.

The Acidale scene and the act 4 masque, though set in a
pastoral landscape, celebrate a courtly idyll. Spenser's Mount
is a richly imaginative version of an idealized court where a
queenly paragon like Elizabeth might "dispose / Her selfe to
pleasaunce." It is inhabited by an elite; no "wilde beast" or
"ruder clowne" is allowed to be present. It leaves the sense of
an isolated, genteel, perfectly orchestrated style of life, a
courtly style of life. The masque in *The Tempest* is a more
specifically courtly phenomenon, though there is no court
properly so called in the play. Masques were courtly entertainments, and the blessings asked for Ferdinand and
Miranda—honor, riches, and "long continuance" of their
posterity—make more sense for a courtly than for a pastoral
couple. Its morality—with temperate nymphs in charge, not
"Mars' hot minion" Venus—fits neatly with the restraint
Prospero has preached. And most of this masque's content,
mythological figures, and special effects relate it strongly to
the actual court masques that were enjoying a vogue in London at the time.

The importance of these episodes, however, is that they represent periods in the respective actions of *The Tempest* and book 6 when the harassment of evil is stayed. As canto 10 opens, the poet asks:

> Who now does follow the foule *Blatant Beast*,
>   Whilest *Calidore* does follow that faire Maid,
>   Unmindfull of his vow and high beheast,
>   Which by the Faery Queene was on him laid,
>   That he should never leave, nor be delayd
>   From chacing him, till he had it attchieved?
> (6.10.1)

After the catastrophe, so to speak, of the Acidale episode we recognize that Spenser has fashioned this courtly vanity only to undermine it. Calidore would wish to remain in this state of felicity, his eyes forever filled with beauty. His fond hope is very much like Ferdinand's:

> Let me live here ever;
> So rare a wonder'd father and a wise
> Makes this place Paradise.
> (4.1.122–24)

In both cases, however, paradise must necessarily be lost if overriding political goals are to be reached. Calidore's high behest finally draws him away from the pleasures of the pastoral idyll, just as Prospero's project brings the masque to a mordant end. Just as certainly as Gonzalo's utopia is undercut, so the enticing but dangerously distracting visions presided over by Colin and Prospero are also undermined.

The "atchievement of the Blatant Beast" is the goal of book 6, while Prospero's goal is to gain power over all his enemies and renovate the dukedom of Milan. The description of Calidore's subjugation of the Beast should remind us of Prospero standing over his "thing of darkness":

207

> Yet greatly did the Beast repine at those
>> Straunge bands, whose like till then he never
>>> bore,
>> Ne ever any durst till then impose,
>> And chauffed inly, seeing now no more
>> Him liberty was left aloud to rore:
>> Yet durst he not draw backe; nor once withstand
>> The proved powre of noble *Calidore*,
>> But trembled underneath his mighty hand,
> And like a fearefull dog him followed through the
>> land.
>
> (6.12.36)

Such is the fate of Caliban in the end—groveling before the power of Prospero's nobler reason. Like the Beast, Caliban is not killed: the dangers of *furor, seditio,* and civic *violentia* are ever-present and may burst forth unless the Calidores and Ferdinands at court are vigilant. The Blatant Beast and Caliban thus reflect the moral image of evil to which these courtly heroes are opposed.

Ignorance and the Dame

Caliban bears remarkable resemblance to a figure from the antimasque of *The Masque of Queenes* (1609). In it a group of witches attempts to establish misrule. They are led by a "Dame" who exhorts:

> Mixe Hell, with Heaven; and make *Nature* fight
> Within her selfe; loose the whole henge of Things;
> And cause the Endes runne back into their Springs.
>
> (VII, 289)

This Dame is modeled after the *furor* figure Até, as Jonson explains in a note: "This *Dame* I make to beare the person of *Ate,* or *mischeife* (for so I interpret it) out of *Homer's* description of her: *Iliad* I. where he makes her swift to hurt Mankind" (VII, 286). After much fulmination the Dame calls for a helper who, I think, should remind us of Caliban:

208

> First, then, advance
> My drowsy Servant, stupide *Ignorance*,
> Known by thy scaly vesture.
>
> (VII, 287)

Ignorance leads in the figures of Suspicion, Credulity, False-hood, Murmur (i.e., rebellion), Malice, Impudence, Slander, Execration, Bitterness, Rage, and Mischief. Jonson thus explains his intentions:

> In the chaining of these *vices*, I make, as if one linke produc'd another, and the *Dame* were borne out of them all . . . Nor will it appeare much violenc'd, if their *series* be considered, when the opposition to all *vertue* begins out of *Ignorance*. That *Ignorance* begets *Suspicion* (for Knowledge is ever open, & charitable); That *Suspicion credulity* . . . Out of this *Credulity* springs *Falshood*, which begetts *Murmure;* and that *Murmure* presently growes *Malice*, which begetts *impudence;* That *Impudence slander;* That *Slander execration; Execration bitternesse; Bitternesse fury;* and *Fury Mischeife.*[19]

All these vices are embodied in Caliban.

It is plausible, as well, to speculate that Caliban in the first performances of *The Tempest* might have worn a costume of "scaly vesture" like that of Ignorance. The editor of the New Arden *Tempest* thinks "there should be no fishiness about his appearance" (note, p. 62), but he adduces no evidence to sup-

---

[19]Jonson then proceeds to offer ancient support for this symbolism; we are thus led back to classic *furor* figures: "Now for the personall praesentation of them [the vices], the Authority in *Poetry* is universall. But, in the absolute *Claudian* there is a particular, & eminent place, where the *Poet* not only produceth such persons, but almost to a like purpose. *in Ruf. lib. I.* where *Alecto,* envious of the times . . . with many other, [is] fit to disturbe the world" (VII, 287). The idea that ignorance was the root of all "mischiefe" is repeated by La Primaudaye in his *French Academy* (p. 12): "Ignorance of mans selfe (saith Lactantius) and the want of knowledge . . . is the cause of error, of evil."

port his view. I feel there is enough in the play to suggest that Caliban might have worn something of ichthyological aspect:

> A fish: he smells like a fish; a very ancient and fish-like smell; a kind of, not of the newest Poor-John. A strange fish!
>
> (2.2.25–28)

> Why, thou debosh'd fish . . . Wilt thou tell a monstrous lie, being but half a fish and half a monster?
>
> (3.2.25–28)

> One of them
> Is a plain fish, and, no doubt, marketable.
>
> (5.1.265–66)

Schücking went so far as to say Caliban is "really a monster of the sea" because "he has claws, is apparently covered with scales . . . has arms like fins and exhales a penetrating odor of fish."[20] Herford and Simpson note, in reference to Jonson's "scaly vesture," a passage from Pierio's *Hieroglyphica* that also reflects on Caliban: "Ignorance. A certain kind of fish endowed with scales and a little fin. . . . the scales of ignorance are a hieroglyphic; these scales can be shaken off and removed with the service and benefit of knowledge."[21] There is also a relevant and telling association of words in Thersites's description of Ajax in *Troilus and Cressida:* "He's grown a very land-fish, languageless, a monster" (3.3.263).

There are more forceful ties between Jonson's Ignorance and Caliban in their respective natures. Caliban's greatest fault is his ignorance:

> A devil, a born devil, on whose nature

---

[20]L. L. Schücking, *Character Problems in Shakespeare's Plays* (London, 1922), p. 253.

[21]Jonson, *Works,* X, 502 (my translation). Translated material is from Giovanni Pierio Valeriano's *Hieroglyphica* (Lyon, 1595), fol. 223.

Nurture can never stick; on whom my pains,
Humanely taken, all, all lost, quite lost.

(4.1.188–90)

One can follow Jonson's chain of vices in Caliban—his
malice, bitterness, execration, rebellious murmuring. All
these lead to the rage and, finally, the mischief of his plot to
become his "own king." Caliban has not only the outer garments of a monster but also the full panoply of inner vices to
make him the balancing-weight for Prospero's virtues. How
close to Caliban in attitude and blatancy is the exhortation of
Ignorance's mistress to prevent a golden age:

Joine, now, our hearts, we faithfull Opposites
To *Fame*, & *Glory*. Let not these bright Nights
Of Honor blaze, thus, to offend our eyes.
Shew our selves truely envious; and let rise
Our wonted rages. Do what may beseeme
Such names, and natures. *Vertue*, else, will deeme
Our powers decreas't, and thinke us banish'd earth,
No lesse then heaven. All her antique birth,
As *Justice, Faith*, she will restore: and, bold
Upon our sloth, retrive her *Age of Gold*.
We must not let our native manners, thus,
Corrupt with ease. Ill lives not, but in us.
I hate to see these fruicts of a soft peace,
And curse the piety gives it such increase.

(VII, 288)

In Shakespeare's play Caliban and his plot-doubled shadow,
Antonio, take this attitude to the established order. In Caliban
we see the cumulative effects of ignorance reach their climax
in a figure "capable of all ill!" There is an amusing irony in
finding a possible source for the "servant monster" Jonson
complained about in *Bartholomew Fair* in one of his own
masques. Perhaps the import of Jonson's criticism was that
such an allegorical figure might be acceptable in a masque, but

211

not on the dramatic stage. True to the insulating nature of courtly art, the evil threatened by Caliban, the Dame, and her helper Ignorance is more rhetorical than real: the obstacles they throw up to a new world order are quickly dispatched— in the play by Prospero and in the masque by Heroic Virtue.

Caliban, the Blatant Beast, and the Dame are all cynosures in their respective imaginative environments of the self-willed attitude that creates civil strife. They are embodiments of the homilist's "ambitious and malicious" social misfits. Because they are enemies of a king and his court, they are enemies of (and in) the courtly aesthetic. Figures like Caliban can be found in virtually every prominent genre of this aesthetic. Since drama is our present interest, however, I want to canvass here some of Caliban's kin from the pastoral dramatic tradition. He is reflected, for instance, in Tasso's *Aminta* by Satyr, who is intended to represent primitive sensuality in opposition to platonic love. Satyr's idea of courtship is similar to Caliban's: "I will seize by force and ravish what this ungrateful maid denies me as the reward for my love." Tasso's character is duplicated in Guarini's *Il pastor fido*. There, Satyr is the rejected lover of Corisca (the play's feminine *furor* figure). As in *The Tempest*, the scenes involving Satyr and Corisca exist solely to make the virtues of the heroine more resplendent.

Mucedorus, a public play with courtly pretensions, has an intriguing prologue figure called Envy—"a monstrous uglie hagge"—who is made an outcast by the figure of Comedy. A "wild man" named Bremo also makes a short, distasteful foray in this pleasing comedy. He seizes the heroine Amadine with rape in mind but is quickly killed by Mucedorus, after many imprecations about his "savage and unhumane deedes." In Gervase Markham's *The dumbe Knight* (1608) the Duke of Epire is defeated in a tilting match and becomes that play's Até figure:

I am resolved . . . henceforth to prove
A villaine fatall, blacke and ominous . . . (C$_3$^{r})
Revenge now rules soveraigne of my bloud . . . (E$_4$^{v})
The blackest thoughts Ile study to excell. (G^r)

And like Caliban, Epire is silent and impotent at the play's
end. The King of Cypress, while calling Epire "this monster,
this my tempting divell," nevertheless forgives him.

The character of Pharamond in *Philaster*, far from being a
wild man, is a Spanish prince betrothed to the heroine. But his
attitude toward courtship and ceremony marks him as a *furor*
figure. Arguing with Arethusa for some precipitate sex, he
says,

> let us not wait
> For dreaming form, but take a little stolen
> Delights, and so prevent our joys to come.

ARETHUSA: If you dare speak such thoughts, I
must withdraw in honour. *Exit.*
PHARAMOND: The constitution of my body
will never hold out till the wedding; I must seek
elsewhere. *Exit.*

(1.2.199–205)

The woman Pharamond seeks out is Megra, this play's
feminine *furor* figure (her name is meant to remind us of
Megaera, one of the Furies). As a courtier Pharamond is
clearly of Caliban's ilk. Finally subdued and displayed like a
tamed animal at the end of the play, Pharamond has one
meager line, and that is one of submission like Caliban's "I'll
be wise hereafter." The Montanus of Daniel's *Hymen's
Triumph* (1615) is also a distant relative of Caliban. He is a
cankered figure, a "rude savage swain," who attempts to spoil
this courtly comedy by stabbing the hero. A miraculous cure,

however, revives the victim in act 5, and in the sweeping joy of the denouement even Montanus is forgiven.

There is also something of Caliban in the figures of Ignorance and the two malcontents in Peele's *Descensus Astraeae,* and in Dekker's Lord Mayor's Show of 1612, *Troia-Nova Triumphans*, where the figure of Envy, as "chiefe Commandresse" of hell, attempts to subvert all virtue. Like all *furor* figures in courtly artistic environments, she and her band are easily banished. The "two horrid monsters" banished by the "glorious presence" of the king at the Conduit Street triumphal arch also serve a function similar to Caliban's: they exist as a means of demonstrating legitimate power justly exercised. In the arch at Temple Bar, representing the Temple of Janus, were five pairs of figures exhibiting the theme of erect virtue ascendant over supine vice: at the feet of Peace "lay Warre groveling," and the four Caliban-like abstractions Tumult, Servitude, Danger, and Unhappiness lay at the feet of Quiet, Liberty, Safety, and Felicity, respectively. In the four corner panels of Rubens's *Whitehall Ceiling* these same themes are repeated (Plate 1): Liberality subjugates Avarice; Temperance crushes Profligacy to earth; Heroic Virtue defeats Rebellion; and Wisdom defeats Lust.

The image of vice in these entertainments and paintings is not unlike that implied in the relationship between Prospero and Caliban. Like the masques, the triumphal arches, the Lord Mayor's shows, and the *Whitehall Ceiling*, *The Tempest* has as one purpose the explication of the benefits of good government—of civilization—and to achieve this it was salutary to present *furor* rendered impotent. Caliban's presence in the play is largely explained by this artistic intention.

· VII ·

CHARACTERS OF THE
COURTLY AESTHETIC:
PROSPERO

*J*N THE FOUR CORNER PANELS of the Rubens Ceiling at Whitehall—the finest painterly monument to the Stuart myth of royal power—the erect, potent figures of Wisdom, Temperance, Heroic Virtue, and Liberality stand in triumph over the crumpled forms of Lust, Profligacy, Rebellion, and Avarice, respectively (Plate 1). The dichotomy between social virtue and vice allegorized in the Rubens paintings is present in the relationship between Prospero and Caliban. As *The Tempest* ends, Prospero becomes the focus of social wisdom, prudent rule, and magnanimous virtue, and the promiser (through the hymeneal masque) of abundance and fertility. Having explored Caliban's background, we are now in a position to study the positive values of the courtly aesthetic embodied in Prospero. Caliban is the rebel capable of all ill; Prospero is Shakespeare's vision of the ruler capable of all good. He becomes in act 5 a paragon born of the intrinsic polarity of the courtly aesthetic.

The Tempest's central character is one of the most elusive and illusive figures in dramatic literature. The various forms into which he has been moulded by scholars and directors would, alone, convince us of the rich imaginative potentialities he encompasses. The reasons for this complexity are many. As we shall see, Prospero is a highly allusive exemplar

215

of the Renaissance allegorical tradition that scholars like Rosemond Tuve have explored, namely, a tradition marked by free association of symbols, iconographic imagery, and eclecticism rather than by rigorously extended philosophical or poetic architecture. Prospero's complexity, though a typical product of the workings of the creative mind in the Renaissance, is confused and confusing to modern sensibilities. Phrases from Rosemond Tuve's *Allegorical Imagery* stand as a warning to students of Shakespeare's Late Plays: "interrupted and interwoven structure," "flowing meanings," "eclectic amalgamation," "intermittent allegorical significance." This oscillating indirection of *The Tempest* will appear as we consider Prospero and his shadowings of the Renaissance Saturn.

The difficulty of "fixing" Prospero's nature is partly attributable to the several levels on which the play operates. Prospero is, as it were, Shakespeare's *nodus continuationis* between these various levels of meaning—the political, moral, aesthetic (i.e. relating to the epistemology of the theatrical experience), topical, and autobiographical. The significance of each level invariably reflects back on Prospero, and the resulting multiple images blur the outline of his character. Or perhaps one should say they lead to a vivid three-dimensionality unparalleled in Shakespearean drama.

Prospero's titular functions are numerous. He is a father, a governor of men and spirits, a learned humanist and mage, a semi-divine figure, and an authorial persona. He is a "lord high everything else" in the play. Prospero's meanings are multiple, confusing, and one might even say contradictory, because he is the product of a typical Renaissance fusion of realms, genres, and influences, of an intentional authorial confusion of perspectives, and of a confusion that derives from the play's sheer inclusiveness. I will here explore some of the sources of Prospero's resonance, the remarkable extent to which he is a fictional composite, and the way he balances on the side of virtue the courtly polarity basic to *The Tempest*.

PROSPERO AS MAGE

> In ancient times, when any man sought to
> shadowe or heighten his Invention, he had
> store of feined persons readie for his pur-
> pose, as *Satyres, Nymphes,* and their like:
> such were then in request and beliefe
> among the vulgar. But in our dayes, al-
> though they have not utterly lost their
> use, yet finde they so litle credit, that our
> moderne writers have rather transfered
> their fictions to the persons of Enchaunters
> and Commaunders of Spirits, as that excel-
> lent Poet *Torquato Tasso* hath done, and
> many others. . . . In imitation of them
> (having a presentation in hand for Persons
> of high State) I grounded my whole Inven-
> tion upon Inchauntments and several trans-
> formations.
>
> THOMAS CAMPION

As Campion suggests in his preface to *The Earl of Som-
erset's Maske* (1614), writers seeking after refined inventions
for a courtly audience ("Persons of high State") often turned
to figures of magicians. Though as late as 1604 both houses of
Parliament passed a statute prohibiting "any invocation or
conjuration of any evil or wicked spirit," the time had arrived
when magicians were more important in literature and *theatralia spectacula* than in real life. Because of their illusionistic
powers magicians naturally presided over an aesthetic that
depended upon novel stage effects, spectacular richness, and
romantic wish-fulfillment. Courtly artists, of course, relied
upon the practitioners of natural magic, not the Circean sor-
cery that parts men from their rational powers. The distinction was crucial. Those who had occasion, for artistic or scientific reasons, to move in the extensive realms then associated
with magic were scrupulous to make clear the difference between good (white) and evil (black) magic. The distinction

217

figures in Daniel's *Vision of the Twelve Goddesses*, where the presenter Sleep enters with a black wand and a white wand. Because this is to be a courtly delight, Daniel notes that Sleep "did here use his white Wand, as to infuse significant Visions to entertain the Spectators."[1] The white wand rules in the magical world of the courtly aesthetic. There is a kinship between Sleep's white wand and Prospero's staff. Indeed, a general kinship exists between Prospero and mage figures from many genres prominent in the courtly aesthetic—epyllion, episodic and epic romance, masque, and tragicomedy. Three particular courtly mages from among Prospero's fictional ancestors, contemporaries, and successors, discussed below, help us better to understand the function of magic in *The Tempest*.

In epic romances mages often performed functions relating to the overarching poetic structure and to the underlying morality preoccupying their authors. These magicians were more than mere plot devices and often uncovered the moral fruit that lay sheathed in concealing layers of artifice, indirection, and *materia*. Prospero is such a magician; his advice and actions go directly to the essence of the play's morality. It is worth comparing him in this respect with a figure in Tasso's *Gerusalemme liberata*, since the moral commonplaces in the play and in a sequence of events from cantos 14 through 16 of the epic are so much alike.

[1]Samuel Daniel, *Complete Works* (London, 1885), III, p. 193. Note Guarini's observations (*Il pastor fido,* [Venice, 1602]) upon the connection between "mad" poets and "perfida maga": "I maghi erano altresì nomi honorati, quando la sapienza loro usarono in buona parte; ma poiche cominciarono, a farsi negromanti, il nome loro divenne [sic] infame: Nè qui voglio tacere, che tutte le magie non sono cattive" (p. 81ʳ). Most pertinent is the chapter on "Festal Magic in Renaissance Masking" in Angus Fletcher's *The Transcendental Masque*. Relevant studies of Renaissance magic are: Paolo Rossi, *From Magic to Science;* D. P. Walker, *Spiritual and Demonic Magic from Ficino to Campanella;* Wayne Shumaker, *The Occult Science in the Renaissance;* and Peter French, *John Dee: The World of an Elizabethan Magus.*

In Tasso a white mage presides over a symbolic event that is based on the metaphor of the labyrinth and its solution through the humane magic of reason. In canto 14 the knights Ubaldo and Carlo are confronted by Armida, a *furor* figure in the epic. Her palace presents the dangers of a maze:

> The pallace great is builded rich and round,
> And in the center of the inmost hold,
> There lies a garden sweet, on fertile ground,
> Fairer than that where grew the trees of gold:
> The cunning sprites had buildings rear'd around,
> With doores and entries false a thousand fold,
> A labyrinth they made that fortresse brave,
> Like *Dedals* prison or *Porsennaes* grave.
>
> (16.1, Fairfax translation, 1600)

To help the two knights meet this challenge Tasso has them meet an "old wisard," who observes that they stand in great need "of a cunning guide" and who then takes them to his "cell." The wizard there explains the distinction between black and white magic, his omniscience, and the necessity of bowing to the knowledge of God. He then offers them a map to guide them through Armida's palace:

> The house is builded like a maze within,
> With turning staires, false doores and winding wayes,
> The shape whereof plotted in velam thin
> I will you give, that all those sleights bewrayes,
> In midst a garden lies, where many a gin
> And net to catch fraile harts, false *Cupid* layes.
>
> (14.76)

Ubaldo and Carlo bid their "grave host" farewell and put the map to the test:

> As through his chanell crookt *Meander* glides
> With turnes and twines, and rowles now to now fro,
> Whose streames run foorth there to the salt sea sides,
> Here backe returne, and to their springward go:

Such crooked pathes, such wayes this pallace hides;
Yet all the maze their mappe described so,
   That through the labyrinth they got in fine,
   As *Theseus* did by *Ariadnaies* line.

(16.8)

Tasso explains the meaning of this passage in his note on "The Allegorie of the Poem." It is primarily that "humane wisedome, when it is directed of the superior or more high vertue, doth deliver the sensible soule from vice, & therein placeth morall vartue." This passage, like the entire poem, shows that the "soveraigne part of the minde" ought to be "armed with reason against concupiscence." The "mappe" that solves the maze is wisdom, or reason.[2]

The Tempest, likewise, revolves upon the resolution of the erring and mazelike human experience through a magician's

---

[2]The map should be compared with the book Melissa gives to Astolfo in canto 15 of Ariosto's *Orlando Furioso:*

> But chiefly to this English Duke she gave
> Of secret skill a little written booke
> Containing many a precept wise and grave.
>
> (15.9)

Harington's gloss on this passage is: "By the booke is signified wisedome, whereby all charmes and toyes are discovered" (p. 119). In canto 22 Astolfo "dissolves" Atlanta's "inchanted pallace" with the aid of the book. Harington's note: "Astolfo, that with helpe of his booke dissolves the inchaunted pallace and with his horne drave away those that assaulted him and put him in great danger, signifieth allegorically . . . how wisdome with the helpe of eloquence discovereth the craftiest and tameth the wildest" (p. 249).

In *Des Ballets,* Ménestrier analyzes the equivalent of Armida's palace in *Orlando,* the palace of Alcina, along similar lines:

> The palace of Alcina is the image of human life, in which most men seek with great effort that imaginary happiness they flatter themselves to think can be found there. They never do find it, because Providence has seen to it that happiness is not placed in that palace . . . . Worldly things appear greater to us than they are. Ruggiero, who wanders in this palace with some other knights, is the symbol of our mind [esprit] which, confused in this labyrinth of the world, is unable to find a pathway out. Bradamante, concerned solely to rescue Ruggiero, signifies Reason, which seeks to retrieve the mind

220

"reason." After traversing a part of the island, Gonzalo wearily complains,

> By'r lakin, I can go no further, sir;
> My old bones ache: here's a maze trod, indeed,
> Through forth-rights and meanders!
>
> (3.3.1–3)

And again in act 5, after the island's mysterious charms have been dissolved, Alonso exclaims: "This is as strange a maze as e'er men trod" (5.1.242). Confused by the island's strange forces, the mariners have good reason to liken it to a labyrinth. The association of *confusion* and *labyrinth* is also

---

from its disorders, protests to it, and urges the fulfillment of its responsibilities. Scarcely are these knights reconciled with their reason than they discover quickly the snares and delusions that have been created to deceive them. In this way we easily discern the evil schemes the world holds out for us.

(pp. 316–37 [pp. 315–23 are mispaginated 216–23], my translation)

Ménestrier's interpretation might apply to *The Tempest:* the figures who wander through Ariosto's labyrinthine poem are like the mariners wandering around Prospero's island maze; Bradamante's (reason) deliverance of Ruggiero (soul) is parallel to Prospero's over-seeing of the return to "reasonable shores"; the "snares and delusions" of Ménestrier recall the ideas expressed in the Revels Speech; and the "evil schemes" are equivalent to the plots of Antonio and Caliban.

Angus Fletcher discusses poetic uses of the labyrinth in his book on Spenser, *The Prophetic Moment* (Chicago, 1971), pp. 24–34. Note also in this regard Isabel MacCaffrey's assertion in *Spenser's Allegory* that "Spenser's name for Truth is Una, and his poem is a great labyrinth with a single center. The labyrinth is made up of efforts to transcribe humanity's sense of its own meaning: in actions, in words, in images, in institutions, in edifices, in prayers (the poem ends, like *The Tempest,* with a prayer)" (p. 75). MacCaffrey has occasion in the same work to quote another contemporary *locus classicus* for labyrinthine symbolism, a passage from Francis Bacon's *Great Instauration:* "The universe to the eye of the human understanding is framed like a labyrinth, presenting as it does on every side so many ambiguities of way, such deceitful resemblances of objects and signs, natures so irregular in their lines, and so knotted and entangled. And then the way is still to be made by the uncertain light of the sense, sometimes shining out, sometimes clouded over, through the woods of experience and particulars" (p. 34).

reflected in the word *amazement* (Shakespeare made the connection before in "Venus and Adonis" [l. 684], and "The Rape of Lucrece" [l. 1151]). Ariel flames "amazement"; Gonzalo feels that "All torment, trouble, wonder, and amazement / Inhabit here"; the crew is led in "amazedly." Only Prospero, above the action, is able to say with assurance, "No more amazement." Those words, spoken to Miranda in act 1, reflect the tenor of his speeches in act 5, when the mariners and royal party are led out of a charmed sleep. As his powers evanesce, as the characters regain their reason, their amazement and confusion vanish. The maze is solved. Put another way, Prospero's fury changes to magnanimity; the maze evanesces. "What, lost in the labyrinth of my fury?" asks Thersites elsewhere in Shakespeare. In such a labyrinth have the men of sin been lost.

The "maze" of the play's action is solved by a presiding mage and the wisdom he displays:

> Yet with my nobler reason 'gainst my fury
> Do I take part: the rarer action is
> In virtue than in vengeance.
>
> (5.1.26–28)

Evil can be overcome only when men who have lost themselves regain "reasonable shores"—only when rulers subjugate their fury with "nobler reason." Edward Guilpin's rhetorical question might stand as a brief synopsis of the morality of the play:

> R[e]ason thou art the soules bright *Genius*,
> Sent downe from *Joves* throne to safe conduct us
> In this lifes intricate *Daedalian* maze:
> How art thou buffuld?
>
> (*Skialetheia*, 1598, $D_8{}^r$)

Prospero performs this guiding and moderating task of Tasso's old wizard for the mariners, whose reason has been baffled by human frailty, greed, and ambition. The mariners' maze is ultimately of their own making, and Prospero's project has been to cure them of this "affliction" through the power of reason. Shakespeare's allegory is the same as Tasso's: reason (Tasso's "soveraigne part of the minde") is the only true guide in the labyrinth of human experience. Of Tasso, Shakespeare, and Shakespeare's Prospero one might say, as Fulke Greville said of Sidney: the end of their works "was not vanishing pleasure alone, but morall Images, and Examples (as directing threads) to guide every man through the confused *Labyrinth* of his own desires, and life" (*Life of Sidney*, p. 223).

The trend of deepening allegorical significance continues as we turn to the court masque. Here too we find numerous figures who perform the same symbolic functions as Prospero. One character is of particular interest, since the masque in which she appears—Jonson's *Hymenaei* (1606)—may have influenced Shakespeare. The symbolic hinge of the masque shows profound similarities to that of *The Tempest* just outlined in the discussion of *Gerusalemme liberata*, namely, the subjugation of the contentious humors and affections by "the soveraigne part of the minde." Holding sway in Jonson's masque is Reason, "a venerable personage, her haire white and trailing to her waste, crowned with starres, lights, her garments blue, and semined with starres, girded unto her with a white bend, fill'd with Arithmeticall figures." Her servant is Order, similarly attired.

Four Humors and four Affections, according to Jonson, "drew their swords, and offered to encompass the [bridal] Altar, and disturbe the Ceremonies." At this point Hymen invokes Reason's assistance, which she gives. Reason continues:

So want of *knowledge*, still, begetteth jarres,
When *humourous* earthlings will controll the starres.
Informe your selves, with safer reverence,

To these mysterious *rites*, whose mysticke sence,
REASON (which all things, but it selfe, confounds)
Shall cleare unto you, from th'authentique grounds.

(VII, 214)

At the sight of Reason, the Humors and Affections "sheathed their swords, and retired amazed to the sides of the stage, while Hymen began to ranke the Persons, and order the Ceremonies." As Reason stands in relation to the Humors and Affections, so Prospero stands in unquestioned control over the "humourous earthlings" in *The Tempest*. Prospero also functions as the voice of reason and social ritual. In the last act, as in the masque, the forces of evil are "amazed" and powerless.

If the court masque's influence on Shakespeare is ever to be "proved," *Hymenaei* (along with *Oberon* and *Love Freed from Ignorance and Folly*) will be crucial to that demonstration. Aside from the similar attire of Reason, Order, and Prospero, other parallels are worth noting:

1. The "contentious musique" accompanying the Humors and Affections has the same effect as the "confused noise" accompanying the ruin of the act 4 masque.

2. There is a descent of Juno and Iris in both works.

3. Caliban's speech (3.2.133) upon the sound-effects and visual delights on the island might remind us of this description from the masque: "Here, the upper part of the Scene, which was all of Clouds, and made artificially to swell, and ride like the Racke, began to open. Juno, sitting on a Throne . . . beneath her the rainebowe, Iris, and on the two sides eight ladies attired richly . . . all full of splendor, sovereignty, and riches." The imagery is also relevant to the Revels Speech.

4. At the end of the masque: "Here they danc'd their last dance . . . and in their latter straine, fell into a faire orbe, or circle; Reason standing in the midst." Is there a possible reflection of this dance symbolism in the stage direction in act 5,

"they all enter the circle which Prospero has made, and there stand charm'd"?

5. Jonson speaks of the masque's power to "surprize with delight" and of the "rapture of the beholders." Compare this with the effect of the masque on Ferdinand: "This is a most majestic vision, and / Harmonious charmingly."

Jonson's *Hymenaei* is the most apt indication of the strong influence of courtly expectations and beliefs on *The Tempest*. While the masque is a prime example of courtly spectacle metamorphosed into drama, the similarities in the moral content and basic structure of the action in the masque and play—the magical movement from chaos to order—are enough to suggest a more than casual relation. In both, *pietas* crushes *furor*; in both, potent virtue renders vice impotent. The courtly polarity is perfectly biased in both masque and play. Magic was a common theatrical means for effecting the representation of this bias.

Taking yet another perspective on Prospero's magical powers, we should observe that they are also Shakespeare's metaphor for the fictive nature of the theatrical experience. Part of Prospero's magic is the magic of the stage itself; it permits him to transcend the normal bounds of the dramatic transaction and gives him a special dramaturgical omnipotence. His magic gives *The Tempest* its extraordinary complexity. No theatrical figure better aids us in exploring Prospero as stage magician than Alcandre in Corneille's *L'Illusion comique* (1635), another intricate, carefully controlled confusion of theatrical "space."[3] The action of *L'Illusion comique* is

---

[3]Pierre Corneille, *L'Illusion comique, édition intégrale* by Colette Cosnier (Paris, n.d.). Cosnier likens the play to a set of Japanese boxes encasing each other (p. 15). Jean Rousset makes many remarks about the play relevant to *The Tempest* in *La Littérature de l'age Baroque en France* (Paris, 1954): "the work turns out to have several centres"; the "action and the work itself do not coincide exactly"; the play has "great zones of shadow"; it manifests a "duplicity of action—comedy, phantasmagoria, buffoonery, tragedy"; the

presided over by the magician Alcandre, whose powers are comparable to Prospero's. As Corneille's play develops we are treated to various vanities of Alcandre's art, and to a subtle exploration of the nature of theatrical illusion. Alcandre is the play's *metteur en scene* and virtuoso manipulator of perspectives. He is, like Prospero, also the dramatist's surrogate.[4]

Prospero and Alcandre signal the end of belief in magic and the ascendancy of artistic and theatrical magic. The power of illusion had finally transferred from the hands of actual sorcerers to the hands of artists skilled in the manufacture of majestic visions. King James warned in his *Daemonologie:* "May not the devil object to [i.e. project himself into] their fantasie, their senses being dulled, and as it were a sleepe, such hilles & houses within them, such glistering courts and traines, and whatsoever such like wherewith he pleaseth to

---

play exposes the "opposition between reality and appearance." See also in this regard Imbrie Buffum's discussion of Corneille in *Studies in the Baroque from Montaigne to Rotrou* (New Haven, Conn., 1957).

[4]Here is a description of Alcandre's great feats (compare Prospero's "Ye elves of hills" speech, 5.1.33–50):

> I shall not tell you how he governs the thunder,
> Makes the sea to swell, and the earth to quake;
> How battalions to fight his enemies from the air he takes,
> Mustering a thousand whirlwinds;
> Nor how the unknown powers of his knowing words
> Transport huge boulders, make the clouds descend,
> And the brightness of two suns blaze in the night;
> Of miracles of that sort you have no need;
> For you it will suffice that he reads one's thoughts,
> Knows the future, and the deeds of the past;
> For him there are no secrets in all the universe,
> And our destinies for him are but open books.
>
> (1.1; my translation)

Cosnier includes the comments of two critics who describe Corneille's highly selfconscious play on the ambiguity of theatrical illusion. These comments suggest to me that Shakespeare and Corneille were thinking along similar lines as they wrote these plays:

> Corneille has forced . . . ambiguity to the extremes precisely by attempting to keep his distance with regard to the baroque, in

delude them."[5] But this did not mean that he and his wife could not patronize theatrical visions of "glistering courts and traines." Men who could project such visions were no longer looked upon with suspicion, but admired as Ferdinand admires Prospero. Alcandre praises this spectacular kind of theater at the end of *L'Illusion comique:*

> [The theater] today is the love of all good wits,
> The talk of the town, the provinces' dream,
> The sweetest diversion of our rulers,
> The gentry's pleasure, the people's delight,
> It takes the first place among their pastimes.
> Even those we behold with most profound sagacity
> Preserving by their illustrious care the entire world
> Find in the sweet pleasures of such delightful sights
> Rest from their so heavy burdens.
> Even our great king, that lightning bolt of war,
> Whose very name is feared to all ends of the earth,
> His forehead crowned with laurels, deigns from time
> to time

---

which the literature of the time was immersed. He mocked this willfully excessive literature but at the same time expressed better than anyone its most profound intention, which was to denounce everything that is ephemeral and deceptive in the world . . . . If illusion, if the theater possess any virtue, it is because they denounce the illusions of the world, because they transform the real world into a spectacle all the more subject to derision, since it is clothed in insubstantial finery [oripeaux magnifiques].
(André Alter, quoted in the Cosnier edition, p. 126,
my translation)
We perceive that Pierre Corneille is the real poet of the theatrical illusion. For nothing that is ever presented to us is real; the actors themselves are nothing but phantoms in the shadow of the cave, as the magician Alcandre explains. The world of Corneille's youthful comedies (which is so perfectly captured in the scenes with Clindor, Lyse, and Isabelle), the more dense and resistant world inhabited by Matamore and the jailer—these are here nothing but images in a mirror.
(Robert Brasillach, *Corneille* [1938], quoted in Cosnier,
p. 124, my translation)

[5]*Daemonologie* (1597; ed. G. B. Harrison, London, 1924), p. 74.

Lend eye and ear to the French theater,
For there Parnassus spreads forth its marvels.
(5.5; my trans.)

Alcandre's pride of creation, so well received by the sophisticated, is also reflected in the artistic hauteur of Prospero in
The Tempest. Shakespeare's play, too, appeared at a time when
the court and king gave special luster and impetus to the arts
of theatrical spectacle. Both plays, dominated by magicians
who possess awesome illusionistic powers, embody self-
conscious praise of the magic of the theater.

PROSPERO AND THE PRESENCE

Perhaps the most important aspect of Prospero's magic
remains to be examined, namely, its function on the play's
political level. His magic should also be viewed as a surrogate for the power of the royal Presence and the attending
protocols that demanded scrupulous behavior in the vicin-
ity of the monarch.[6] The Presence required the most careful
attention to decorum and forbade, among other things, the
drawing of weapons. "Your wrathful weapons drawn / Here
in our presence?" the king asks in *2 Henry VI; "Dare you be
so bold?"* (3.2.237–38). Wherever the ruler went the Presence
established a protective inner sanctum; as the loyalist War-
wick says, "My sovereign's presence makes me mild" (*2
Henry VI,* 3.2.219). Honesty, too, was obligatory in the
king's Presence. It is the height of iniquity in Wolsey—
Shakespeare's finest essay on the powerful and evil courtier in
a peacetime context—that

---

[6]Depending upon the royal Presence for their consummation, court
masques frequently celebrated the symbolic power of the Presence. For typical references to the royal spectators in Jonson's masques, see his *Works,* VII,
171, 241, 304, 351, 388.

> I' th' presence
> He would say untruths, and be ever double
> Both in his words and meaning.
>
> (*Henry VIII*, 4.2.37–39)

And it is the height of kingly prescience to see through the sycophancy that inevitably fills the atmosphere of the Presence. Thus, the idealized Henry VIII rebukes Gardiner,

> I come not
> To hear such flattery now, and in my presence
> They are too thin and base to hide offenses.
>
> (5.2.158–60)

The "politics" of the Presence were a crucial part of government, a *sine qua non* for effective royal leadership. This lesson is manifest in Shakespeare's plays, as it was in the real-life Presence of Elizabeth and James. Indeed, Henry IV's lecture to his son upon the artful and the foolish ways of filling the royal Presence in *1 Henry IV* might be used to describe, with considerable historical accuracy, the respective deportment of these two monarchs within the magic circle of the Presence. Of his own carriage, Henry says:

> Thus did I keep my person fresh and new,
> My presence, like a robe pontifical,
> Ne'er seen but wond'red at, and so my state,
> Seldom but sumptuous, show'd like a feast,
> And wan by rareness such solemnity.
>
> (3.2.55–59)

Anyone familiar with Elizabeth's court will find something of that shrewd, deft queen in these lines.[7] If any monarch knew

---

[7]John Clapham wrote of Elizabeth in 1603: "In her latter time, when she showed herself in public, she was always magnificent in apparel, supposing haply thereby, that the eyes of her people, being dazzled with the glittering aspect of those accidental ornaments would not so easily discern the marks of age and decay of natural beauty" (*Certain Observations concerning the Life and*

the way to work the peace of the Presence, it was she. Her insistence upon the strictest observation of the Presence ritual, her demand for moderate behavior from her courtiers (except in honoring their queen), and her extraordinary concern to focus attention upon her royal person through elaborate habiliment and jewelry—all helped to make her court a relatively peaceful one internally.

What Henry then says of Richard II applies with even more plausibility to the court of James:

> The skipping King, he ambled up and down,
> With shallow jesters, and rash bavin wits,
> Soon kindled and soon burnt, carded his state,
> Mingled his royalty with cap'ring fools,
> Had his great name profaned with their scorns.
>
> (3.2.60–64)

The enormous influx of Scots knights, James's private predilections, the manifest prodigality of the king and his satellites, and the king's inability to cope with British counselors and institutions—all these had their reflection in his royal Presence, which was far more sprawling, promiscuous, and extravagant than his predecessor's.

The control of the Presence—whether illusory or genuine—was both metaphor and microcosm for the control of the realm, and in Shakespeare's royal tragedies the decline of the power of the Presence is an important way of showing the decline of the ruler's actual power. The theme is part of *Richard II*—

> We are amaz'd, and thus long have we stood
> To watch the fearful bending of thy knee,
> Because we thought ourself thy lawful king;

Reign of Queen Elizabeth [1603; rpt. Philadelphia, 1951] p. 86). See also Roy Strong, *Portraits of Queen Elizabeth* (Oxford, 1963), and Roy Strong and Julia Trevelyan Oman, *Elizabeth R* (London, 1972).

And if we be, how dare thy joints forget
To pay their aweful duty to our presence?

(3.3.72–76)

—as it is a crucial factor in the early scenes of *King Lear*, where the father unwisely attempts to retain his titular "authority" or Presence without the real power that vitalizes it. When we first meet Prospero, he has already learned through harsh experience that the power of the Presence and the power actually to govern are inseparable. *State* in the Renaissance signified both the realm and the ruler's own physical trappings of majesty, his throne itself. When Prospero admits that he "to my state grew stranger," we recognize that he had grown stranger to his Presence as well. By casting government on his brother and retiring to pursue "secret studies," by relinquishing public responsibilities ("temporal royalties"), Prospero allowed his domain to shrink to the walls of his study: "Me, poor man, my library / Was dukedom large enough." For Antonio, who becomes accustomed to "executing th' outward face of royalty / With all prerogative" and desires to be in name what he is in fact, the solution is treachery. Like Lear's, Prospero's Presence becomes insensibly but ineluctably impotent; both figures find their regnal powers grow "most faint" and are eventually "o'erthrown."

King Lear, of course, is a tragedy. Lear is doomed never to see his powers made whole again. But *The Tempest* is a royal comedy, and Prospero will again become "absolute" duke of Milan. Bereft of the political power of the Presence and exiled from his realm, Prospero is first discovered exercising wondrous magical arts newly won through further study. These arts provide him with a surrogate Presence in his new seignory, the barren island. His magic in effect provides a "Presence in exile" and is also the means of regaining his natural power in Milan. What Jonson wrote of James in *Oberon*—

Before his presence, you must fall, or flie,
He is the matter of vertue, and plac'd high.

> His meditations, to his height, are even:
> And all their issue is a kin to heaven.
>
> (VII, 353)

—is reflected in Prospero's magical "presence" in *The Tempest*. He achieves many effects of the historical Presence protocol, which enjoins true conflict or, in formal terms, inhibits genuine dramatic development. Swords raised in anger are harmless against this Presence:

> The elements,
> Of whom your swords are temper'd, may as well
> Wound the loud winds, or with bemock'd-at stabs
> Kill the still-closing waters, as diminish
> One dowle that's in my plume: my fellow-ministers
> Are like invulnerable. If you could hurt,
> Your swords are now too massy for your strengths,
> And will not be uplifted.
>
> (3.3.61–68)

Ariel's haughty denunciation vividly indicates how legitimate power was felt to radiate its presence and render impotent the men of sin who sought to undermine it. In reality, of course, the Presence may have been a mere custom at best and a deceptive fraud at worst, yet the concept was alive in Shakespeare's time and in his plays. Through the symbolism of Prospero's potent art, it becomes a vital idea in *The Tempest*. He finally does work "the peace of the presence" (1.1.22). When Prospero regains the dukedom, his art has served its interregnal purposes. To retain his magical powers would be supererogatory, for he can now assert the power of the right duke of Milan, that is to say, the power of the Presence that inheres to those responsibly wielding right power. His power to enchant is no longer necessary; his "temporal royalties" give him that power now. He may "discase" his magic robes and present himself as "sometime Milan"; his magic staff can now be broken and buried "deeper than did ever plummet sound."

How, then, does the concept of the Presence work in the theatrical context of the play? Fortunately, we have in a controversy surrounding Ben Jonson's *Every Man out of His Humour* (1599) a suggestive answer to this question. At the first performance Jonson arranged for the climax of his play a miraculous transformation of the cynical central figure Macilente (who shares something in tone with Jacques, Thersites, and Autolycus) by the sudden appearance of an actor impersonating Elizabeth in full state. Official reaction was immediate and adverse, and Jonson was forced to rewrite the end. But he added a preface to the quarto edition justifying his original *coup de théâtre*. Because the concluding harmonizing action and "most high miracle" of *The Tempest* are paralleled in Jonson's play, some of the reasons Jonson adduces in his defense are worth quoting in full:

> *Macilente* being so strongly possest with Envie, (as the *Poet* heere makes him) it must bee no sleight or common *Object*, that should effect so suddaine and straunge a cure upon him, as the putting him cleane *Out of his Humor*.
>
> (III, 602)

> His [the poet's] greedinesse to catch at any *Occasion*, that might expresse his affection to his *Soveraigne*, may worthily plead for him.
>
> (III, 602)

> There was nothing (in his examin'd *Opinion*) that could more neare or truly exemplifie the power and strength of her Invaluable *Vertues*, than the working of so perfect a *Miracle* on so oppos'd a *Spirit*, who not only persisted in his *Humor*, but was now come to the *Court* with a purpos'd resolution (his Soule as it were

new drest in *Envie*) to maligne at any thing that
should front him; when sodainly (against expectation, and all steele of his *Malice*) the verie wonder of
her *Presence* strikes him to the earth dumbe, and as-
tonisht.

(III, 602–3)

What Jonson failed to achieve, perhaps for being too obvious
and for demeaning the Presence protocol on the public stage
(this sort of conceit would have worked quite happily in a
masque at Whitehall, with the sovereign "actor" present),
Shakespeare managed more smoothly and subtly in *The Tempest*.[8] Through magical symbolism he used the Presence to a
moral end: he defended the "power and strength" of right
rule; he showed in effect how Prospero's Presence strikes
dumb and impotent the "opposed spirits" who may inhabit a
court; he achieved a perfect "miracle" whose repercussions
are ultimately political. The magical influence Prospero exerts
upon the royal party in act 5 is very like the influence Jonson
intended his impersonated queen to have upon Macilente.
This is the magical influence of the royal Presence.

---

[8]George Chapman caused a similar difficulty when, in *The Conspiracy
and Tragedy of Byron,* he brought the Queen of France onto the public stage.
The French ambassador, in a letter dated 5 April 1608, wrote: "I caused certain players to be forbidden from acting the history of the Duke of Byron;
when, however, they saw that the whole Court had left the town, they per-
sisted in acting it; nay, they brought upon the stage the Queen of France . . . .
At my suit three of them [i.e. the players] were arrested, but the principal
person, the author, escaped" (quoted by T. M. Parrott in his edition of *The
Plays of Chapman,* "The Tragedies" [1910, rpt. New York, 1961], Volume II,
p. 591). Lope de Vega wrote in his little treatise, "I understand that King
Philip the Prudent, King of Spain and our lord, was offended at seeing a king
in them [the plays], either because the matter was hostile to art or because the
royal authority ought not to be represented among the lowly and vulgar"
(*The New Art of Writing Plays* [1609; ed. B. Dukore, New York, 1974], p.
200).

PROSPERO AND THE
RENAISSANCE SATURN

This is no mortal business.

The Tempest

A sound magician is a mighty god.

Dr. Faustus

To the Renaissance mind, those who relinquished the
rule of reason and indulged baser appetites descended to the
bestial; those who exercised reason were likened to gods. As
the homilist wrote, the man whose reason was not corrupted
was "made altogether like unto God." Part of Prospero's
meaning lies in this equating of virtue with divinity, and an
introduction to his "complicated multiform nature" (a phrase
from Tuve) should include a consideration of his godlike
status in *The Tempest*. Gonzalo cries out:

> Look down, you gods,
> And on this couple drop a blessed crown!
> For it is you that have chalk'd forth the way
> Which brought us hither.

> (5.1.201–4)

But we know that a theatrical god and his mercurial satellite
have in fact chalked forth the action.[9] Prospero, whose ser-

[9]The scope of the present study does not permit a full examination of the
mythology of Mercury, the winged messenger of the gods, and his presence
in Ariel's fictional genealogy. But a few references will suggest the possibilities that such an approach to the dutiful "chick" might open. For instance, the description of Mercury in Nathaniel Baxter's *Sir Philip Sidney's
Ourania* (London, 1606) seems to reflect on many of Ariel's traits:

Mercurie fraught with sophistication.
Nimble, ingenious, busie as the Bees,
Wittie, as an Ape, to follow what he sees.
In each thing some skill, in full Arte no bodie:
Thus whirleth about this Mercurial nodie.

vants are "ministers of Fate," can order at will the music of
the heavens, and is in Miranda's unwitting words a "great god

---

> Prate like a Perrot and readie of tongue,
> At dice, Cards, and gaming all the day long.
> Of wit sharpe and subtile, of quick apprehention,
> Fit to exploite any rare mad invention.
>
> (C_4^v)

Mercury also figures allegorically in a manner parallel to Ariel in the
Beaujoyeulx *Balet comique:*

> Mercure vagabond, muable & insensé,
> De soudian mouvement deçà dela poussé,
> Sans chois & sans conseil
>   est foible & sans puissance,
> Si Pallas ne luy donne
>   advis & asseurance.
>
> (26^r)

Ariel's relation to the magic of Prospero is important, and a study of
what Renaissance mages thought about Mercury might throw light on Ariel.
Mercury was a crucial symbolic figure for John Dee, a Renaissance mage who
has been associated with Prospero by some critics, notably Frances Yates.
According to the translator of Dee's alchemical treatise *Monas Hieroglyphica,*
the mercurial symbol represented "in its broadest interpretation . . . the principle of transmutation itself, that principle of which Mercury is the universal
agent and of which mercurial man, i.e. the true alchemist or *magus,* as a fit
recipient of that influence, is the noblest subject" (p. 103). Dee calls Mercury
Spiritus purissimus magicus (purest magic spirit, p. 164) and *Hieroglyphicus nun-
cius* (hieroglyphic messenger, p. 163). See Peter French, *John Dee: The World
of an Elizabethan Magus* (London, 1972) and Jean Seznec's discussion of Mercury in *The Survival of the Pagan Gods* (1940; trans. Barbara Sessions, New
York, 1953).
    Ariel has often been identified with the faculty of imagination or fancy.
For men of the Renaissance this would also have led to a mercurial connotation. One commendatory verse of the time speaks of "Shakespeare, that nimble *Mercury* thy braine" (Munro, *Shakespeare Allusion Book,* I, p. 245), and Ben
Jonson tells in his encomium how Shakespeare came "like Mercury to
charme" his age. We might see a motto for Ariel in these lines from Sonnet
44: "For nimble thought can jump both sea and land / As soon as think the
place where he would be."
    A final remark: study of this kind seems much more promising as a way
of understanding Ariel's meanings than studies that cling solely to prior stage
figures or traditions.

236

of power" and "some god o' th' island." He is a figure of
surrogate divinity, a creator or god. This aspect of Prospero's
character has frequently been observed, particularly in speculation about the staging of the play,[10] but I wish to make a
specific Olympian connection with Saturn.

The divine afflatus that surrounds Prospero relates again
to the political meaning of the play. Prospero is a political
archetype created during the reign of James. Both in art and
literature and in actual courtly life of the time, the praise of
magnanimous rulers often took the form of supernatural
parallelism based either on classical-humanist mythology or
Biblical dogma.[11] What had for a long time been a common
artistic conceit became under James political dogma, for he
was the first English monarch to propound aggressively and
unequivocally the concept of the divine right of kings. God,
he wrote to his son Henry in *Basilikon Doron*, "made you a
little GOD to sit on his Throne."[12] The celebration of political
wisdom in an absolute monarchy required the search for
metaphors of perfection: for artists, ecclesiasts, courtiers, and
statesmen—be they neoplatonists or Protestants—the theme
of the ruler's surrogate divinity often fueled their flattery.

[10]See, for example: John Adams, "The Staging of *The Tempest*, III, iii,"
Review of English Studies 14 (1938): 404–19; George Kernodle, *From Art to
Theatre* (Chicago, 1944); F. D. Hoeniger, "Prospero's Storm and Miracle,"
Shakespeare Quarterly 7 (1956): 33–38; Harry Berger, "Miraculous Harp: A
Reading of Shakespeare's *Tempest*," *Shakespeare Studies* 5 (1969): 253–83.

[11]Consider the opening of John Williams's sermon *Great Britains Solomon* (London, 1625), delivered at James's funeral on 7 May 1625: "*Solomon*
wàs a *Type* of *Christ* himselfe, and by consequence a *Paterne* for any *Christian*.
I doe therefore in these *three Verses* [Kings 11:41–43] observe *three parts*, the
Happy Life, the *Happy Raigne*, and the *Happy End* of this great King Solomon" (p. 3). See also the central panel of the Whitehall Ceiling depicting the
apotheosis of James (Plate 1).

[12]James I, *Political Works*, p. 12. In his study *The House of Commons,
1604–1610*, Wallace Notestein wrote: "That he [James] was a kind of god on
earth and in touch with a Higher Power was implied more than once" ([New
Haven, Conn., 1971], p. 504).

This fundamental form of courtly praise finds notable expression in Portia's lines:

> Mercy is above this sceptred sway,
> It is enthroned in the hearts of kings,
> It is an attribute to God himself;
> And earthly power doth then show likest God's
> When mercy seasons justice.
>
> (*Merchant of Venice*, 4.1.193–97)

Much complimentary courtly art sought to show that the exercise of virtues such as mercy turned human kings into worldly gods. The purpose was, in Jonson's words, "to shew, his [James's] rule, and judgement is divine" (VII, 241).

The classical palladium in particular offered many "hinges" upon which flattering theatrical or poetic structures turned. The speech addressed to James himself in Jonson's *Oberon* (1611), in its tacit reference to the Saturn myth of the golden age and in its paraphrase of the Virgilian prophecy (*Aeneid* 6) written for another deified ruler, Augustus, exemplifies the form:

> He is a god, o're kings; yet stoupes he then
> Neerest a man, when he doth governe men;
> To teach them by the sweetnesse of his sway,
> And not by force. H[e] is such a king, as thay,
> Who are tyrannes subjects, or ne're tasted peace,
> Would, in their wishes, forme, for their release.
> 'Tis he, that stayes the time from turning old,
> And keepes the age up in a head of gold.
>
> (VII, 353)

Prospero's divinity is analogous to the divinity attributed by Jonson to James; it is the divinity of the governmental paragon. Prospero's divinity is one of Shakespeare's means of setting his protagonist and perfected ruler above what Gonzalo calls the "human generation" (3.3.33) of corruptible men.

Prospero is a "god o' th' island" just as the idealized James was the "little GOD" ruling over the English island.

Shakespeare did not consciously create Prospero with Saturn in mind. But Prospero is an archetypal figure who performs many functions and carries many significations dictated by a world-view that drew much from saturnine mythology. The common Renaissance themes of death and regeneration, the return of the golden age, and of mutability all bear strong ties to the Saturn myth. Further, Saturn had meaning on different levels in the Renaissance, and if reference to this god can foster a conviction that Prospero's implications as a stage figure are also multiple, then this present exploration will serve its purpose.

The saturnine traits recognized in the Renaissance are numerous and not free from contradiction.[13] We find in these traits some clues to Prospero's own self-contradictory nature. Vincenzo Cartari's well-circulated iconology *The Fountaine of Ancient Fiction*, translated into English by R. Linche in 1599, opens up the spectrum. According to him Saturn "painfully instructed them [the Trojan exiles] in the perfect knowledge of the nature of each soile, and how, and by what industrious meanes of art any ground (fruitlesse of it self by nature) might become fertile and rich" (D₂ʳ). Prospero's art of rendering the barren fruitful is not manifest so much on the island itself

---

[13]In *The Myth of the Golden Age in the Renaissance,* Harry Levin suggests that this confusion was the result of long development: "Saturn . . . remains an elusive and self-contradictory figure, probably because of his syncretic origin and his checkered past, his dethronement in Greece and apotheosis in Rome. As Kronos, he has been heavily involved in conflicts with parents and with children. With a slight alteration of his name, he becomes Chronos, the god of time, which is of the essence in our myth. When he crosses over from Crete to Italy and is fused with Saturnus, he is forced into several contradictions. As a founding figure and a civilizer, he instructs the Latins . . ." ([Bloomington, Indiana, 1969], p. 27). Jean Seznec notes a similar disparity in *The Survival of the Pagan Gods,* (1940; trans. Barbara Sessions, New York, 1953), p. 248.

(we know from Caliban that it was already luxuriant) as symbolized in the "industrious meanes" by which he makes his dynasty and the social system fertile again. The wedding masque is the culminating expression of civil fertility—of which Ceres in the masque is a symbolic extension.

Like Saturn, Prospero is a god of "perfect knowledge" whose wisdom ultimately makes civilization possible, a feat far more wonderful than merely controlling the island world with his "rough magic." Cartari observes also that "other writers there are, that would have him signifie Time" ($D_2{}^r$), and this I will elaborate shortly. Physically, Saturn is often seen "in the shape of a very aged man" ($D_2{}^r$), a trait that Prospero should probably reflect to some degree. He is a father-figure in the play and (like Ulysses or Gaunt) something of a wise graybeard.

Another common feature that Cartari observes in Saturn, the placement of two wings on his head, brings us to the god's central and crucial significance. Cartari says these wings demonstrate

> by one of them the excellencie and perfection of the mind, and by the other . . . mans sence and understanding. For say the Naturalists, the soule of man when she entreth into the humane bodie, bringeth with her from the spheare of Saturne the force of knowledge and discourse, so that the Platonickes understand by Saturne, the mind, and the inward contemplation of things celestiall, and therefore called the time wherein hee lived the golden age, as a time, entertaining quiet, concord, and true content.[14]

[14]Vincenzo Cartari, *The Fountaine of Ancient Fiction,* sig. $D_3{}^r$. It may not be too far-fetched to suggest that Prospero's winged assistant Ariel is, by extension, related to the wings of Cartari. The relationship between the powers of the mind and the winged head-dress also points to another aspect of Prospero as the semidivine artist, who was often thus attired. See the *impresa* for *furor poetico,* with wings, quill and tablet, in Ripa's *Iconologia* (1610), and Inigo Jones's design for the character of Entheus in Campion's *Lords' Masque*

This passage bears on Prospero, for *The Tempest* is organized around the "force [i.e., art, power] of knowledge" he possesses. Prospero represents the "mind" as Saturn does—that is, the power of nobler reason to rule. Like the god, he is a figure of inward contemplation, the ruler of "things celestiall." The new age he projects in act 5 is clearly burnished in golden tones, promising a future of "quiet, concord, and true content." The similarities here are encouraging but do not exhaust the possibilities that the Renaissance found in saturnine myth.[15] Cartari offers at best an impressionistic overview. In order to make the present point we must consider separately certain important and generally accepted saturnine traits.

In the Renaissance, Saturn was associated with melancholy: "Those men to Melancholie given, we Saturnists do

---

(1613). Other comments by Cartari are of more than passing interest. What he observes about Saturn as a correcting force may remind us of Ariel's speech to the men of sin about "powers delaying, not forgetting": "And *Macrobius* among the rest of his descriptions sayth, That his feet are tied together with the threds of woll, agreeing thereby with the Proverbe of the Latines, saying, That the gods doe not any thing in hast, nor make any forced speed to castigate the iniquities of men, but proceed with a slow and unwilling progression, as giving them time and leisure of amendment" (D₃ʳ).

[15]Compare Francis Sparry's 1591 translation (a quarto appeared in 1608 also) of *The Geomancie of Maister Christopher Cattan:*

> They called ♄ the Father of the gods, the temperatour of times, saying that he was high and a great Lorde, sage, prudent, wise, foreseeing & wittie, antient, and of great profoundnesse in knowledge and understanding, knowing the thoughts of men, and boldening them in high enterprises and actes valiant, the keeper of things secret and hid, and a great Lord over life and death.
>
> (p. 25)

E. K. notes other characteristics of those born under Saturn in *The Shepheards Kalender* (1604) that also seem relevant to Prospero:

> full of law and vengeance, and will never forgive till they be revenged of their quarrel . . .
>
> beare malice long in their mindes . . .
>
> they looke to be obeyed and to have great reverence . . .
>
> (Mᵛ)

call."[16] One can observe in Shakespeare's treatment of melancholy throughout his career a movement toward its more profound embodiment: from the sonnets (melancholy as a poetic conceit), *Love's Labour's Lost* (melancholy the object of caricature) through *As You Like It* (still amusing, but with some dark hints), *Hamlet* (melancholy as a necessary existential response to an evil world), to *King Lear* and *Timon of Athens* (melancholy exploding into misanthropy). From the extremes of trivial or feigned melancholy in the early plays and the obsessive melancholy of the later tragedies issued the tempered and mature melancholy of Prospero in *The Tempest*. In Prospero is the sadness of the inward eye (Cartari calls it "inward contemplation"), the melancholy of a social being who sees a necessary retirement before him, and an artist who sees an inevitable end to his powers. Prospero feels the oppression of "perfect knowledge."

When La Primaudaye comes to defend Saturn and the planet's intellectual influence, he sketches such a melancholic as we see in Prospero: "The childe increasing in yeeres and judgement may addict himselfe to studie and contemplation of high and divine things, which are the delights of him, who leadeth a solitarie life: and doubtlesse hee shall perceive that Saturne is not evill, but doth rather favour him with a good influence."[17] Is not this the Prospero, "all dedicated / To closeness and the bettering of my mind," who requires solitude after the Revels Speech? Is this not what Ben Jonson called "that best melancholy which does not run madde after trifles"?

Prospero's melancholy is born of serious issues. He is a figure of philosophical and poetic profundity—a figure

---

[16]*Englands Parnassus* (London, 1600), p. 205. This was commonly accepted and can be found in Shakespeare: *Titus Andronicus,* 2.3.31; Sonnet 45. See G. B. Harrison's "Essay on Elizabethan Melancholy," prefatory to his edition of Breton's *Melancholike Humours* (London, 1929).

[17]La Primaudaye, *The French Academy* (1601 edition), III, p. 143.

worthy of comparison with Albrecht Dürer's richly symbolic engraving of *Melencolia*.[18] How natural that only at the end of his career should Shakespeare finally create a character whose melancholy is aroused, not by trifles, but by realities that every man, every citizen, and every artist must face. What was decorative in his youth—

> For when these quicker elements are gone
> In tender embassy of love to thee,
> My life being made of four, with two alone
> Sinks down to death, oppress'd with melancholy
>
> (Sonnet 45)

—becomes vital in just a few fleeting lines of *The Tempest*. One thinks of Caliban crying to dream again, Prospero's abjuration of his powers, his retirement where "every third thought shall be my grave," his fond farewell to Ariel, and of course his admission that the "ending is despair" without the aid of others. There are disconcerting things of darkness in the play, glancing blows of sadness, and intimations of mortality. Even the glorious masque has its dismal obverse side; the vanity of Prospero's art becomes through its own epilogue, the Revels Speech, a reminder, *et in arcadia ego*.[19] An undercurrent of melancholy runs through the play. For Prospero as a man it is the melancholy of maturity; for Prospero the artist the melancholy is one of achieved mastery.

Saturn was called by Macrobius the *auctor temporum* and by Cattan the "temperatour of times." Ben Jonson notes in his *Hymenaei* that "Truth is fained to be the daughter of *Saturne*: who, indeed, with the Ancients, was no other then

---

[18]See the exhaustive treatment of the meanings of Saturn in the medieval and Renaissance periods and of Dürer's engraving in *Saturn and Melancholy* by Erwin Panofsky, Fritz Saxl, and Raymond Klibansky (London, 1964).

[19]See Douglas Peterson, *Time, Tide, and Tempest* (San Marino, Calif., 1973), p. 240. For a more general discussion of the theme *et in Arcadia ego* in Renaissance art, see Panofsky's pioneering essay in *Meaning and the Visual Arts* (Garden City, N.Y., 1955).

Time, and so his name alludes" (VII, 233). Prospero is also a temperator of time, and the latinity of the phrase draws attention to a crucial word-cluster in the play centering upon *temperance, season (tempestas), temporal, time (tempus), tempest,* and *temper.* To see Prospero as the theatrical focus of these words, Leo Spitzer's etymology for *temperare* is helpful:

> I submit as the *ultimate* etymology a derivation from *tempus* . . . that is to say, from *tempus* in the meaning, "the right time"; this is one of the meanings of Greek καιρός = "the right measure," "convenience," "the right time," and we may assume that *tempus* also took over nontemporal meanings of καιρός. Accordingly *temperare* would mean an intervention at the right time and in the right measure, by a wise (σώφρων) "moderator" who adjusts, adapts, mixes, alternatively softens or hardens (wine, iron, etc.). Any purposeful activity which proceeds with a view to correcting excesses was called *temperare*.[20]

This etymology points to Prospero, a wise moderator whose project is to correct and prevent excesses of human behavior. As his project gains momentum, he adjusts, intervenes, and prepares. Prospero frequently expresses a sense of urgency and "the right time":

'Tis time
I should inform thee farther.
(1.2.22–23)

The hour's now come;
The very minute bids thee ope thine ear.
(1.2.36–37)

I find my zenith doth depend upon
A most auspicious star, whose influence

[20]Leo Spitzer, *Classical and Christian Ideas of World Harmony* (Baltimore, Maryland, 1963), p. 82.

If now I court not, but omit, my fortunes
Will ever after droop.

(1.2.181–84)

The time 'twixt six and now
Must by us both be spent most preciously.

(1.2.240–41)

Now does my project gather to a head:
My charms crack not; my spirits obey; and time
Goes upright with his carriage.

(5.1.1–3)

Prospero is the *auctor temporum;* he specifies the time within
which the action must be consummated. But he also feels the
tyranny of time. Like all creative artists, he has set himself
limitations and must be governed by them. This tyranny is
most sorely felt when the masque is cut short because (and we
tend to overlook the fact in our expectation of the Revels
Speech) time presses: "the minute of their plot / Is almost
come." Those "distemper'd" thoughts that follow are in one
respect an anguished statement that time destroys all things:
tempus edax rerum. The Revels Speech refers obliquely to
Saturn as the symbol of time and its ineluctable power. Prospero presides as a Saturn figure over the demise of his own
"vanity."

For the end of the masque *Love Freed from Ignorance and
Folly* (1611), Jonson wrote a song that, in its reference to
Saturn and in its melancholy tone, could easily conclude the
masque of act 4:

What just excuse had aged *Time,*
    His wearie limbes now to have eas'd,
And sate him downe without his crime,
    While every thought was so much pleas'd!
For he so greedie to devoure
    His owne, and all that hee brings forth,

245

Is eating every piece of houre
Some object of the rarest worth.

(VII, 370)

A similarly moving statement was occasioned by the passing glory of the 1604 triumphal arches. Dekker reported:

> Behold how glorious a Flower, Happinesse is, but how fading. The Minutes (that lackey at the heeles of *Time*) run not faster away then do our joyes. What tongue could have exprest the raptures on which the soule of the Citie was carried beyond it selfe, for the space of manie houres? What wealth could have allurde her to have closde her eyes, at the comming of her King, and yet See, her Bridegrome is but stept from her, and in a Minute (nay in shorter time, then a thought can be borne) is she made a Widdow.
>
> (*Works*, II, 301)

As with the masque and the triumphal arch, the true ruler of *The Tempest* and of Prospero's art is time. "Time's the king of men" (*Pericles*, 2.3.45).

Saturn was also considered a dispenser of knowledge. Cartari associated him with agricultural science, and in Heywood's *Golden Age* (1611) we find him a teacher of "Art / Of Architecture, yet unknowne till now." His knowledge was also esoteric; Lomazzo called him the "auctor of secret contemplation" and Cattan "the keeper of things secret and hid." This bears on Prospero's magic. Renaissance defenses of natural magic contain many references to the useful and beneficent arts associated with Saturn. Reginald Scot defends "naturall magic" because it teaches "manie good and necessarie things, as times and seasons to sowe, plant, till, cut, etc; and divers other things"; Cornelius Agrippa reinforces this defense in his *Three Books of Occult Philosophy:* "But those things which are for the profit of man, for the turning away of evil events, for the destroying sorceries, for the curing of diseases, for the exterminating of phantasmes, for the preserving of life, honor, fortune, may be done without offence to God."[21] Such are Prospero's achievements in the play; indeed, when Agrippa comes to specifics, he forcefully recalls to us the Ovidian speech in which Prospero boasts of his magical powers:

> Rocks have been cut off, and Vallies made, and Mountains made into a Plain, Rocks have been digged through, Promontories have been opened in the Sea, the bowels of the Earth made hollow, Rivers divided, Seas joined to Seas, the Seas restrained, the bottome of the Sea been searched, Pools exhausted, Fens dried up, new Islands made, and again restored to the continent, all which, although they may seem to be against nature, yet we read have been done.

> (p. 169)

These are the miracles made possible by a magician who knows the "Mechanicall arts," such arts as might have been learned by Prospero in his "secret studies." The knowledge contained in his books gives him the power to create the "most high miracle" of the action and gives him, in Bacon's words, the secret knowledge to perform wonderful operations.[22]

Just as many have suggested that *Hamlet* and *King Lear* are Shakespeare's most Montaignesque dramas, *The Tempest* is his most Baconian. The play mounts in theatrical dress Bacon's arguments for the advancement of useful knowledge. The characterizations of the play are virtually all reflected in Bacon's theorem that true learning "doth make the minds of

[21]Reginald Scot, *The Discoverie of Witchcraft* (1584; rpt. Carbondale, Ill., 1964), p. 245; Cornelius Agrippa, "To the Reader" (1531; English edition London, 1651), sig. Aᵛ.

[22]Bacon defined magic thus: "the science which applies the knowledge of hidden forms to the production of wonderful operations" (*De Augmentis, Works*, IV, pp. 366–67).

men gentle, generous, maniable, and pliant to government; whereas ignorance makes them churlish, thwart, and mutinous" (III, 273). Prospero's power over Caliban lies in the civilizing "nurture" of his learning, and the servant monster is therefore naturally adamant that the rebellion he is planning with Stephano and Trinculo begin with the seizure of Prospero's books, the symbol of that learning:

> Remember
> First to possess his books; for without them
> He's but a sot, as I am, nor hath not
> One spirit to command: they all do hate him
> As rootedly as I. Burn but his books.
>
> (3.2.89–93)

Even more Baconian is the play's emphatic conclusion that the best knowledge is not won by those who become "transported / And rapt in secret studies" (1.2.76–77). Rather, the best knowledge gives us power to understand the "infinite doings of the world" more perfectly and then to shape a more perfect world. To gain and use such knowledge requires balancing the *vita contemplativa* with the *vita activa*. Or as Bacon writes, bringing us back again to Saturn: "This is that which will indeed dignify and exalt knowledge, if contemplation and action may be more nearly and straitly conjoined and united together than they have been; a conjunction like unto that of the two highest planets, Saturn the planet of rest and contemplation, and Jupiter the planet of civil society and action" (III, 294). Prospero's potency on the island is due to just such a conjunction. Only when he can retire from "civil society" with an easy mind may he let the planet of rest and contemplation gain the ascendancy.

Renaissance humanists symbolized the two-edged nature of knowledge in Saturn. Knowledge has its obvious dangers: those given great "profoundnesse in knowledge" (Cattan) run a risk that it may weigh upon them and, as La Primaudaye

said, make "the spirit and minde darkish." Prospero's studies
have given him power, but they have also given him unique
distress:

> Sir, I am vex'd;
> Bear with my weakness; my old brain is troubled:
> Be not disturb'd with my infirmity:
> If you be pleas'd, retire to my cell,
> And there repose: a turn or two I'll walk,
> To still my beating mind.
>
> (4.1.158–63)

The burden of the saturnine and melancholic is that the mind,
like the heart, will beat on. "His imagination is never idle,"
Overbury said of the melancholy man. Lear is Shakespeare's
great dramatization of this idea, and there is something of
Lear in Prospero—the pain of special sensitivity in a world
where evil exists. To know too much carries its own punish-
ment.

Knowledge also gives the power to produce the "wonderfull operations" of art. As Harry Levin points out, the
power of art was associated with Saturn: "The ancient as-
trologers had consigned the artists and men of letters to the
planetary sphere of Mercury; but the Renaissance transferred
them to the sphere of Saturn."[23] Saturn's two-edged nature is
reflected yet again in the theme of the power and vanity of
art—of art as the means of creating majestic visions and of art
as a trap for the unwary.

For Renaissance artists, Saturn was perhaps the most expansive mythological god, as Lomazzo's capsule summary
indicates:

> His effects here below: Wise, Intelligent, Ingenious,
> the seede of great profundity, the auctor of secret
> contemplation, the imprinter of waighty thoughts in

---

[23]Levin, *The Myth of the Golden Age in the Renaissance*, p. 28.

men, a destroyer and preserver, the subverter of power and might, the keeper of hidden thinges, and the auctor of finding and losing.[24]

For Shakespeare's most expansive and all-inclusive dramatic figure Lomazzo's summary might do service. Prospero is everything specified —a figure of power, insight, profundity, a moral teacher, and above all the author of finding and losing. We can learn much about Prospero from the Panofsky and Saxl study of Albrecht Dürer's *Melencolia*, for this engraving is also the profound work of a person who exercised, like Shakespeare and his Prospero, supreme artistic power.[25] The figure of Saturn/Melancholy presides over the deeper meanings of *The Tempest* that run to the nature of art itself. Panofsky and Saxl call Dürer's figure "a being whose thoughts have reached the limit" (p. 345). In the Revels Speech and in the epilogue we have Prospero, another figure whose thoughts have reached the limit.

PROSPERO'S REVELS SPEECH

He that buildes Castles in the ayre, in hope
of a new world, may breake his necke, ere
hee come to half his age.

NICHOLAS BRETON

. . . all our beauty and our trim decays,
Like courts removing, or like ended plays.

JOHN DONNE

---

[24]Paolo Lomazzo, "Of the Motions Procured by the Seven Planets," *Tracte,* trans. Richard Haydocke (London, 1598), chap. 7, II, p. 17.

[25]Panofsky, Saxl, and Klibansky, *Saturn and Melancholy:* "'Power,' therefore, is what Dürer considered the end and essence of artistic capacity; and thereby the apparently casual sentence [in Dürer's description of the engraving] 'keys signify power' acquires a new and deeper meaning . . . Is not Melencolia herself the presiding genius of art?" (p. 341).

The Tempest is at once about the power and the vanity of art. In his Revels Speech, Prospero makes the point that only through art can dramatic "trim" like paint, deal board, and scene-cloth be made to live, and only when we see these things rationally (after the manner of a Hamlet, Marston, or Greville) rather than imaginatively, do they die. Here is one of the great statements in literature of the ambivalence between the realms of reality and of art, the fabric of life and the fabrication of the artist.

The Revels Speech takes us, as it were, backstage—just as in *A Midsummer Night's Dream* Shakespeare describes through the duke the imaginative processes of the poet. We see something more astonishing than the masque vision itself; we see how the miracle is achieved. In his *Elements of Architecture*, Wotton described a splendid painting as an "admirable *Object* because it comes neere an *Artificiall Miracle* to make diverse distinct *Eminences* appeare upon a *Flat*, by force of *Shadowes*" (p. 83). This is exactly what Prospero is saying to Ferdinand and to the audience; by the force of his art he has with his shadows wrought the artificial miracle of the wedding masque. To perform artistic miracles was a common task of the court-influenced artist. "Such tricks hath strong imagination!"

The Revels Speech expresses the power of the dream of art. Jonson invokes this power at the opening of his masque *The Vision of Delight* (1617):

> Breake, *Phant'sie*, from thy cave of cloud,
>   and spread thy purple wings;
> Now all thy figures are allow'd,
>   and various shapes of things;
> Create of airie formes, a streame;
>   it must have bloud, and naught of fleame,
> And though it be a waking dreame;
>   Yet let it like an odour rise

> to all the Sences here,
> And fall like sleep upon their eyes,
> or musick in their eare.
>
> (VII, 464–65)

The cloud imagery might remind us of those clouds that open to Caliban and show riches.[26] Such are the clouds of Prospero's speech; his spirits are airy; they fall like sleep upon the beholder. Prospero, too, is speaking of the power of a waking dream created through art.

Though the speech may seem a derogation of his art, it is also a defense of its *fictional* power. So often in the Renaissance the artistic license to move "beyond the life" was expressed through the imagery of the dream. Visionary or spectacular escapes beyond the reality of conscious life frequently called to use the imagery of sleep. In the first Jacobean masque, Daniel based his entire conceit on the fictive powers of the dreaming mind.[27] The Revels Speech correlates the "meerely fictive" dreams of art and life. As human beings we cope pathetically with the reality of our own vanity—much as Bottom copes with his dream, which is the vanity of Oberon's art. In his dream Bottom is indeed an ass, but Shakespeare's wordplay suggests that he is as a man an ass—a mortal fool. The rude mechanic cannot fathom the significance of his rare vision and so it remains for him bottomless. But when

---

[26]One of the 1604 arches had a similar effect on an observer: "But the glorie of this show, was in my eye as a dreame, pleasing to the affection, gorgeous and full of joy, and so full of show, and variety, that when I held down my head as wearied with looking so hie, me thoght it was a griefe to me to awaken so soone" (Gilbert Dugdale, *The Time Triumphant* [London, 1604], sig. B₃ᵛ). Angus Fletcher captures the ambivalent responses generated by courtly entertainments in *The Transcendental Masque:* "Only the element of ritual keeps the occasional nature of [the] masque from being a depressant" (p. 6).

[27]"In this project of ours, *Night & Sleepe* were to produce a Vision—an effect proper to their power, and fit to shadow our purpose, for that these apparitions & shewes are but as imaginations, and dreames that protend our affections" (Daniel, *The Vision of Twelve Goddesses, Works,* III, p. 192).

Prospero's majestic vision dissolves, we are asked to ponder its bottom. We are not asked, as Oberon puts it, to

> think no more of this night's accidents
> But as the fierce vexation of a dream.
>
> (4.1.68–69)

Rather, we are taken the further step and are shown the cause of Prospero's vexation ("Sir, I am vex'd").

Indeed, the word *vexation* is crucial to an understanding of Prospero's vision. On one level he feels the anguish of the artist:

> The vexations of art are certainly as the bonds and handcuffs of Proteus, which betray the ultimate struggles and efforts of matter. For bodies will not be destroyed or annihilated; rather than that they will turn themselves into various forms.[28]

Part of Prospero's struggle is to keep the "form" of his project—to prevent it from relaxing into mere farce, romance, or even tragedy. The play's instances showing this struggle are obvious enough. On another level is the anguished sense of the limitations under which Prospero must work, that is, the time within which his power and servants are available and potent. More deeply, there is a feeling for the limitations of art, whose power must end at last, leaving not a rack behind. Finally and most fierce is the vexing recognition that as dreams, even the dreams of the most potent artists, pass quickly, so passes the life of man:

> Swift as a shadow, short as any dream,
> Brief as the lightning in the collied night
> That, in a spleen, unfolds both heaven and earth;
> And ere a man hath power to say "Behold!"
> The jaws of darkness do devour it up:
> So quick bright things come to confusion.[29]

[28]Francis Bacon, *Translation of the Parasceve, Works,* IV, p. 257.
[29]Shakespeare, *A Midsummer Night's Dream,* 1.1.144–49. Allusions to

The Revels Speech reiterates this idea that bright things come unalterably to dissolution, as man comes to death.[30] The speech is a painful but necessary reminder set amid a very bright thing—precisely like the anamorphosed death's-head in Holbein's splendid embodiment of Renaissance humanist confidence, "The Ambassadors" (Plate 9). Among the picture's symbols of the liberal arts and of civilization itself hovers Holbein's symbolic reflection of the sense of an ending—and death—we find in the Revels Speech.

As a play written with extraordinary concern for "artificial contexture," *The Tempest* stands as an example of the courtly aesthetic in the public theater. However, containing a critique of that aesthetic, it goes beyond and reaches a unique level of self-conscious artistry. The courtly aesthetic bore fruit in magnificent illusion. This aesthetic created a dream world which, though exceedingly pleasant and uplifting, had its at-

---

experiences as dream-like constitute one of the play's important themes. In addition to lengthy passages like the Revels Speech, the Antonio–Sebastian dialogue (2.1.203–12), and Caliban's dream (3.2.133–41), note:

MIRANDA	'Tis far off,
	And rather like a dream.
	(1.2.44)
FERDINAND	My spirits, as in a dream, are all bound up.
	(1.2.489)
BOATSWAIN	Even in a dream, were we divided from them.
	(5.1.239)

[30]Nearing her death, even Queen Elizabeth finally saw the pleasures of the courtly aesthetic fade. Her response to some light-hearted poems offered to her by Harington was: "When thou dost feel creeping time at thy gate, these fooleries will please thee less: I am past my relish for such matters" (quoted in J. E. Neale, *Queen Elizabeth* [London, 1934], p. 390). Prospero's Revels Speech should be compared with Berowne's ending the revels in *Love's Labour's Lost*:

MARCADE	The King your father—
PRINCESS	Dead, for my life!
MARCADE	Even so: my tale is told.
BEROWNE	Worthies, away! the scene begins to cloud.
	(5.2.719–21)

tendant dangers. Shakespeare alludes to the vulnerability of "royal" psychology in his Sonnet 114:

> 'tis flatt'ry in my seeing,
> And my great mind most kingly drinks it up;
> Mine eye well knows what with his gust is 'greeing,
> And to his palate doth prepare his cup.

If one took courtly dreams too seriously, one might flatter oneself to think that evil does not exist in this world, or, if it does, that it can be easily and invariably controlled. The courtly aesthetic, indeed, could not have existed without the conviction that the forces of evil *were* conquerable. This is why the wedding masque is brought to a sad end: all is possible so long as the spell is not marred; once it is, the life of courtly art is jeopardized. The scene begins to cloud. The courtly aesthetic could not thrive in a world where evil was admitted to be at large, both because great imaginative leaps are more difficult in the face of evil and because evil can have its most devastating effect when ignored or masked over by idealism—either political or artistic. The incursion of political

---

Also in the mordant key and ending the revels of *A Midsummer Night's Dream* is Puck's speech:

> Now the hungry lion roars,
> And the wolf behowls the moon;
> Whilst the heavy ploughman snores,
> All with weary task foredone.
> Now the wasted brands do glow,
> Whilst the screech-owl, screeching loud,
> Puts the wretch that lies in woe
> In remembrance of a shroud.
> (5.1.371–78)

This might also be compared with a beautiful speech from the later courtly drama, *Argalus and Parthenia* (1629) by Francis Quarles. Its last lines are:

> Delights vanish; the morne o're casteth,
> The frost breaks, the shower hasteth;
> The towre falls, the hower spends;
> The beauty fades, and man's life ends.
> (*Works* [Edinburgh, 1818],
> III, p. 285)

9. *The Two Ambassadors*, portrait of Jean de
Dinteville and Georges de Selve, by Hans Holbein
the Younger (1533). Reproduced by courtesy of
the Trustees, the National Portrait Gallery,
London.

and economic realities undermined the vanity of courtly art just as Caliban's plot brought the masque to an end.

Candid observers saw this danger in the tendencies of courtly taste. Thomas Elyot, under Queen Mary, warned the prince to "declare thy magnificence not in such sumptuous expences, that ghostly doo vanishe, but onely in the thinges before expressed: that is to say, in the adourning or garnishinge of thy possessions."[31] While Breton's comment in the epigraph above may have special portent for Charles I, the dangers he alludes to were already being courted under James: exercise of the magical art that gives Prospero the power to build "Castles in the ayre" entails some risk. Bacon advised well in his essay "Of Building": "Leave the goodly fabrics of houses, for beauty only, to the enchanted pallaces of the poets; who build them with small cost" (VI, 481).

This danger is further hinted by the age's most eminent realist. In his *De Augmentis* Bacon had occasion to defend magic, "which has been long used in a bad sense." His modern-minded definition of magic might well be used to describe the Continental theatrical innovations that appeared in England under James: "I however understand it [magic] as the science which applies the knowledge of hidden forms to the production of wonderful operations" (IV, 366–67). Such was the purpose of the knowledge of stage perspective, scenic transformation, *periaktoi* and *scena versatilis*, cloud-machines, and the more elaborate lighting techniques—to produce wonderful operations. Unfortunately, these magical new stage technologies had just the effect upon audiences that Bacon criticized in the "false and ignoble" astrological or alchemical magic. Such magic, he felt, thrived on "credulous and superstitious traditions and observations concerning sympathies and antipathies, and hidden and specific prop-

[31]From Thomas Elyot's translation of Isocrates' oration delivered to Nicocles, titled by Elyot *The Doctrinal of Princes* (1533; facs. rpt. ed. Lillian Gottesman, Gainesville, Florida, 1967), p. 15.

erties, with experiments for the most part frivolous" (IV, 367). These effects amounted, in Bacon's mind, to an obfuscation of *real* knowledge, a fatal departure from real experience, and a relinquishment of rational means of exploring for truth:

> So they who are carried away by insane and uncontrollable passion after things which they only fancy they see through the clouds and vapours of imagination, shall in place of works beget nothing else but empty hopes and hideous and monstrous spectres. But this popular and degenerate natural magic has the same kind of effect on men as some soporific drugs, which not only lull to sleep, but also during sleep instil gentle and pleasing dreams. For first it lays the understanding asleep by singing of specific properties and hidden virtues, sent as from heaven and only to be learned from the whispers of tradition; which makes men no longer alive and awake for the pursuit and inquiry of real causes, but to rest content with these slothful and credulous opinions; and then it insinuates innumerable fictions, pleasant to the mind, and such as one would most desire,—like so many dreams.[32]

Such was the magic of courtly art that it instilled gentle and pleasing dreams of security, unquestioned power, and opulence in its royal and aristocratic audience.[33] *The Vision of Twelve Goddesses* (1603) was based on the nature of dreams as

[32]Bacon, *De Augmentis Scientiarum* (Book 3, Chap. 5), *Works,* IV, p. 367.

[33]Jonson makes a glancing attack on the illusory nature of courtly life in *Cynthia's Revels* (IV, 89):

> The strangest pageant, fashion'd like a court,
> (At least I dream't I saw it) so diffus'd,
> So painted, pied, and full of rainbow straines,
> As never yet (either by time, or place)
> Was made the food to my distasted sence.

Jonson's "Expostulation with Inigo Jones," though, is the most concentrated and powerful poetic attack upon the courtly aesthetic we have. Angus Fletcher discusses the poem in *The Transcendental Masque,* pp. 87–115.

Bacon describes it, and it is symbolic of much Jacobean courtly art, which encouraged the king's complacency toward the "real causes" of his nation's ills and which helped to delay until too late an inquiry into his difficulties with Parliament and the English economy. The magic of the courtly aesthetic was designed to insinuate "innumerable fictions, pleasant to the mind," but they all finally proved to be baseless and insubstantial fictions. Like Prospero's Revels Speech, Bacon's statement warns of the dangers of theatrical magic.

In one of the period's most popular moral treatises, La Primaudaye's *French Academy*, the dangers of the courtly aesthetic are put in certain terms in a chapter "Of Superfluitie, Sumptuousness, Gluttonie, and wallowing in delightes":

> Now, if Princes and governors of Common-wealths, in steade of abridging superfluous charges, take delight therein themselves, from thence proceedeth the necessity of charging and overcharging their people with imposts and subsidies to maintaine their excesse, and in the end cometh the overthrow and subversion of the one and the other.[34]

A better assessment of the fundamental ills of the Stuart reign could scarcely be found. These kings, failing to heed common sense or the advice of more candid, even cynical advisers, began to take seriously the dream of art that was created for them:

LYSIPPUS   What think'st thou of a maske, will
                            it be well?

[34]La Primaudaye, *The French Academy* (1614 edition), p. 206. La Primaudaye further comments, in words prophetic of the events of the 1640s, "Now let us speake of those that propound . . . unto themselves the vaine glory of outward shew . . . through frivolous, unprofitable and superfluous expences . . . . This is that which at length stirreth up civill wars, seditions, and tyrannies within cities, to the end that such voluptuous men, & ambitious of vaine glory, fishing in a troubled water, may have wherewith to maintaine their foolish expences, and so come to the end of their platformes" (pp. 203–4).

STRATO   As well as masks can be.
LYSIPPUS   As masks can be?
STRATO   Yes, they must commend their King, and
                                   speak in praise
           Of the assembly, bless the Bride and
                                   Bridegroome,
           In person of some god, they're tied to rules
           Of flatterie.[35]

The courtly artistic world was tied to rules of flattery, and it appears that James began to take this world seriously. As Wallace Notestein concluded in his study of the early reign, "he deceived himself and lived much of the time in a dream world."[36] Courtly art helped to make this dream world possible, and Charles I was even more incorrigibly self-imprisoned in the courtly aesthetic, as a perusal of the last great Caroline masques would suggest.

It is fascinating to wonder to what extent the "privie marke of Ironie" is present in the Revels Speech, that is, whether it comments subversively on the Jacobean artistic pageant that sparkled during the playwright's last creative years. Did Shakespeare, like Fulke Greville, sense the folly of the majestic visions that were meant to celebrate James's government?[37] The court of James was fascinated by the power of

[35]Beaumont and Fletcher, *The Maid's Tragedy* (circa 1608–11), 1.1.6–11 (*Dramatic Works*, II, p. 29). Compare *Othello*, 1.3.18–19: "'Tis a pageant/ To keep us in false gaze."

[36]Notestein, *The House of Commons, 1604–1610*, p. 504. This psychology led to elaborate artistic expressions of courtly wish-fulfillment. Romance literature was especially suitable to these expressions—for reasons made clear in Northrop Frye's discussion of "The Mythos of Summer: Romance" in *Anatomy of Criticism:* "The romance is nearest of all literary forms to the wish-fulfillment dream" (p. 186). See also Frye's essay "Romance as Masque," in *Shakespeare's Romances Reconsidered,* edited by Carol Kay and Henry Jacobs (Lincoln, Nebraska, 1978), pp. 11–39.

[37]A good but impressionistic description of the court of James is G. V. Akrigg's *The Jacobean Pageant, or The Court of King James I* (Cambridge, Mass., 1962).

While there is profound self-deprecation in the Revels Speech, I suspect

art to create illusion, but wiser heads, especially those who
worked behind the scenes or had to pay the Revels accounts,
must have sensed the vanity of it all. For these men, where the
spectacle was most sublime, so was the sense not only of its
evanescence but also of its social cost most deep.
Though *The Tempest* celebrates the power of art to create
the vision of the good courtly life, it also suggests that the
dream must be relinquished. This lesson, though applicable to
every aspect of experience, has in Prospero's case been applied
to the creation of the artist. All art is insubstantial—a potent
thought reflected in a passage from *Aeneid* 1, in which the
hero studies the murals in the Temple of Juno:

> . . . animum pictura pascit inani
> multa gemens, largoque umectat flumine voltum.
>
> (1.464–65)

(He feasts his soul on the unsubstantial picture, sigh-
ing oft-times, and his face wet with a flood of tears.)

These lines, like Prospero's speech, encompass the nature of
artistic creation, its powers and limitations. The paradox of
the phrase *pictura pascit inani*, which is that Aeneas could
nourish himself upon the "baseless" picture, is the most wonderful paradox of art. That *The Tempest* addresses this
paradox is not the least source of its wonder: while in both
form and content it celebrates the courtly aesthetic, the play

---

there is also the kind of irony Fulke Greville found in the work of the supreme Elizabethan courtier, Sir Philip Sidney, "that hypocritical figure *Ironia,*
wherein men commonly (to keep above their workes) seeme to make toyes of
the utmost they can doe" (*Life of Sidney*, p. 154). That Shakespeare could keep
this (and so many more) possibilities open in the Revels Speech is a "most
high miracle" of dramaturgy. This equivocation cannot be sufficiently emphasized, especially in the light of a passage from Lope de Vega's *New Art of
Writing Plays* (1609): "To deceive the audience with the truth is a thing that
has seemed well . . . . Equivoque and the uncertainty arising from ambiguity
have always held a large place among the crowd, for it thinks that it alone
understands what the other one is saying" (pp. 202–3). We have in *The Tempest* just this intentional and fascinating authorial equivocation.

moves beyond and offers a sobering perspective on it.[38] One is reminded of the poignantly sad closing lines of Shakespeare's first courtly play, *Love's Labour's Lost:* "The words of Mercury are harsh after the songs of Apollo." Prospero's Revels Speech, following as it does upon the exultation of the masque, also reflects mercurial harshness as it expresses the transience not only of courtly art but also of human life.

[38]The Revels Speech has sent scholars scurrying to the ancients. The 1892 Variorum alone mentions Pindar, Aeschylus, Sophocles, Aristophanes, and Euripides. But these Greek names seem unlikely. More plausible, especially for the present discussion, is the name of Virgil. A passage from *Aeneid* 6 bears a significant similarity to the Revels Speech. Whereas Prospero is explaining that a glorious vision is not real, Anchises is explaining that the scene of terror in Hell is likewise unreal:

> In the midst an elm, shadowy and vast, spreads her boughs and aged arms, the home which, men say, false Dreams [*somnia vana*] hold in throngs, clinging under every leaf. And many monstrous forms besides of various beasts are stalled at the doors . . . . Here on a sudden, in trembling terror, Aeneas grasps his sword, and turns the naked edge against their coming: and did not his wise companion warn him that these were but *faint, bodiless lives, flitting under a hollow semblance of form,* he had rushed upon them and vainly cleft shadows with the steel.
>
> (6.282–94, emphasis added)

The lesson Aeneas must learn is to discern appearance from reality, and this is the point Prospero makes in the Revels Speech. Both Anchises and Prospero are addressing themselves to the illusion of dreams, and their conclusion is the same: dreams must cease to affect us (either with fear or delight) when we see them "rationally." Their phrases echo each other: *tenuis*/insubstantial; *cava sub imagine formae*/baseless fabric of this vision; *sine corpore vitas*/all spirits.

· VIII ·

BEYOND THE JACOBEAN
COURTLY AESTHETIC

*I*N THE FOREGOING CHAPTERS I have attempted to identify characteristics of an aesthetic that was a major
and hitherto neglected influence on Shakespeare. Reference to
other literary genres than drama and to other arts than literature was unavoidable, for the *Gesamtkunstwerk* of a royal court
was always the result of a collective artistic effort. Shakespeare, Jonson, Jones, Ferrabosco, Campion, Hilliard, and
Rubens—not to mention myriad nameless artisans—all
played a part in the phenomenon of artistic royalism.

By way of drawing back from my focus on one king's
court and of summarizing my thoughts on *The Tempest* as, in
many significant respects, a product of the courtly aesthetic
(and hence as a work that bears kinship to all courtly art), I
wish to compare the play with an indubitably courtly work
from another art, another realm, and another age: *Las Meninas*
or *The Ladies in Waiting* by Diego Velázquez (Plate 10). A
comparison of these two works—rich in biographical, historical, and aesthetic parallels—will provide the broadened horizons apt for an envoi. This subjective exercise, like Prospero's
epilogue, may ask indulgence, but it will permit a summary
of many of the suggestions made in preceding chapters about
Shakespeare's play and its artistic environment. The picture
and the play are masterpieces of their time, both require the
same patience for full appreciation, both are products of royal
servants, and both go beyond their courtly métier to examine

10. *Las Meninas* (*The Ladies in Waiting*),
by Diego Velázquez (1656).

the creative process itself. And, most important, we are here
confronting supreme artists at the height of their powers.[1]
   Though a generation separated Velázquez (1599–1660)
and Shakespeare, they had much in common. From what little
we know about each man, they both led relatively quiet and
uneventful lives, Shakespeare dying at fifty-two and Velázquez at sixty-one. Both were successful in their lifetime:
Shakespeare retired to Stratford a wealthy man, and Velázquez eventually attained noble orders (celebrated by his attire
in the picture) and the distinguished post of *aposentador* in the
royal household of Philip IV. Both lived much of their creative lives under royal protection or patronage. *The Tempest*
and *Las Meninas* also stand in similar biographical contexts as

[1]My personal view is that *The Tempest* is Shakespeare's richest, most
allusive, and most controlled play—attributes that may by now be obvious.
That *Las Meninas* is the painter's finest work is an all but unanimous opinion.
J. A. Emmens ("Les Ménines de Velázquez: Miroir des Princes pour Philippe
IV," *Nederlands Kunsthistorisch Jaarboek* 12 (1961): 51–79) calls it "cette com-
position exceptionelle" and a picture "qui comte parmi les oeuvres maîtresses
de la peinture du dix-septième siècle." In his great early work Acisclo
Palomino devotes a chapter to this painting: "In which the most famous
work of Don Diego Velázquez is described" (*Las Vidas de los Pintores* . . .
Eminentes Españoles [Madrid, 1726], III, p. 342). Francisco Cantón, in *Las
Meninas y sus personajes* (Barcelona, 1943), calls it "one of the principal works
in the history of painting." Like views are expressed by Hugo Kehrer in *Die
Meninas des Velázquez* (Munich, 1966) and Kurt Gerstenberg, *Diego Veláz-
quez* (Munich, 1957). William Stirling, in his *Annals of the Artists of Spain*
(London, 1848), calls it Velázquez's "last great work . . . his masterpiece."
   The Velázquez painting still exerts a remarkable fascination in this cen-
tury: Picasso was particularly drawn to it (see his *Variations on Velázquez's
Painting "The Maids of Honor,"* [New York, 1957]. A rather precious discus-
sion of the painting figures in the introduction to Michel Foucault's *Les
Mots et les choses (The Order of Things)* (New York, 1970). *Las Meninas* has
figured in recent literary criticism also: Leslie Epstein, "Beyond the Baroque:
The Role of the Audience in the Modern Theater," *Tri-Quarterly* 12 (1968):
215–19; Alvin Kernan, "Shakespeare's Essays on Dramatic Poesy," in *The
Author and His Work,* ed. Louis Martz (New Haven, Conn., 1978), p. 176;
Ernest Gilman, *The Curious Perspective* (New Haven, Conn., 1978), pp.
209–15; Alvin Kernan, *The Playwright as Magician* (New Haven, Conn.,
1979), pp. 148–49.

the last great works these men produced. Shakespeare wrote his play about six years before he died; in 1656, four years before his death, Velázquez painted *Las Meninas*. As nearly final and supreme works, *The Tempest* and *Las Meninas* possess a special gravity that partially derives from interior allusions to their creators. It cannot be wholly coincidental that both men were motivated in these works to allude to themselves as artists and to the creative process. Their careers drawing to a close, they saw fit to allow the beholder behind the tiring-house façade and into the atelier for a glimpse of the act of creation—the power to create the "forms of things unknown." *Las Meninas* is the only extant authenticated self-portrait of Velázquez, and in *The Tempest* we have the closest approach to a self-portrait in the Shakespearean canon. What Cantón says of the painting—"It is the last, most important, and the most faithful of his self-portraits" (p. 15)—might well apply to the character of Prospero. Both works are in a sense portraits of the man as mature artist.

Both are reflections of real-life courtly drama. Velázquez portrays what Cantón calls "the scenario of a courtly anecdote." Cantón then analyzes the painting as a brief courtly drama. He describes the "cast" of eleven and observes that the "spectators"—the king and queen—are reflected in the mirror at the back of the atelier. The picture is all the more allusive, for the central portrait of the infanta reminds us of the many adolescent likenesses the painter produced during his nearly half-century tenure as servant to the doting royal father. This scene must have occurred, with mundane variation, countless times in the painter's career.

No clear topical courtly allusions have been discerned in *The Tempest*. Nonetheless, the play reflects courtly life with considerable fidelity. An air, if not of the anecdotal, at least of the occasional pervades the act 4 masque, a Shakespearean attempt to recreate a frequent courtly event under James. The pointed allusions for Ferdinand and Miranda in the hymeneal masque were just the kind constantly insinuated in masques at Whitehall for the royal family or honored nuptial participants. Though masques appear frequently in plays of the period, they usually exist for ulterior dramatic purposes—as a vehicle for assassination, for instance, in *The Malcontent*. Excepting the masque in *The Maid's Tragedy*, the masque in *The Tempest* is the only one that has the *feel* of an actual Jacobean masque. It exists essentially though not solely for its own beauty, the wonder it creates, and the celebration of that central festive event at any court, the marriage of future rulers. In real life the masque would have concluded in the tenor of the last act of the play itself, where Prospero (as symbolic ruler of the masquing world) performs the royal act of unifying and harmonizing. The action of *The Tempest* requires a slight detour and delay in act 5, but the profound congeniality of act 5 is the same plangent, ebullient effect that signals the end of many a Jacobean masque.[2]

Perhaps most important in our comparison is the cluster of themes focusing on the artistry of these respective masterpieces—the ideas of art portraying art, the interplay of the perspectives of art and reality, the ambivalence of artistic power—themes I have previously mentioned. A famous story, reported by Palomino, relates that when the court painter Luca Giordano (1628–1704) was asked his opinion of *Las Meninas*, he replied: "It is the theology of painting." Giordano must have meant that it was essentially a visual treatise on the epistemology of the "divine" art of painting. The painting certainly is, aside from its ostensible purpose of portraying members of the Spanish royal family and their entourage, a portrait of the artist, his method, his atelier. It is a portrait, in short, of his professional life. Ortega y Gasset perhaps put the laminated implications of the work most suc-

---

[2]See, for example, the closing Epithalamium of Jonson's *Haddington Masque* (VII, 261), the end of *Hymenaei* (VII, 240–41) and of *Love Freed from Ignorance* (VII, 371).

cinctly when he said that in it "a portraitist is portraying the portrayal."[3] This effect, which is similar to a set of Chinese boxes, is also present in *The Tempest*, where Shakespeare has dramatized a figure who is himself creating a drama (and a masque within that drama as well). It is a play that shows the audience the composition of a play. Isabel MacCaffrey has described *The Faerie Queene* in her *Spenser's Allegory* as a poem that "looks at itself and offers an eloquent argument for its own existence" (p. 9). For their respective art forms, *Las Meninas* and *The Tempest* perform the same functions.

As in *The Tempest*, the organization of perspectives and "planes of reality" is crucial to *Las Meninas*. We are able to see something (the king and queen) that is, as it were, outside the frame. Put differently, we the viewers are standing in the place of figures who are reflected in the painting. Furthermore, we are able to "see" in our mind what is in fact being painted on the unseen canvas to the left.[4] As well, though probably requested to paint a portrait of the infanta, Velázquez also included the patrons, the artist himself, and other lowly satellites in the final product. The organization is more complex than that of a mere painting within a painting, so numerous are the possible central focuses of the work.[5] Is the infanta, Philip, Velázquez, or—as Ortega y Gasset has suggested—the central *space* itself the true protagonist? Vel-

[3]José Ortega y Gasset, "Introduction to Velázquez," in *Velázquez, Goya and the Dehumanization of Art* (1943; trans. Alexis Brown, New York, 1972), p. 106.

[4]Even here there is some doubt. Carl Justi (*Diego Velázquez and His Times* [London, 1889]), among others, has suggested that Velázquez is painting a double portrait of the king and queen, though there is no record of such a painting. Gerstenberg rejects this idea (*Diego Velázquez*, p. 191) for the usual one that the infanta is the sitter, and that she has momentarily turned to address her parents (thus presenting her pose as Velázquez is actually painting it).

[5] "There is a superfluity of frames in the picture—frames of the mirror, of the door, of the easel, many (all of these black) of oil paintings . . . . Yet no picture is more calculated than this to make us forget that it is a picture" (Justi, *Diego Velázquez*, p. 418).

ázquez delicately sustains the central ambivalence, and in just this way, I have sought to show, Shakespeare maintains the central oscillation of reference to Prospero as ruler, as theatrical mage, as creative intellect, and as his own shadowed persona. This is not all. We have not plumbed the complexity of the Velazquian mystery, just as Prospero's mystery can never be plucked out. *Las Meninas* not only contains within it riddling and delectable play on normal perspective and the normal "distance" between creator and viewer, but also reaches out beyond the quadrature in an ironical and engaging fashion.[6] And we *see* the author of this fascination looking out upon us. Shakespeare performs this same feat in a dramatic context through the dexterous play upon different perspectives.[7] Hence, this statement by Cantón about the painting says

[6]In his study Kurt Gerstenberg makes the following relevant analysis of *Las Meninas:*

> What a remarkable breakthrough or, even more, a doubling of the levels of being is reached by it! Here, the ultimate conclusions in Baroque painting are drawn, as Bernini drew them in the area of sculpture, namely, the reaching out from the plane of representation into that of reality, the greatest animation of the optical process in the joining and collaborating of the beholder. Insofar as the boundaries of the picture seem to have been broken through in the direction of the foreground, the partition between the representation and the viewer is set aside. The end of a development has been reached here . . . insofar as the sphere of the painting reaches forward and pulls the beholder within.
> (pp. 196–98, my translation)

[7]Compare Robert Adams's statement in *Strains of Discord* (Ithaca, New York, 1958):

> Many of Shakespeare's late plays seem to make use of an analogous [open] structure . . . . By deliberately overstepping the boundary between the aesthetic sphere and that of "real life," they seek to convince us, not that the aesthetic is fraudulent, but that it is more real than reality itself . . . . By means of *trompe-l'œil* the artist mingles and contrasts different levels of representation . . . . A figure painted within a frame may be depicted as reaching across the frame to claim existence in a third dimension . . . . The device is essentially that of the overstepped or obliterated frame; its effect is

something about *The Tempest* too: "When one contemplates the painting alone, after the first moments the gaze is caught in the bewitching illusion and is finally unable to determine where the painting ends and where the reality of the room begins. It almost suggests the possibility of entering the scene of this courtly anecdote" (p. 29). Hence the complexity of the two works and the sheer time they require for their shimmering implications to insinuate themselves into our imaginations. Justi said of *Las Meninas:* "All this dawns only gradually on the eye. Few pictures demand such continuous study" (p. 420). And few plays require such sustained reflection as *The Tempest.* If of all Shakespeare's plays *King Lear* demands the greatest imagination, *The Tempest* asks for the greatest contemplation.

These works, in their self-conscious complexity and flair of execution, are vanities of their creators' art. The power of Velázquez's brush is amply demonstrated in the painting, and the play celebrates the power to create majestic visions out of thin air. Both works display the magic of artistic illusion and the power of the artist to organize it in an entrancing way. We see from behind the easel of the painter—which is to say we see the baseless and insubstantial materials on which he painted his fictions. We see how, in Wotton's words, the "artificial miracle" of a painting is achieved. Our view of the atelier is paralleled by the view Prospero divulges in the Revels Speech. Just as Prospero reminds us that the "charms" of art are transitory, so does the view of Velázquez at work remind us that *Las Meninas* is itself but another fiction and once lay half-completed on the easel before which we see the artist working.

Shakespeare and Velázquez create in these works a captivating vision and at the same time force us to observe that

to surprise by the incongruity or to impress by the depth of representational levels; and though less frequent in literature than in the plastic arts, it does have an existence on the printed page.

(pp. 52–53)

only through their artistic power have these works been created—out of nothing. *Las Meninas* and *The Tempest* are uniquely expansive masterpieces; they traverse the normal limitations of their respective genres. If I were to venture an explanation for their enduring fascination, I would say it is their fusion of realms—the realms of appearance and reality, of the king and his artistic servant, of the artwork and its audience, of traditional and individual expression, of their own time and of the timelessness of all great art. Though products of courtly preoccupations and aesthetics, both works transcend what is merely courtly and address more abiding truths.[8] If they are finely, intentionally ambiguous, it is not because something has been left out, but because they include—with their own secret harmony and integrity—all that is possible.

[8]Max Raphael's observations on prehistoric cave paintings apply also to *Las Meninas* and *The Tempest*: "The work of art closest to perfection is both most profoundly determined by its time and goes furthest beyond it into timelessness" (*Prehistoric Cave Paintings* [New York, 1945], p. 17).

BIBLIOGRAPHY

Place of publication is London unless
otherwise indicated.

PRIMARY SOURCES

Agrippa, Heinrich Cornelius. *Three Books of Occult Philosophy*
(1531). Translated by John Freake. 1651.

———. *Of the Vanitie and uncertaintie of Artes and Sciences.*
Translated by James Sanford (1569). Edited by Catherine
Dunn. Northridge, California, 1974.

Alberti, Leone Battista. *On Painting* (*De pictura,* circa 1435).
Translated by Cecil Grayson. 1972.

———. *Ten Books on Architecture.* Translated by James Leoni
(1755). Reprint edited by Joseph Rykwert. 1955.

Amadis de Gaule (1508–11). Translated by Anthony Munday.
1619 edition.

Ariosto, Ludovico. *Orlando Furioso.* Translated by John
Harington (1591). Edited by Robert McNulty. Oxford,
1972.

Bacon, Francis. *The Works.* 15 volumes. Edited by James
Spedding. 1857–74; rpt. Stuttgart, 1963.

Baxter, Nathaniel. *Sir Philip Sidney's Ourania.* 1606.

Beaujoyeulx, Baltasar de. *Balet comique de la royne* (1581). Facsimile reprint edited by Giacomo Caula. Torino, 1965.

Beaumont, Francis, and John Fletcher. *Philaster.* Edited by
Andrew Gurr. 1969.

———. *The Dramatic Works of Francis Beaumont and John
Fletcher.* 4 volumes. General editor, Fredson Bowers.
Cambridge, England, 1976.

Boccaccio, Giovanni. *Boccaccio on Poetry.* (*Genealogy.*) Translated by Charles Osgood. Princeton, 1930.

Brathwaite, Richard. *Sonnets or Madrigals* (annexed to the 1611
edition of Brathwaite, *The Golden Fleece*). 1611.

———. *The Prodigals Teares.* 1614.

Breton, Nicholas. *Melancholike Humours* (1600). Edited, with an essay on Elizabethan melancholy, by G. B. Harrison. 1929.

Calderón de la Barca. *La vida es sueño*. Edited by Albert Sloman. Manchester, 1961.

Campion, Thomas. *The Works*. Edited by Walter Davis. Garden City, New York, 1967.

Cartari, Vincenzo. *The Fountaine of Ancient Fiction*. Translated by R. Linche. 1599.

Cartigny, Jean de (John Carthenay). *The Voyage of the Wandering Knight* (1607). Edited by Dorothy Evans. Seattle, 1951.

Case, John. *The Praise of Musicke*. 1586.

Castiglione, Baldassare. *The Book of the Courtier*. Translated by Sir Thomas Hoby. Edition introduced by W. H. D. Rowse and annotated by W. B. Henderson. 1928.

Cattan, Christophe de. *The Geomancie of Christopher Cattan*. Translated by Francis Sparry. 1591.

Cervantes Saavedra, Miguel de. *The Historie of the valorous and wittie Knight-Errant, Don Quixote*. Translated by Thomas Shelton. 1612.

Chapman, George. *The Plays*. Edited by T. M. Parrott (1910). 2 volumes. Reprint, New York, 1961.

———. *Poems*. Edited by Phyllis Bartlett (1941). Reprint, New York, 1962.

———. *The Revenge of Bussy d'Ambois*. Facsimile reprint, Menton, England, 1968.

———. *The Whole Works of Homer* (1616). 2 volumes. Edited as *Chapman's Homer* by Allardyce Nicoll. New York, 1956.

Chester, Robert. *Loves Martyr: or, Rosalins Complaint* (1601). Edited by Alexander Grosart. 1878.

Clapham, John. *Certain Observations concerning the life and Reign of Queen Elizabeth* (1603). Reprint edited by E. P. Read as *Elizabeth of England*. Philadelphia, 1951.

Corneille, Pierre. *L'Illusion comique* (1635). Edited by Colette Cosnier. Paris, n.d.

Cornwallis, Sir Charles. *A discourse of the most Illustrious Prince Henry*. 1641.

———. *The Life and Death of our Late most Incomparable and Heroique Prince Henry* (1641). Reprint with an appendix by J. Morgan. 1738.

Cousin, Jean de. *Livre de Pourtraiture*. Paris, 1618.

Daniel, Samuel. *The Complete Works*. 5 volumes. Edited by Alexander Grosart. 1885.

Dee, John. "Mathematicall Praeface." In *The Elements of Geometrie of Euclid of Megara* (1570). Edited and introduced by Allen Debus. New York, 1975.

———. *Monas Hieroglyphica* (1564). Translated by C. H. Josten. *Ambix* 12 (June and October, 1964): 84–221.

Dekker, Thomas. *The Gull's Hornbook* (1609). Ed. R. B. McKerrow (1904). Reprint New York, 1971.

———. *The Dramatic Works*. 4 volumes. Edited by Fredson Bowers. Cambridge, England, 1953–61.

———. *The Non-dramatic Works*. 5 volumes. Edited by Alexander Grosart (1885). Reprint, New York, 1963.

Donne, John. *Devotions upon Emergent Occasions* (1624). Edited by John Sparrow. Cambridge, England, 1923.

———. *The Sermons of John Donne*. 10 volumes. Edited by George Potter and Evelyn Simpson. Berkeley, 1957.

Drayton, Michael. *The Works*. 6 volumes. Edited by J. W. Hebel. Oxford, 1961.

Dugdale, Gilbert. *The Time Triumphant*. 1604.

Du Jon, François. *The Painting of the Ancients*. 1638.

Elyot, Thomas. *The Doctrinal of Princes* (1533). Facsimile reprint edited by Lillian Gottesman. Gainesville, Florida, 1967.

Englands Parnassus (1600). Compiled by Robert Allot. Edited by Charles Crawford. Oxford, 1913.

Estienne, Henri. *The Art of Making Devises*. Translated by Thomas Blount. 1650.

———. *A World of Wonders*. 1607.

Feltham, Owen. *Resolves, or Excogitations: A Second Centurie*. 1628.

Fletcher, John. *See* Beaumont, Francis, and John Fletcher.

Gelli, Giovanni. *Circe* (1549). Translated by H. Iden. 1557.

Gesta Grayorum. Edited by W. W. Greg (1914). Reprint, Liverpool, 1968.

Gordon, John. *ΕΝΩΤΙΚΟΝ, or A Sermon of the Union of Great Brittannie.* 1604.

Gosson, Stephen. *Playes Confuted in five Actions.* 1582.

Greville, Fulke. *The Life of Sir Philip Sidney* (1652). Edited by Nowell Smith. 1907.

————. *The Remains.* Edited by G. A. Wilkes. 1965.

Guarini, Giovanni Battista. *Il pastor fido.* Venice, 1602.

————. *Il pastor fido.* Translated by Richard Fanshawe (1647). Bilingual edition by J. H. Whitfield. Austin, Texas, 1976.

Guilpin, Edward. *Skialetheia* (1598). Reprint edited by D. Allen Carroll. Chapel Hill, 1974.

Heywood, Thomas. *The Dramatic Works* (1874). 5 volumes. Reprint, 1964.

————. "Oenone and Paris." In *Elizabethan Minor Epics,* edited by Elizabeth Donno. New York, 1963.

Hilliard, Nicholas. *A treatise concerning the arte of limning.* Edited by Philip Norman. Walpole Society 1. 1911.

Holinshed, Raphael. *Holinshed's Chronicles of England, Scotland, and Ireland.* 1586.

James I, King of England. *Daemonologie* (1597). Edited by G. B. Harrison. 1924.

————. *The Political Works of James I.* Edited by Charles McIlwain. Cambridge, Mass., 1918.

Jonson, Ben. *The Works.* 11 volumes. Edited by C. H. Herford, Percy and Evelyn Simpson. Oxford, 1925–52.

Kalender, The Shepheards. 1604.

Lacroix, Paul, ed. *Ballets et Mascarades de Cour . . . 1581–1652.* 6 volumes. Geneva, 1868–70.

La Primaudaye, Pierre de. *The French Academy.* Translated by T. Bowes. 1614 edition.

————. *The Second Part of the French Academy.* 1594.

————. *The Third Volume of the French Academy.* Translated by R. Dolman. 1601.

Leonardo da Vinci. *The Literary Works.* 2 volumes. Edited by Jean Paul Richter. 1970.

Lomazzo, Paolo Giovanni. *A tracte containing the artes of curious paintinge.* Translated by Richard Haydocke. Oxford, 1598.

Marcelline, George. *The Triumphs of King James the First.* 1610.

Markham, Gervase. *The dumbe Knight.* 1608.

———. *The Second and last part of the first booke of the English Arcadia.* 1613.

Marston, John. *The Plays.* 3 volumes. Edited by H. H. Wood. Edinburgh, 1934–39.

Ménestrier, Claude-François. *Des Ballets anciennes et modernes selon les règles du Théâtre* (1682). Reprint, Geneva, 1972.

———. *Des Représentations en musique anciennes et modernes* (1681). Reprint, Geneva, 1972.

Middleton, Thomas. *The Works.* 8 volumes. Edited by A. H. Bullen. Boston, 1885.

Montaigne, Michel de. *The Complete Essays.* Translated by Donald Frame. Stanford, California, 1957.

More, Thomas. *The English Works.* 2 volumes. Edited by W. E. Campbell. New York, 1931.

Mucedorus. 1606.

Munday, Anthony. *Sidero-Thriambos or Steele and Iron Triumphing.* 1618.

Niceron, Jean François. *La Perspective curieuse ou Magie Artificiele des effets merveilleux.* Paris, 1638.

Nichols, John. *The Progresses, Processions, and Magnificent Festivities of King James the First.* 4 volumes. 1828.

Nixon, Anthony. *The Dignitie of Man.* 1612.

Ortuñez de Calahorra, Diego. *The second part of the first Booke of the Mirrour of Knighthood.* Translated by Robert Parry. 1585.

Peacham, Henry, the Elder. *The Garden of Eloquence* (1577). Facsimile reprint of the 1593 edition, by William Crane. Gainesville, Florida, 1954.

Peacham, Henry, the Younger. *The Gentlemans Exercise.* 1612.

Peele, George. *The Life and Works of George Peele.* Edited by David Horne. New Haven, 1952.

Pelletier, Thomas. *Discours politicque à tres-hault et tres-puissant Roy Jacques premier* . . . . 1603.

Primaleon of Greece, The History of. Translated by Anthony Munday. 1619 edition.

Puttenham, George. *The Arte of English Poesie* (1589). Edited by Gladys Willcock and Alice Walker (1936). Reprint, 1970.

Quarles, Francis. *The Complete Works.* 3 volumes. Edited by Alexander Grosart. Edinburgh, 1881.

Rinuccini, Camillo. *Descrizione delle feste fatte nelle reali nozze . . . di Cosimo de' Medici.* Florence, 1608.

Scot, Reginald. *The Discoverie of Witchcraft* (1584). Reprint edited with an introduction by H. R. Williamson. Carbondale, Illinois, 1964.

Serlio, Sebastiano. *The Firste Booke of Architecture.* Translated by Robert Peake (1611). Facsimile reprint introduced by A. E. Santaniello. New York, 1970.

Sermons or Homilies, Certaine. Edited by John Griffiths. Oxford, 1859.

Sermons or Homilies, Certaine. Facsimile reprint of the 1623 folio edition, edited by Mary Rickey and Thomas Stroup. Gainesville, Florida, 1968.

Shakespeare, William. *The Riverside Shakespeare* (complete works). Textual editor, G. Blakemore Evans. Boston, 1974.

———. *The Tempest.* New Variorum edition by H. H. Furness (1892). Facsimile reprint, New York, 1964.

———. *The Tempest.* New Arden edition by Frank Kermode. Cambridge, Mass., 1954.

Shirley, James. *The Dramatic Works and Poems.* 6 volumes. 1833.

Sidney, Sir Philip. *Prose Works.* 4 volumes. Edited by Albert Feuillerat (1912). Reprint, 1962.

Spenser, Edmund. *The Works of Edmund Spenser.* 8 volumes. Variorum edition by Edwin Greenlaw *et al.* Baltimore, 1938.

Stow, John. *The Annales, or Generall Chronicle of England.* 1615 edition.

Tasso, Torquato. *Aminta*. Edited by Ernest Grillo. 1924.
———. *Godfrey of Bulloigne, or The Recoverie of Jerusalem (Gerusalemme liberata)*. Translated by Edward Fairfax. 1600.
———. *Prose*. Edited by Ettore Mazzali. Milan, 1959.
Thomas, Thomas. *Dictionarium linguae Latinae et Anglicanae* (1588). Seventh edition, 1606.
Thornborough, John. *A discourse plainely proving the evident utilitie and urgent necessitie of the desired happie Union of the two famous Kingdomes.* 1604.
———. *The Joyefull and Blessed Reuniting.* Circa 1604.
Tottel, Richard. *Tottels Miscellany* (1557). Facsimile reprint, revised by Hyder Rollins. Cambridge, Mass., 1965.
Vega, Lope Felix de. *The New Art of Writing Plays* (1609). Translated by William Brewster. Included in *Dramatic Theory and Criticism*, edited by Bernard Dukore. New York, 1974.
Vergilius Maro, P. *The Aeneid.* 2 volumes. Translated by H. R. Fairclough. New York, 1930.
Vinci, Leonardo da. *See* Leonardo da Vinci.
Vitruvius Pollio. *Vitruvius on Architecture.* 2 volumes. Translated by F. Granger. New York, 1931–34.
Walkington, Thomas. *The Optick Glasse of Humours.* 1607.
Webster, John. *The Complete Works.* 4 volumes. Edited by F. L. Lucas. 1927.
Williams, John. *Great Britains Solomon.* 1625.
Wotton, Henry. *The Elements of Architecture* (1624). Facsimile reprint edited by Frederick Hard. Charlottesville, Virginia, 1968.
———. *Reliquiae Wottonianae.* 1651 edition.
Wright, Thomas. *The Passions of the minde in generall.* 1604.

SELECTED SECONDARY SOURCES

Adams, John C. "The Staging of *The Tempest*, III, iii." *Review of English Studies* 14 (1938): 404–19.
Adams, Robert. *Strains of Discord: Studies in Literary Openness.* Ithaca, New York, 1958.

Adelman, Janet. *The Common Liar: An Essay on Antony and Cleopatra*. New Haven, 1973.

Akrigg, G. V. *The Jacobean Pageant, or The Court of King James I*. Cambridge, Mass., 1962.

Alexander, Peter, ed. *Studies in Shakespeare*. 1964.

Allen, Don Cameron. *Mysteriously Meant*. Baltimore, 1970.

Anglo, Sydney. *Spectacle, Pageantry, and Early Tudor Policy*. Oxford, 1969.

Ashton, Robert, ed. *James I by His Contemporaries*. 1969.

Baldwin, T. W. *Smalle Latine and Lesse Greeke*. 2 volumes. Urbana, Illinois, 1944.

Barkan, Leonard. "The Imperialist Arts of Inigo Jones." *Renaissance Drama*, new series 8 (1976): 257–86.

Barton, Anne (Anne Righter). "He that plays the King: Ford's *Perkin Warbeck* and the Stuart History Play." In *English Drama: Form and Development*, edited by Marie Axton and Raymond Williams. Cambridge, England, 1977.

———. *Shakespeare and the Idea of the Play*. 1962.

Bazin, Germain. *The Baroque*. New York, 1968.

Bender, John. "The Day of *The Tempest*." *ELH* 47 (1980): 235–58.

———. *Spenser and Literary Pictorialism*. Princeton, 1972.

Bentley, G. E. *The Profession of the Dramatist in Shakespeare's Time*. Princeton, 1971.

———. "Shakespeare and the Blackfriars Theatre." *Shakespeare Survey* 1 (1948): 38–50.

———. *Shakespeare and Jonson*. Berkeley, 1945.

Berger, Harry. "Miraculous Harp: A Reading of Shakespeare's *Tempest*." *Shakespeare Studies* 5 (1969): 253–83.

Bergeron, David. *English Civic Pageantry, 1558–1642*. Columbia, South Carolina, 1971.

———. *Twentieth-Century Criticism of English Masques, Pageants, and Entertainments: 1558–1642*. San Antonio, Texas, 1972.

Berry, Francis. "Word and Picture in the Final Plays." In *Later Shakespeare*, edited by J. R. Brown and Bernard Harris. *Stratford-upon-Avon Studies* 8 (1966): 81–101.

Bethell, S. L. *The Winter's Tale: A Study*. 1947.

Brockbank, Philip. "With a saving grace." *Times Literary Supplement*, 26 November 1976, 1470–71.

Brower, Reuben. *The Fields of Light: An Experiment in Critical Reading*. New York, 1951.

———. *Hero and Saint: Shakespeare and the Graeco-Roman Heroic Tradition*. New York, 1971.

Brownlow, F. W. *Two Shakespearean Sequences*. Pittsburgh, 1977.

Buffum, Imbrie. *Studies in the Baroque from Montaigne to Rotrou*. New Haven, 1957.

Burke, Kenneth. *A Rhetoric of Motives*. New York, 1950.

Buxton, John. *Elizabethan Taste*. 1963.

Cantón, Francisco. *Las Meninas y sus personajes*. Barcelona, 1943.

Chambers, E. K. *The Elizabethan Stage*. 4 volumes. Oxford, 1923.

———. *William Shakespeare: A Study of Facts and Problems*. 2 volumes. Oxford, 1930.

Chambers, R. W. *Man's Unconquerable Mind*. 1939.

Clark, Arthur. *Thomas Heywood* (1931). Reprint, New York, 1967.

Coleridge, Samuel T. *Inquiring Spirit*. Edited by Kathleen Coburn. 1951.

———. *Coleridge's Writings on Shakespeare*. Edited by Terence Hawkes. New York, 1959.

Colie, Rosalie. *The Resources of Kind: Genre-Theory in the Renaissance*. Edited by Barbara Lewalski. Berkeley, 1973.

Cope, Jackson. *The Theater and the Dream*. Baltimore, 1973.

Cox, John D. "*Henry VIII* and the Masque." *English Literary History* 45 (1978): 390–409.

Cruttwell, Patrick. *The Shakespearean Moment*. 1954.

Doebler, John. "Bibliography for the Study of Iconography in English Renaissance Literature." *Research Opportunities in Renaissance Drama* 22 (1979): 45–55.

Doran, Madeleine. *Endeavors of Art: A Study of Form in Elizabethan Drama*. Madison, Wisconsin, 1954.

Dowden, Edward. *Shakespeare: A Critical Study of His Mind and Art* (1875). Reprint, 1967.

Dukore, Bernard, ed. *Dramatic Theory and Criticism.* New York, 1974.

Ebner, Dean. "*The Tempest:* Rebellion and the Ideal State." *Shakespeare Quarterly* 16 (1965): 161–73.

Edgerton, Samuel Y., Jr. *The Renaissance Rediscovery of Linear Perspective.* New York, 1975.

Edwards, Philip. "Shakespeare's Romances: 1900–1957." *Shakespeare Survey* 11 (1958): 1–18.

Egan, Robert. *Drama within Drama.* New York, 1975.

———. "This Rough Magic: Perspectives of Art and Morality in *The Tempest.*" *Shakespeare Quarterly* 23 (1972): 171–82.

Ellis-Fermor, Una. *The Jacobean Drama.* 1936.

———. *Shakespeare the Dramatist and Other Papers.* Edited by Kenneth Muir. 1961.

Emmens, J. A. "Les Ménines de Velázquez: Miroir des Princes pour Philippe IV." *Nederlands Kunsthistorisch Jaarboek* 12 (1961): 51–79.

Evans, Bertrand. *Shakespeare's Comedies.* Oxford, 1960.

Felperin, Howard. *Shakespearean Romance.* Princeton, 1972.

Fletcher, Angus. *The Transcendental Masque: An Essay on Milton's Comus.* Ithaca, New York, 1971.

———. *The Prophetic Moment.* Chicago, 1971.

Foucault, Michel. *Les Mots et les choses* (1966). English translation as *The Order of Things.* New York, 1970.

Fraser, John. "*The Tempest* Revisited." *The Critical Review* 11 (Melbourne, 1968): 60–78.

French, Peter. *John Dee: The World of an Elizabethan Magus.* 1972.

Frost, David. *The School of Shakespeare.* Cambridge, England, 1968.

Frye, Northrop. *Anatomy of Criticism.* Princeton, 1961.

———. "My Credo." *Kenyon Review* 13 (1951): 92–110.

———. "Romance as Masque." In *Shakespeare's Romances Reconsidered*, edited by Carol Kay and Henry Jacobs. Lincoln, Nebraska, 1978.

Gerstenberg, Kurt. *Diego Velázquez.* Munich, 1957.

Gilman, Ernest. *The Curious Perspective: Literary and Pictorial Wit in the Seventeenth Century.* New Haven, 1978.

Goldberg, Jonathan. "James I and the Theater of Conscience." *ELH* 46 (1979): 379–398.

Gombrich, Ernst. *Art and Illusion*. New York, 1960.

———. *Symbolic Images: Studies in the Art of the Renaissance*. 1972.

Gordon, D. J. *The Renaissance Imagination*. Edited by Stephen Orgel. Berkeley, 1975.

Guillén, Claudio. "On the Concept and Metaphor of Perspective." In *Comparatists at Work*, edited by Stephen Nichols Jr. Waltham, Mass., 1968.

Gurr, Andrew. *The Shakespearean Stage: 1574–1642*. Cambridge, England, 1970.

Hale, David. "*Coriolanus:* The Death of a Political Metaphor." *Shakespeare Quarterly* 22 (1971): 197–202.

Hankins, John. "Caliban the Bestial Man." *PMLA* 62 (1947): 793–801.

Harbage, Alfred. *Shakespeare and the Rival Traditions* (1952). Rpt. Bloomington, Indiana, 1970.

Harrison, G. B. *A Jacobean Journal*. 1941.

———. *A Second Jacobean Journal*. Ann Arbor, 1958.

Hart, Alfred. *Shakespeare and the Homilies*. Melbourne, 1934.

Hartwig, Joan. *Shakespeare's Tragicomic Vision*. Baton Rouge, 1972.

Held, J. "Rubens's Glynde Sketch and the Installation of the Whitehall Ceiling." *Burlington Magazine* 112 (1970): 274–81.

Heninger, S. K., Jr. *Touches of Sweet Harmony: Pythagorean Cosmology and Renaissance Poetics*. San Marino, California, 1974.

Herrick, Marvin. *Tragicomedy*. Urbana, Illinois, 1955.

Hill, Christopher. "The Many-Headed Monster in Late Tudor and Early Stuart Thinking." In *From the Renaissance to the Counter-Reformation: Essays in Honor of Garrett Mattingly*, edited by Charles Carter. New York, 1965.

Hoeniger, F. D. "Prospero's Storm and Miracle." *Shakespeare Quarterly* 7 (1956): 33–38.

———. "Shakespeare's Romances since 1958: A Retrospect." *Shakespeare Survey* 29 (1976): 1–10.

Howard, Donald. *The Idea of the Canterbury Tales*. Berkeley, 1976.

Hoy, Cyrus. "Artifice and Reality and the Decline of Jacobean Drama." *Research Opportunities in Renaissance Drama* 13 (1970): 169–80.

Jacobs, Henry. *See* Kay, Carol, and Henry Jacobs, eds.

Jacquot, Jean, ed. *Les Fêtes de la Renaissance.* 3 volumes. Paris, 1956–75.

——. *Le Lieu théâtrale à la Renaissance.* Paris, 1964.

James, D. G. *The Dream of Prospero.* Oxford, 1967.

Javitch, Daniel. *Poetry and Courtliness in Renaissance England.* Princeton, 1978.

Johnson, Paula. "Jacobean Ephemera and the Immortal Word." *Renaissance Drama*, new series, 8 (1977): 151–71.

Johnson, Samuel. *Johnson on Shakespeare.* 2 volumes. Edited by Arthur Sherbo. New Haven, 1968.

Justi, Carl. *Diego Velázquez and His Times.* Translated by A. H. Keane. 1889.

Kaplan, Joel, ed. *Drama and the Other Arts. Renaissance Drama*, new series 7 (1976).

Kay, Carol, and Henry Jacobs, eds. *Shakespeare's Romances Reconsidered.* Lincoln, Nebraska, 1978.

Kehrer, Hugo. *Die Meninas des Velázquez.* Munich, 1966.

Kermode, Frank. *Shakespeare, Spenser, Donne.* 1971.

Kernan, Alvin. *The Playwright as Magician.* New Haven, 1979.

Kernodle, George. *From Art to Theatre.* Chicago, 1944.

Kipling, Gordon. "Triumphal Drama: Form in English Civic Pageantry." *Renaissance Drama*, new series, 8 (1977): 37–56.

Kirsch, Arthur. "*Cymbeline* and Coterie Dramaturgy." *English Literary History* 34 (1967): 285–306.

——. *Jacobean Dramatic Perspectives.* Charlottesville, Virginia, 1972.

Klibansky, Raymond. *See* Panofsky, Erwin, Fritz Saxl, and Raymond Klibansky.

Knight, G. W. *The Crown of Life.* 1947.

——. *The Shakesperian Tempest.* 1932.

Knights, L. C. *Public Voices: Literature and Politics.* Totowa, New Jersey, 1972.

Kott, Jan. "The *Aeneid* and *The Tempest,*" *Arion,* new series, 3 (1976): 424–51.

———. "*The Tempest,* or Repetition." *Mosaic* 10 (1977): 9–36.

Leech, Clifford. *The John Fletcher Plays.* 1962.

———. "Masking and Unmasking in the Last Plays." In *Shakespeare's Romances Reconsidered,* ed. Carol Kay and Henry Jacobs. Lincoln, Nebraska, 1978.

Levin, Harry. *The Myth of the Golden Age in the Renaissance.* Bloomington, Indiana, 1969.

———. "The End of Elizabethan Drama." *Comparative Drama* 3 (1971): 275–81.

MacCaffrey, Isabel. *Spenser's Allegory: The Anatomy of Imagination.* Princeton, 1976.

McFarland, Thomas. *Shakespeare's Pastoral Comedy.* Chapel Hill, North Carolina, 1972.

McGowan, Margaret. *L'Art du Ballet de Cour en France, 1581–1643.* Paris, 1963.

Mack, Maynard. "The Jacobean Shakespeare." *Jacobean Theatre,* edited by J. R. Brown. *Stratford-upon-Avon Studies* 1 (1960): 11–42.

Mehl, Dieter. *The Elizabethan Dumbshow.* Cambridge, Mass., 1965.

Mincoff, Marco. "*The Faithful Shepherdess:* A Fletcherian Experiment." *Renaissance Drama* 9 (1966): 163–77.

———. "Shakespeare, Fletcher and Baroque Tragedy." *Shakespeare Survey* 20 (1967): 1–15.

Morris, Christopher. *Political Thought in England: Tyndale to Hooker.* 1953.

Mowat, Barbara. *The Dramaturgy of Shakespeare's Romances.* Athens, Georgia, 1976.

Munro, John, ed. *The Shakespeare Allusion Book* (1909). 2 volumes. Reprint, 1932.

Murrin, Michael. *The Veil of Allegory.* Chicago, 1969.

Nagler, A. M. *Theatre Festivals of the Medici, 1539–1637.* New Haven, 1964.

Neale, J. E. *Queen Elizabeth*. 1934.

Nosworthy, J. M. "The Narrative Sources of *The Tempest*." *Review of English Studies* 24 (1948): 281–94.

Notestein, Wallace. *The House of Commons, 1604–1610*. New Haven, 1971.

Orgel, Stephen. *The Illusion of Power: Political Theater in the English Renaissance*. Berkeley, 1975.

————. *The Jonsonian Masque*. Cambridge, Mass., 1965.

————. "The Poetics of Spectacle." *New Literary History* 2 (1971): 367–390.

————, and Roy Strong. *Inigo Jones: The Theatre of the Stuart Court*. 2 volumes. Berkeley, 1973.

Orr, David. *The Italian Renaissance Drama in England before 1625*. Chapel Hill, 1970.

Ortega y Gasset, José. *Velázquez, Goya and the Dehumanization of Art*. Translated by Alexis Brown. New York, 1972.

Otis, Brooks. *Virgil: A Study in Civilized Poetry*. Oxford, 1963.

Palme, Per. *The Triumph of Peace*. Stockholm, 1956.

Palomino de Castro y Velasco, Acisclo. *Vida de los Pintores . . . Eminentes Españoles*. Madrid, 1726.

Panofsky, Erwin. *Meaning and the Visual Arts*. Garden City, New York, 1955.

————, Fritz Saxl and Raymond Klibansky. *Saturn and Melancholy: Studies in the History of Natural Philosophy, Religion, and Art*. 1964.

Pater, Walter. *Appreciations* (1889). Reprint, 1924.

Patrides, C. A. "The Beast with Many Heads: Renaissance Views of the Multitude." *Shakespeare Quarterly* 16 (1965): 241–46.

Patterson, Annabel M. *Hermogenes and the Renaissance: Seven Ideas of Style*. Princeton, 1970.

Paul, Henry. *The Royal Play of Macbeth*. New York, 1950.

Peterson, Douglas. *Time, Tide, and Tempest*. San Marino, California, 1973.

Pöschl, Viktor. *The Art of Vergil: Image and Symbol in the Aeneid* (1950). Translated by Gerda Seligson. Ann Arbor, 1962.

Rabkin, Norman. "Rabbits, Ducks, and *Henry V.*" *Shakespeare Quarterly* 28 (1977): 279–96.

―――. *Shakespeare and the Common Understanding.* New York, 1967.

Rebhorn, Wayne. *Courtly Performances: Masking and Festivity in Castiglione's Book of the Courtier.* Detroit, 1978.

Ribner, Irving. *Jacobean Tragedy: The Quest for Moral Order.* 1962.

Richmond, H. M. *Shakespeare's Political Plays.* New York, 1967.

Righter, Anne. *See* Barton, Anne.

Rockett, William. "Labor and Virtue in *The Tempest.*" *Shakespeare Quarterly* 24 (1973): 77–84.

Rossi, Paolo. *Francis Bacon: From Magic to Science* (1957). Translated by Sacha Rabinovitch. Chicago, 1968.

Rousset, Jean. *La Littérature de l'age Baroque en France.* Paris 1953.

Russell, Conrad. *The Crisis of Parliaments: English History, 1509–1660.* 1971.

Saxl, Fritz. *See* Panofsky, Erwin, Fritz Saxl and Raymond Klibansky.

Schücking, L. L. *Character Problems in Shakespeare's Plays.* 1922.

Seznec, Jean. *The Survival of the Pagan Gods* (1940). Translated by Barbara Sessions. New York, 1953.

Shumaker, Wayne. *The Occult Sciences in the Renaissance.* Berkeley, 1972.

Skinner, Quentin. *The Foundations of Modern Political Thought.* 2 volumes. Cambridge, England, 1978.

Smith, Bruce. "Landscape with Figures: The Three Realms of Queen Elizabeth's Country-house Revels." *Renaissance Drama*, new series, 8 (1977): 57–115.

Smith, Hallett. *Shakespeare's Romances: A Study of Some Ways of the Imagination.* San Marino, California, 1972.

Solomon, Maynard. *Beethoven.* New York, 1977.

Spencer, T. J. B., ed. *A Book of Masques in Honour of Allardyce Nicoll.* Cambridge, Mass., 1967.

Spitzer, Leo. *Classical and Christian Ideas of World Harmony.* Baltimore, 1963.

Stauffer, Donald. *Shakespeare's World of Images.* Bloomington, Indiana, 1949.

Steadman, John M. *The Lamb and the Elephant: Ideal Imitation and the Context of Renaissance Allegory.* San Marino, California, 1974.

Stirling, William. *Annals of the Artists of Spain.* 3 volumes. 1848.

Strong, Roy. *The English Icon: Elizabethan and Jacobean Portraiture.* New York, 1969.

———. *Portraits of Queen Elizabeth.* Oxford, 1963.

———. *Splendour at Court: Renaissance Spectacle and the Theatre of Power.* Boston, 1973.

———, and Julia Trevelyan Oman. *Elizabeth R.* 1972.

———, and Stephen Orgel. *See* Orgel, Stephen, and Roy Strong.

Tillyard, E. M. W. *Shakespeare's Last Plays.* Reprint, 1964.

Tobias, Richard, and Paul Zolbrod, eds. *Shakespeare's Late Plays: Essays in Honor of Charles Crow.* Athens, Ohio, 1974.

Tonkin, Humphrey. *Spenser's Courteous Pastoral.* Oxford, 1972.

Tuve, Rosemond. *Allegorical Imagery: Some Medieval Books and Their Posterity.* Princeton, 1966.

Vawter, Marvin. "*Julius Caesar:* Rupture in the Bond." *Journal of English and Germanic Philology* 72 (1973): 311–28.

Waddington, Raymond. *The Mind's Empire: Myth and Form in George Chapman's Narrative Poems.* Baltimore, 1974.

Walker, D. P. *Spiritual and Demonic Magic from Ficino to Campanella.* 1948.

Weimann, Robert. *Shakespeare and the Popular Tradition in the Theater.* Baltimore, 1978.

Wellek, René. "The Concept of Baroque in Literary Scholarship." *Journal of Aesthetics* 5 (1946): 77–109.

Welsford, Enid. *The Court Masque: A Study in the Relationship between Poetry and the Revels.* Cambridge, England, 1927.

Whitaker, Virgil. "Shakespeare the Elizabethan." *Rice University Studies* 61 (1974): 141–51.

Wickham, Glynne. *The Early English Stages, 1300–1660*. 3 volumes. 1959–72.

———. "Masque and Anti-masque in *The Tempest*." *Essays and Studies* 28 (1975): 1–14.

———. "Shakespeare's Investiture Play." *Times Literary Supplement*, 18 December 1969, p. 1456.

Wilson, F. P. "The Elizabethan Theatre." *Neophilologus* 39 (1955): 40–58.

———. *Elizabethan and Jacobean*. Oxford, 1945.

Wölfflin, Heinrich. *Renaissance and Baroque* (1888). Translated by Kathrin Simon. 1964.

Yates, Frances. *Astraea: The Imperial Theme in the Sixteenth Century*. 1975.

———. "Queen Elizabeth as Astraea." *Journal of the Warburg and Courtauld Institutes* 10 (1947): 27–82.

———. *Shakespeare's Last Plays: A New Approach*. 1975.

———. *Theatre of the World*. Chicago, 1969.

Young, Alan R. "Prospero's Table: The Name of Shakespeare's Duke of Milan." *Shakespeare Quarterly* 30 (1979): 408–10.

Zimbardo, Rose Abdelnour. "Form and Disorder in *The Tempest*." *Shakespeare Quarterly* 14 (1963): 49–56.

Zolbrod, Paul. *See* Tobias, Richard, and Paul Zolbrod, eds.

INDEX

Designer: Wolfgang Lederer
Compositor: Interactive Composition Corporation
Printer: Thomson-Shore
Binder: Thomson-Shore
Text: VIP Bembo
Display: VIP Bembo
Cloth: Holliston Roxite C57503
Paper: 55 lb. P&S Offset